9-16-71

Priming the German Economy

PRIMING THE

GERMAN ECONOMY

AMERICAN OCCUPATIONAL POLICIES

1945 – 1948

JOHN H. BACKER

DUKE UNIVERSITY PRESS
DURHAM, N.C., 1971

© 1971 Duke University Press
LCC Card Number 70–142289
ISBN 0–8223–0243–8

Printed in the United States of America
by the Kingsport Press, Inc., Kingsport, Tennessee

1654813

To Evelyn

ACKNOWLEDGMENT

I should like to express my gratitude to the members of the staff at the National Archives and at the Federal Records Center for their assistance in the course of my research. I am particularly indebted to Mr. Thomas E. Hohmann whose help in locating relevant files and in declassifying the extracted documents was indeed invaluable— without his understanding and cheerful support I would not have been able to overcome the numerous obstacles which research in governmental archives entails.

Preface

This book is an attempt to describe the reconstruction of the German economy under the auspices of the American Military Government as observed from its working level by the writer. Other books have dealt with America's long-range policies for postwar Germany, often reaching the conclusion that they were at best ambivalent.

By contrast, and in a more pragmatic vein, this study is primarily concerned with the onerous responsibility of the American Military Government to prevent the starvation of several millions of Germans. Because it was recognized at an early date that the agriculture of West Germany would be unable to provide sufficient food for its inhabitants, a program had to be developed to feed the German people through imports of food. And since American and British taxpayers could not be expected to shoulder this burden indefinitely, German industry had to be revived so that the proceeds of its exports would pay for the necessary imports. American official rhetoric and unofficial interpretations to the contrary notwithstanding, only two Allied policies were permitted to interfere with this basic approach: denazification and reparations. The economic impact of these two programs will be discussed in the third chapter.

By the force of circumstances, most of the initiative for the reconstruction of the German economy had to come initially from the United States; Great Britain was too weak economically to assume a proportionate share of the burden, and Germany at that time was spiritually and economically too exhausted to play much more than a passive role.

Accordingly a small group of American public servants—in uniform or in civilian garb—was called upon to do the necessary spadework. In the face of impossible odds, they worked ceaselessly and devotedly as if the welfare of their own country rather than that of a recent enemy were at stake. Their efforts and the obstacles they had to overcome will be described in the following pages.

J. H. B.

CONTENTS

List of Abbreviations

ACA	Allied Control Authority
AGWAR	Adjutant General, War Department
BICO	Bipartite Control Office
CAD	Civil Affairs Division
CA/MG	Civil Affairs/Military Government
CCS	Combined Chiefs of Staff
CEEC	Committee of European Economic Cooperation
ECA	Economic Cooperation Administration
ERP	European Recovery Program
FEA	Foreign Economic Administration
GARIOA	Government and Relief in Occupied Areas
HICOG	High Commissioner for Germany
IARA	Inter-Allied Reparations Agency
IEFC	International Emergency Food Council
JCS	Joint Chiefs of Staff
OEEC	Organization for European Economic Cooperation
OMGB	Office of Military Government for Bavaria
OMGH	Office of Military Government for Hesse
OMGUS	Office of Military Government for Germany (U.S.)
USFET	United States Forces Europe
US GROUP CC	United States Group, Control Council
VFW	Verwaltungsamt für Wirtschaft

PRIMING THE GERMAN ECONOMY

CHAPTER ONE

THE DRAFTING OF OCCUPATIONAL POLICIES

Disenchanted Americans who ponder current national issues with growing apprehension may find some comfort in reflecting that twenty-five years after the end of hostilities in Europe no consensus on the wisdom of America's World War II policies has yet been reached. This void exists although most of the archives of the period are open and available to historians.

There are writers who strongly disapprove of Franklin Roosevelt's accommodating attitude toward Stalin; on the other hand, there are scholars who, in the president's defense, will point to some of the unknown factors he had to consider: a hurriedly trained and inexperienced army, a general staff to a great extent assembled from civilian life, the real or imaginary possibility of a separate German-Soviet peace settlement tentatively initiated by the Soviet creation of a "National Committee for Free Germany," and American intelligence estimates which predicted a prolonged last-ditch stand in a German redoubt and several years of combat on the Japanese mainland. In a similar division of opinion, there are critics who blame American policy makers in World War II for their belated attention to postwar planning and an almost exclusive concentration on the attainment of victory. On the other side are those who point to General Rommel's preparations on the Normandy coast and the hard and bloody D-Day battle on Omaha Beach. They sympathize with military and civilian leaders who felt that an American victory was by no means a foregone conclusion and who therefore decided to put first things first. Surely, those who participated in the D-Day landings on the coast of France and came through alive appreciated the rationale of Washington policy makers who turned to intensive postwar planning only after the beaches had been secured.

Actually, while Roosevelt's cabinet concentrated on occupational policy only after the successful Normandy landings and the Avranches breakthrough, lower echelons concerned themselves with related problems much earlier. In the State Department an Advisory Committee on Postwar Foreign Policy examined the question of a possible dismemberment of Germany as early as 1942. This body was replaced in the following year by an Interdivisional Country Committee on Germany which prepared drafts of an instrument of German unconditional surrender, as well as proposals for zones of occupation and for the Allied control machinery.[1] At about the same time a Combined Civil Affairs Committee, established by the Combined Chiefs of Staff, also began to draft civil affairs policies, while the War Department's newly formed Civil Affairs Division focused initially on organizational and jurisdictional matters and paid little attention to German affairs.[2]

It was hardly surprising that London became the center of preliminary posthostilities planning. The conduct of any military operation entails contingency planning, and while a sudden German collapse did not appear likely in the spring of 1943, European Theater Headquarters nevertheless considered it necessary to plan for this eventuality, remote as it may have been. Accordingly, a small group of American and British officers went to work with plans for the military occupation of Germany as early as May 1943. They served under Lieutenant General Sir Frederic E. Morgan, chief of staff to the supreme Allied commander, whose headquarters were generally referred to as COSSAC. Inaugurated on April 17, 1943, COSSAC was absorbed in January 1944 by Supreme Headquarters Allied Expeditionary Force,[3] which became the more familiar SHAEF.

Originally, planning for the occupation of Germany was only a part of the general strategy for the defeat of the Axis Powers. The first product prepared by the London planning group along these lines was Operation RANKIN CASE C, a strategic document probably as significant for what it did not cover as for what it contained.[4] In substance, it provided a survey of the strategic areas which would have to be seized by troops based in Great Britain, what forces would be necessary for this task, and how these troops would be moved into position.[5] It contained no provisions for the disposition of the German forces, the recovery and repatriation of displaced persons, the disposal of captured war material, and numerous other matters which soon became the responsibility of the

1. Paul V. Hammond, "Directives for the Occupation of Germany, the Washington Controversy," pp. 317–18.
2. Ibid., p. 321.
3. "Planning for the Occupation of Germany," p. 12.
4. Ibid., p. 22.   5. Ibid., p. 17.

supreme commander. Most important, RANKIN CASE C did not refer to policy or procedure in the fields of civil affairs and military government, an omission which, as the document emphasized, was due to the lack of political guidance for the drafting officers.[6]

The chief objective of the occupation of Germany, according to RANKIN CASE C, was the enforcement of the terms of unconditional surrender; however, since no draft for the terms of surrender existed at SHAEF at the time, the concept of the occupation as expressed in the plan was by necessity vague. The drafters apparently thought that upon the cessation of hostilities there would be a short occupation of Germany. Actually the question of whether there was to be a complete occupation of Germany was settled at the Moscow Foreign Ministers Conference in October 1943, when the partitioning of Germany into three zones was decided upon. Among the London drafters there was considerable discontent about the lack of political guidance—with good reason as it turned out—and General Morgan, when transmitting RANKIN CASE C to the Joint Chiefs of Staff in Washington, tactfully though firmly called their attention to "the essential difficulty in planning operations before the clear establishment of the political policy whence these operations derive their necessity." [7]

In spite of such prodding from the field, Washington was still not prepared to release occupational policy guidance, and for several months RANKIN CASE C remained the only document pertaining to the occupation of Germany. In the spring of 1944, however, the first directive on military government was completed by the Combined Civil Affairs Committee in Washington and, after approval by the Combined Chiefs of Staff, forwarded to General Eisenhower. Known as CCS 551 and entitled "Directive for Military Government in Germany Prior to Defeat or Surrender," it was received in London on April 28, 1944.[8] Although CCS 551 referred only to the period during which military operations would continue, it contained some useful guidance regarding the policies to be followed during the occupation. The directive established some basic principles which were later taken over in substance by subsequent authoritative documents. For the first time it was spelled out that the supreme commander would be responsible for establishing military government, and to that end he was vested with supreme legislative, executive, and judicial authority, including the power to establish military courts for the control of the civilian population. Mili-

6. Ibid., p. 23.   7. Ibid., p. 32.
8. Ibid., p. 44.

tary government was not to be organized by simply staffing the German administration with Americans and Britons, but rather by enlisting for public office the services of acceptable qualified Germans. All political activities in Germany were to cease; exceptions to the rule had to be approved by the supreme commander. The Gestapo and related police agencies were to be dissolved and German courts closed until all Nazi influence had been eliminated.

The extensive economic controls envisaged by the directive primarily entailed the maintenance of production and the collection and distribution of food. Agricultural output was to be maximized, utilities and coal mines kept in working order, and industrial production protected. German regulations governing wages, prices, rationing, and taxes would remain in force. The only permanent political objective of the occupation mentioned in the directive was the destruction of "Nazism-Fascism and of the Nazi Hierarchy"; the temporary objectives listed pertained to maintenance of law and order, assistance to military operations, and the establishment of normal conditions. CCS 551 also established the so-called disease-and-unrest formula, but with a quite different emphasis from that it later received. It prescribed that German food resources be distributed only to the extent necessary to prevent disease and unrest; at the beginning of the occupation the principle not only was extended to relief supplies from abroad but actually became a prime mover of American economic policies in Germany. There was no reference to the complex problems of disarmament, demilitarization in the economic sphere, reparations, restitution, and the establishment of a democratic German Government. These and other issues were studied but not resolved by the European Advisory Commission in London and a related Working Security Committee in Washington. The former, consisting of representatives of the United States, Great Britain, and the Soviet Union, had been established late in 1943 by a Moscow agreement of the three powers. In essence, the commission was a negotiating body, and since all its activities had to have the advance approval of three (later four) governments, its progress was necessarily slow.[9]

The Working Security Committee, formed in December 1943 under the auspices of the Department of State, consisted of representatives of State, War, and Navy and was intended to serve as a central body through which policy papers for the European Advisory Commission could be cleared. A second and often competing policy channel went from the Joint and Combined Chiefs of Staff to General Eisenhower and

9. Ibid., p. 35.

was controlled by the military. Although the Departments of War and State had agreed that the former had to have freedom of action in military matters and the latter would be responsible for the drafting of postwar policies, the practical application of this understanding became a most difficult and often exasperating task. An analytical appraisal of the resulting acrimonious disputes is beyond the scope of this study; it can be found in *American Civil-Military Decisions,* a volume edited by Professor Harold Stein.[10]

With D-Day approaching, the number of planning units concerned with posthostilities issues and the scope of their studies increased considerably. (In March 1944 SHAEF had in preparation thirty-eight studies pertaining to the occupation of Germany, and by the end of April there were seventy-two.) [11] Some of the fundamental problems such as the responsibilities of the supreme commander were settled; the idea originally presented by the G-5 Division of SHAEF of using the German High Command as a channel for transmitting military orders in implementation of the surrender terms was dropped; and it was decided that, contrary to the underlying assumption of RANKIN CASE C, the occupation would not be a jointly administered Anglo-American undertaking.[12] After the landings in Normandy, RANKIN CASE C was replaced by the plan TALISMAN, which in turn eventually became operation ECLIPSE. None of these papers attempted to tackle the primarily civilian aspects of military government because whenever drafting officers strayed into that territory, they were reminded of General Eisenhower's explicit instructions that "emphasis will be placed on the solution of the problem on a military basis." [13]

Eventually, of course, the gap between the military and civilian aspects of an occupation of Germany had to be bridged. The unavoidable confrontation between the necessarily pragmatic approach at Theater Headquarters and the long-range policy considerations at the higher echelons of the American administration came about when an advance copy of the *Handbook for Military Government in Germany,*[14] one of the important products of the posthostilities planners at SHAEF, was sent to Washington for approval by the Combined Chiefs of Staff.

10. Hammond, passim.   11. Ibid., p. 328.
12. "Planning for the Occupation of Germany," pp. 54, 57.
13. Ibid., p. 28.
14. *Handbook for Military Government in Germany,* 15 Aug. 1944. This item is among the records of the Office of Military Government for Germany, United States (OMGUS) that are available at the Federal Record Center, Suitland, Md., in Record Group 260. In the notes below and the bibliography, the term "OMGUS records" directs the reader to this source.

The *Handbook* reached Washington in August 1944, at a time when many Americans, with Henry Morgenthau as their most influential and vocal protagonist, favored a harsh peace for Germany. By contrast, the London draft reflected the thinking of the officers at SHAEF, who were soon to assume responsibility for the American administration in occupied Germany and who, as the following quotations will bear out, had made a realistic, if not prophetic, appraisal of the impending problems:

> This administrative machinery must of course be cleansed of all traces of Nazi Control, but as the first concern of M.G. will be to see that the machine works and works efficiently, it may not be possible to eliminate every Nazi from every position of responsibility at the very outset [Chapter I. 003].
>
> Military Government officers must remember that to dismiss every civil servant because of his previous associations with National Socialists would be to paralyze M.G. at the outset but they must remember at the same time that it is essential that all ardent active Nazis should be eliminated [Chapter III. 163].
>
> But your main and immediate task to accomplish your mission is to get things running, to pick up the pieces, to restore as quickly as possible the efficient functioning of German civil government in the area for which you are responsible [Chapter IX. 5].
>
> The chief factor influencing food and agriculture policy lies in the terms of the projected division of Germany into zones. If there is no transfer of agricultural produce from East to West the food problem in the US/BR zones will be acute. It will therefore be necessary in the absence of a given policy on this all important problem to prepare estimates of requirements for both contingencies and to make alternative arrangements for importing the necessary foodstuffs in order to maintain a ration of 2000 calories [Chapter X. 029].
>
> Having regard to the food goal aimed at, the extent of the prospective decline in production, the disorganization of the system of distribution, and the uncertainties of interzonal exchange of products, more or less substantial food imports may be needed [Chapter XI. 005].
>
> In conjunction with other interested and affected agencies and authorities ensure that steps are taken to
>
> 1) import needed commodities and stores.
> 2) convert industrial plants from war to consumer goods.

3) subsidize essential economic activities where necessary.

4) reconstruct German foreign trade with priority for the needs of the U.N. [Chapter XII. 046e].

In other words, as the Army saw it, it was imperative to do an efficient job in Germany and if this required some shortcuts, such shortcuts should be taken. The secretary of the treasury on the other hand—he had obtained a copy of the *Handbook* in the course of a visit to London [15]—had no sympathy for such a pragmatic attitude which, in his words, would result in a "WPA program for Germany." Deeply perturbed, he and Harry White, the director of the Treasury's Monetary Research Division, took the proofs to the White House, where, according to Drew Pearson, the president threw them down indignantly.[16] A few days later, a scathing letter went out to the secretary of war ordering the *Handbook* rescinded.

Inasmuch as it was ready for distribution, the presidential order caused quite a stir. The Combined Chiefs of Staff, who looked at the *Handbook* in a more rational vein, ruled that it was based upon their directive CCS 551 but actually reflected posthostilities conditions; furthermore they pointed out that it was in conflict with policies regarding the economic rehabilitation of Germany, which at the time were under discussion by the cabinet. For a short period it seemed that in spite of the urgent need for a prompt release, SHAEF would have to block out or rewrite some of the objectionable passages.[17] Eventually, however, after an exchange of numerous cables and several telephone conversations between Washington and London, the dilemma was resolved by the decision to authorize issuance provided every copy contained the following notice:

The Handbook applies only to the pre-defeat period. The following basic principles apply to pre-defeat conditions and supersede any other considerations; no steps toward economic rehabilitation for Germany will be undertaken except as may be immediately necessary in support of military operations. No relief supplies are to be imported or distributed beyond the minimum necessary to prevent disease and such disorder as might endanger or impede military operations. Under no circumstances shall active Nazi or ardent sympathizers be retained in office, or shall any Nazi organi-

15. Henry Morgenthau, "Our Policy Toward Germany," *New York Post,* 26 Nov. 1947, sec. 1, p. 2.
16. *Washington Post,* 21 Sept. 1944, p. 9.
17. "Planning for the Occupation of Germany," p. 75.

zation be permitted to continue in existence for purposes of administrative convenience or expediency.

The authorization to issue the *Handbook* with these modifications reached the rapidly advancing American divisions just in time. On September 11, 1944, their vanguards had crossed the frontier and were fighting on German soil. Couriers were hurriedly dispatched to the front with supplies of the *Handbook* for distribution.[18] At a later date (December 1944) a revised version of the *Handbook* superseding the original one was published; it was in full accord with top-level policies which had been drafted in the meantime. While the *Handbook* incident may seem small in retrospect, it was not only indicative of Morgenthau's aggressive meddling in areas beyond his immediate jurisdiction, but also, as John McCloy remarked to this writer, "a symbol of the trend of policy" prevailing in Washington at the time.

The top-level meetings on occupational policy in the autumn of 1944, to which the Combined Chiefs of Staff had referred in their comments on the *Handbook,* were indeed of far-reaching importance. According to Roosevelt's wishes, a cabinet committee which was to deal with these matters had been formed in August. Composed of Secretary of State Cordell Hull, Secretary of the Treasury Henry Morgenthau, and Secretary of War Henry Stimson, it met for the first time on September 5, 1944. Harry Hopkins joined the committee in its deliberations.

Contrary to some press reports at the time [19] depicting a united front within the cabinet against the tough position of the president and of the secretary of the treasury, there was general agreement among the administration on most of the fundamental policies to be applied to the immediate postwar period. There was unanimous consent that Germany should be treated as a defeated nation, that Nazism had to be eradicated, and that war criminals should be punished. Germany was to be disarmed, demilitarized, and politically decentralized to prevent it from becoming a threat to the peace of the world. In view of the experiences of the United States with the consequences of the financial terms of the Versailles Treaty, there also was agreement that America should not demand reparations and, as far as the Allies were concerned, reparations should be effected only by the transfer of existing German resources and not by future payments or deliveries.

In view of the widespread tendency among contemporary critics to

18. Ibid., p. 81. General Lucius Clay's comment in *Decision in Germany,* p. 8, indicating that the *Handbook* was "suppressed" is erroneous.
19. *Washington Post,* 24 Sept. 1944, p. 1.

attribute to the secretary of the treasury the sole authorship of reparations, restitution, denazification, demilitarization, etc., it ought to be stressed that many of these contemplated measures were in accordance with the views of the administration and also reflected the mood of the American people as it prevailed at the time.

The principal points of disagreement dividing the cabinet committee at the meetings pertained to the methods of war crime prosecution and to the economic and fiscal policies which were to govern the occupation of Germany. In both respects the position of the secretary of the treasury was the most extreme. As to war criminals, he recommended that, upon capture and identification, these men should be shot at once.[20] As we know, a more legalistic approach—with questionable results— was taken in Nürnberg at a later date.

When it came to the drafting of economic policies toward Germany, Morgenthau, in disregard of the findings of American historical research,[21] clung to the cliché that Germany alone was responsible for the outbreak of World War I. His rationale then proceeded along the line that, since the Treaty of Versailles had failed to prevent German industrial rearmament, more drastic measures were needed to insure against a resurgence of Germany as a great military power.[22] He consequently recommended the partition of Germany ino three states: a South German state in customs union with Austria, with the Main River as its northern boundary; a North German state east of the Weser River; and, most important, an international zone reaching from the Danish border to the Main. The last was to include the Ruhr area, which Morgenthau intended to turn into "second rate agricultural land." [23] The Saarland was to be annexed by France.

In connection with these proposals the reader ought to be cautioned against placing the exclusive responsibility for the suggested splitting up of Germany into three states on Morgenthau's doorstep. Public discussion concerning a division of Germany was the topic of the day, and several months earlier even as conservative a diplomat as Sumner Welles had proposed this along with a permanent cession of East Prussia to Poland.[24] On the other hand, while one will appreciate Morgenthau's personal feelings toward Nazi Germany, it is nevertheless difficult to understand how a secretary of the treasury could propose permanent

20. Henry L. Stimson, *On Active Service in Peace and War*, p. 570.
21. Sidney B. Fay, *The Origins of the World War*, 2 : 547–58.
22. Henry Morgenthau, *Germany Is Our Problem*, pp. 1–15.
23. Ibid., photographic copy of Memorandum to the President.
24. Sumner Welles, *Time for Decision*, p. 349.

transformation of part of Europe's industrial heartland into a second-rate pastoral state, a suggestion which at an early stage had been described as "fantastic, childish, and imbecilic." [25]

As far as the destruction of German industry was concerned, Morgenthau's proposals were in part supported by Cordell Hull, and Stimson initially found himself in a dissenting minority of one. After the first committee meeting he recorded his position in a memorandum emphasizing that he was in agreement in principle with most of the State Department's "suggested recommendations on treatment of Germany." His main objections pertained to the last paragraph of the State Department proposals, which suggested that the standard of living of the German people should be reduced to subsistence level; that Germany's economic power be curtailed; and that German economic capacity had to be converted in such a manner that Germany could not reconvert to war production by its own devices. Stimson added that he was especially perturbed by the interpretation of these terms as expressed at the meeting of the cabinet committee. In particular, he was opposed to the proposal that the "great industrial regions of Germany, namely the Ruhr and Saar . . . should be transformed into . . . agricultural land." [26]

There were several additional meetings of the committee in the course of which Cordell Hull changed his position and came to Stimson's support. The president, however, must have been impressed with the Treasury's proposals, for he asked Morgenthau for a written outline of them prior to his departure for a scheduled meeting with Churchill in Quebec. It was submitted to him as a top-secret paper under the indicative heading "Program to Prevent Germany from Starting a World War III." [27]

Composed of fourteen points, the document covered demilitarization, war crimes, the partitioning of Germany, restitution and reparations, political decentralization, economic controls, and several other pertinent topics. Regarding the Ruhr, it proposed that "the area should not only be stripped of all presently existing industries but so weakened and con-

25. This comment of Philip E. Mosely is in the *Morgenthau Diary* (Germany). In a similar vein Henry C. Wallich remarked: "The Morgenthau Plan presented the astonishing spectacle of the Chief Financial Officer of the world's most economically successful nation disregarding what appeared to be obvious facts about the German and European economies." Wallich, *The Mainsprings of the German Revival*, p. 347.

26. Memorandum, Secretary of War to Harry Hopkins, 5 Sept. 1944, on policy recommendations for the treatment of Germany (National Archives, Record Group 107, Office of the Secretary of War).

27. Morgenthau, *Germany*, photographic copy of memorandum to the President.

trolled that it can not in the foreseeable future become an industrial area." Furthermore, it "should be made an international zone to be governed by an international security organization to be established by the United Nations." As to economic controls, the paper recommended that the Military Government should not take any measures for the purpose of maintaining or strengthening the German economy except those considered essential to military operations. The document's last paragraph, reflecting another facet of Morgenthau's lack of political foresight, is quoted in full:

14. *United States Responsibility*

Although the United States would have full military and civilian representation on whatever international commission or commissions be established for the execution of the whole German program, the primary responsibility for the policing of Germany and for civil administration in Germany should be assumed by the military forces of Germany's continental neighbors. Specifically, those should include Russian, French, Polish, Czech, Greek, Yugoslav, Norwegian, Dutch and Belgian soldiers.

Under this program United States troops could be withdrawn within a relatively short time.

Roosevelt left for Canada on September 10. Soon after the conference had begun, the secretary of the treasury was asked to join the president in order to present his views to the two leaders personally. Cordell Hull, who had been invited to accompany Roosevelt, had begged off, indicating that he was too tired.[28] On September 15, Churchill and Roosevelt initialed the following memorandum, from then on often referred to as the "Morgenthau Plan":

At a conference between the President and the Prime Minister upon the best measures to prevent renewed rearmament of Germany, it was felt that an essential feature was the future disposition of the Ruhr and the Saar. The ease with which the metallurgical, chemical, and electrical industries in Germany can be converted from peace to war has already been impressed upon us by bitter experience. It must also be remembered that the Germans have devastated a large portion of the industries of Russia and of other

---

28. Morgenthau, "Our Policy . . . ," *New York Post,* 28 Nov. 1947, p. 18. Cordell Hull explains his absence in his *Memoirs,* p. 1602, with the comment: "The conference was intended to be largely military. I was not well . . . and I told the President I preferred to remain in Washington."

neighboring Allies, and it is only in accordance with justice that these injured countries should be entitled to remove the machinery they require in order to repair the losses they have suffered.

The industries referred to in the Ruhr and in the Saar would therefore be necessarily put out of action and closed down. It was felt that these two districts should be put under some body under the world organization which would supervise the dismantling of the industries and make sure that they were not started again by some subterfuge.

This program for eliminating the war-making industries in the Ruhr is looking forward to converting Germany into a country primarily agricultural and pastoral in its character. The Prime Minister and the President were in agreement upon this program [September 16, 1944].[29]

The Quebec memorandum differed from Morgenthau's "Program to Prevent Germany from Starting a World War III" in several important respects: it did not mention the suggested permanent division of Germany into three states or the customs union of Southern Germany with Austria; furthermore, rather than approving the recommended annexation of the Saar by France, it put this area as well as the Ruhr area under international supervision. On the other hand, it spelled out Morgenthau's aim of making Germany "a country primarily agricultural and pastoral in its character," a suggestion interestingly enough omitted in Morgenthau's top-secret program. It is, of course, noteworthy that the Quebec memorandum was at variance with the Atlantic Charter, which both statesmen had previously signed and which had promised that "the U.S. and the U.K. would further the enjoyment by all States great or small, victor or vanquished, of access on equal terms to the trade and the raw materials of the world which are needed for their economic prosperity."

For anyone unfamiliar with the vagaries of political decisions, the example of the Quebec memorandum should provide a memorable illustration. Churchill, while never formally renouncing his signature, expressed himself at Yalta against a peace for vengeance and later argued at Potsdam that Germany's heavy industries should not be reduced to a point that would require other governments to come to Germany's economic assistance.[30] Roosevelt's attitude was even more

29. Herbert Feis, *Churchill, Roosevelt, Stalin*, pp. 369–70.
30. James F. Byrnes, *Speaking Frankly*, p. 185.

startling. A few days after his return from Quebec, he received two separate memoranda, from Cordell Hull and Henry Stimson. The secretary of state pointed out that the future of Germany would have to be settled on a tripartite basis, that the British government so far had given no indication that it was in favor of the elimination of German industrial capacity in the Ruhr and the Saar, and that the views of the Soviet government on this matter had not been heard. Henry Stimson's memorandum, drafted by John McCloy, was taken to Hyde Park by Harry Hopkins. It raised the rhetorical question as to whether in the long run a group of seventy million educated and efficient people could be held on such a low level of subsistence as the Treasury suggestions contemplated. In conclusion it stated:

> The proposed treatment of Germany would deliberately deprive many millions of people of the right to freedom from want and freedom from fear. Other people all over the world would suspect the validity of our spiritual tenets. . . . The sum total of the drastic political and economic steps proposed by the Treasury is an open confession of the bankruptcy of hope for a reasonable economic and political settlement of the causes of war.[31]

As so often on the American political scene, it was not so much the opposition of key cabinet members as public opinion which decisively influenced the course of events. On September 23 the *Wall Street Journal* published a detailed account of the split in the cabinet, a report which was expanded on the following day by the Associated Press's John M. Hightower. As the American press rallied to the support of Stimson and Hull, the president reacted swiftly. On September 27 he telephoned the secretary of war in order to explain that he really had not intended to make Germany a purely agricultural country and that his main motive was to help England, "which was broke." As Stimson evaluated the conversation, Roosevelt had realized that he had made a mistake and was trying to correct it.[32] On October 3 the two men had lunch together and Stimson brought up the question of the postwar treatment of Germany. The president, in a complete reversal of his original position, remarked that in essence his views were quite similar to those of Stimson and that he never had had the intention of turning Germany into an agricultural state. All he wanted was part of the

31. Memorandum, Secretary of War to the President, 15 Sept. 1944, on policy recommendations for the treatment of Germany (National Archives, Record Group 107, Office of the Secretary of War).
32. Stimson, p. 582.

production of the Ruhr for Great Britain, which needed financial and economic aid; the remainder of the production could remain in Germany. He became so emphatic on this point that Stimson felt obliged to remind him of the Quebec memorandum, actually reading to him verbatim its last paragraph. As Stimson reports, "Roosevelt was frankly staggered by this and had no idea how he could have initialed this; that he had evidently done this without much thought." [33]

The secretary concluded that the president never had the intention of implementing the Treasury's proposals and that the Quebec memorandum really did not represent his matured opinion. As far as Stimson was concerned, the incident of the "pastoral letter" [34] was closed, and the War Department, despite persistent interference on the part of the Treasury, continued preparing for the occupation of Germany. [35]

It seems appropriate at this point to mention the disparate views regarding the authentic text of the Morgenthau Plan. Paul Y. Hammond, in *Directives for the Occupation of Germany,* mentions in this connection the Treasury draft memorandum of September 1, 1944, "Suggested Post-Surrender Program for Germany"; [36] Morgenthau himself refers to the above-cited "Program to Prevent Germany from Starting World War III," whereas other writers have quoted the Quebec memorandum (the "pastoral" letter) as the pertinent document. Although none of these three divergent papers directly or indirectly became an instrument of American foreign policy, [37] the political and psychological impact of the plan's publication can hardly be overestimated. Inaccurate and sensational reports by the news media, of course, made a bad situation worse. The October 2, 1944 issue of *Time,* for instance, carried on the first page the picture of the secretary of the treasury with the caption, "He recalled Carthage and Clemenceau." The accompanying lead story, headlined "The Policy of Hate," said that the "fanatical Naziphobe Morgenthau would reduce Germany from a prewar industrial giant into a fourth-rate nation of small farmers." After listing the key points of the Morgenthau Plan, *Time* then added on its own that "no reconstruction of railroads or factories within Germany would be permitted," that "Germany would be occupied by Russian, British and American troops for a generation," and that "there would be

33. Ibid.
34. A term used by John J. McCloy when discussing the Morgenthau Plan with the writer in November 1967.
35. Stimson, p. 582; Byrnes, pp. 180–85.
36. Hammond, pp. 361–62.
37. Philip E. Mosely refers to the incident as "the Will-o'-the-Wisp of the Morgenthau Plan." Mosely, "The Occupation of Germany," p. 596.

no reparations because Germany would not be allowed to earn payments in the future." The journal concluded that "this was barely above the level to sterilize all Germans and indeed a Carthaginian peace. However, Morgenthau, who has Eleanor Roosevelt's ear, believes that Germany must be destroyed as Carthage was." [38]

Clearly the publicity around the Morgenthau Plan was grist for Dr. Goebbels's propaganda mills. In the first broadcast after the plan's publication, the Berlin radio said that occupation by American and British forces with all its continuous hunger would be worse than the bomb terror. And Hitler's *Völkische Beobachter* added that while Clemenceau had said there were 23 million Germans too many, Morgenthau wanted to see 43 million Germans exterminated.[39]

As far as the image of the United States abroad was concerned, it was most unfortunate that in the forum of world opinion Dr. Goebbels from then on had the floor to himself. There were no official statements from the American side making it clear that the Morgenthau Plan had been dropped nor were any alternative occupational policies published. To the extent that silence is considered consent, the general public in Germany, and for that matter in other parts of the world, was allowed to believe that the United States indeed was preparing for the occupation of Germany in a spirit of hate and revenge. Even the downfall of the Third Reich did not bring about a change because, in spite of the deputy military governor's urgent requests for the removal of the security classification, the U.S. government chose to remain silent on its plans for the occupation. As General Clay pointed out, it was "most difficult to convince American press representatives in Germany that Military Government was not conducting its administration on the basis of expedience." [40] The inept handling of the whole affair might indeed be cited as a textbook example of psychological warfare in the reverse.

By October 1945, when the basic Joint Chief of Staff Directive No. 1067 was finally declassified, the news value of the issue had been largely dissipated and the stereotype of a vengeful American ruling clique was firmly established in the German mind. Also there remained enough people who had a vested interest in keeping this image alive; their ranks were soon to be joined by the foreign minister of the Soviet Union, who, at the Foreign Ministers Conference in Paris in July 1946, sanctimoniously declared that it would be a mistake to plan for Ger-

38. "The Policy of Hate," *Time* 44, no. 14 (2 Oct. 1944), p. 19.
39. *Washington Post,* 26 Sept 1944, p. 4.
40. Clay, p. 17.

many's agrarianization and destruction of its main industrial centers. The Soviet Union's purpose was not to destroy Germany but to transform it into a democratic and peace-loving state which, in addition to its agriculture, would have its own industry and foreign trade.[41]

The first headlines mentioning the Morgenthau Plan had just appeared in the American press when on September 24, 1944, the War Department's Civil Affairs Division submitted to the Joint Chiefs of Staff the draft of a "Directive to the Supreme Commander Allied Expeditionary Force Regarding the Military Government of Germany in the Period Immediately Following the Cessation of Organized Resistance." This was the first version of JCS/1067, the directive which, with major changes imposed by the Potsdam Declaration, was to remain in force for more than two years. The actual drafting process of the document had begun on September 2, 1944, when the three assistant secretaries of war, navy, and state agreed that, regardless of impending high-level discussions, interim instructions for the treatment of Germany should be sent promptly to General Eisenhower and remain in force until a long-term policy was decided upon.[42] In order to avoid later complications, Treasury representatives were invited to participate in the deliberations. In a report to the Joint Chiefs of Staff which accompanied the interim directive, the director of the Civil Affairs Division remarked that the European Advisory Commission was currently working on a tripartite control machinery for Germany, but so far had given no guidance "upon which SHAEF would formulate a program and policies for the Military Government of Germany." In view of the urgency of the situation, the Civil Affairs Division recommended an early approval of the draft by the Joint Chiefs of Staff and its transmittal to the secretary of state with the suggestion that a copy be forwarded to the U.S. Representative in the EAC (Ambassador John Winant) for his information and guidance.

The first version of JCS/1067 emphasized that, pending the receipt of directives with long-range policies, the objectives of the Military Government had to be of short term and military in character in order not to prejudice whatever ultimate policies might later be determined. Listed as the main objectives of the occupation were the elimination of Nazism and militarism, the apprehension of war criminals for punishment, and industrial disarmament. In the section dealing with economic matters, the supreme commander was ordered to assure production, provision, and distribution of supplies essential for preventing disease and civil

41. Byrnes, p. 179.   42. Hammond, p. 371.

unrest, always making maximum use of available supplies and resources in order to limit imports. The production of goods for the prosecution of the war against Japan was to be assured and the dissipation or sabotage of German resources needed for relief, restitution, or repatriation to be prevented. The draft said that no steps were to be taken to rehabilitate, maintain, or strengthen the German economy. The responsibility for such economic problems as price controls, rationing, unemployment, etc., was to remain with the German people. In Appendix D, dealing with relief, the supreme commander was made responsible for the provision and distribution of food supplies for civilian relief only to the extent necessary to prevent disease and such disorder as might endanger or impede military occupation. German consumption was to be held to a minimum "so as to make surplus of agricultural products available to devastated countries of Europe."

It is noteworthy that the original War Department draft would have authorized the supreme commander to control financial institutions, industry, agriculture, utilities, transportation, and communication facilities to maintain the German economy in working order and prevent disease and unrest. Under the influence of the Treasury, however, this authority was drastically curtailed. By contrast a Treasury draft had endeavored to prevent the use of the disease-and-unrest formula as an escape clause by stipulating that positive efforts in behalf of the German economy were permissible only in order to prevent *"epidemic"* or *"serious"* disease and *"serious"* civil unrest (author's italics). Upon the insistence of the War Department, these limiting words were omitted.[43] Interestingly enough, a copy of the interim directive was forwarded by the State Department to John Winant, the American ambassador in London, in his capacity as "officer in charge of the American Mission in the United Kingdom," with the provision that it was "not transmitted for submission to the European Advisory Commission."

The most significant aspects of the document were the broad authority given to the American Zone commander and the establishment of a hands-off policy as far as the German economy was concerned. Both facets were acceptable to the Department of State as long as they pertained only to the first brief period of occupation subsequent to the surrender. For the long term, however, the State Department advocated firm and detailed tripartite agreements which, of course, would have greatly curtailed the authority of the zone commanders.

Probably the most vociferous proponent of the latter course of action

43. Ibid., p. 372.

was the American ambassador in London. Its most influential opponent was the president of the United States, who on October 20, 1944, in a letter to the secretary of state, had the following to say on the subject:

> I think it is all very well for us to make all kinds of preparation for the treatment of Germany but there are some matters in regard to such treatment that lead me to believe that speed on these matters is not essential at the persent moment. It may be in a week, or it may be in a month or it may be several months hence. I dislike making detailed plans for a country which we do not yet occupy. . . . Much of this is dependent on what we and the Allies find when we get into Germany—and we are not there yet.[44]

Accordingly and in spite of considerable pressure exerted by the Department of State, there was little progress during the next six months as far as the negotiation of long-term policies was concerned. During that time the War Department, with the assistance of State and a very influential participation by the secretary of the treasury, proceeded with revisions of the interim directive.

If one wishes to assume—and it is quite an assumption—that in the course of these six months, detailed and effective occupational policies could have been negotiated with the Russians, the British, and finally the French, the presidential policy "of no policy" is open to strong criticism. On the other hand, in the interests of historical objectivity the following points ought to be made. As a prominent American historian wrote, there was doubt as to the authority of the Executive to commit the United States on matters which are usually settled in treaties of peace; and there was also uncertainty regarding the degree to which American public opinion would be willing to maintain responsibility for specific European problems.[45] Furthermore, as the writer can personally testify, there were the bitter battles at Arnheim and in the Ardennes. By the end of September 1944 Field Marshal Montgomery's attempt to outflank the central German armies by crossing the Rhine at Arnheim to bring the war to an early end had aborted, and in December von Rundstedt almost retook Liège. On the American side there was a mad scramble for infantry replacements, U.S. stockades in England being combed for combatants and Air Force personnel being drafted as infantry. At Saint-Vith near Bastogne the major elements of the 106th Infantry

44. The President to the Secretary of State, 20 Oct. 1944, in *Foreign Relations of the United States; The Conferences at Malta and Yalta,* p. 158.
45. Mosely, p. 581.

Division surrendered to the Germans after a brief fight. We indeed were not there yet, and we certainly did not know what we would find. Was there going to be a guerrilla warfare by the Werwolf, as American intelligence estimates indicated, or would we run into a fanatically defended German redoubt in the Bavarian and Austrian Alps? [46]

The original version of JCS/1067 was revised twice. In January 1944 a State-War-Navy coordinating committee of assistant secretaries, after clearance by the Treasury, amended the original paper with the statement that the authority of the Control Council would be paramount and that the commanders would enforce its decisions in their respective zones of occupation. The economic section of the January document also went into greater detail, and the authority to control wages, prices, fiscal and monetary affairs in order to prevent inflation was added.[47] The second and final revision was accomplished in March and April by a newly formed informal policy committee consisting of Army, Navy, State, Treasury, and Foreign Economic Administration (FEA) representatives; in recognition of a possible deadlock of the Control Council, it authorized the American Zone commander to decide policy in the absence of a Control Council agreement. Upon insistence of the Treasury, the authority to control inflation was again curtailed, however, by inserting the following clause: "Prevention or restraint of inflation shall not constitute an additional ground for the importation of supplies, nor shall it constitute an additional ground for limiting removal, destruction or curtailment of productive facilities in fulfillment of the program for reparations, demilitarization and industrial disarmament." [48]

Although JCS/1067 was issued in its final form on May 14, 1945, it was declassified for general publication only on October 17, 1945, that is, five months after the end of hostilities. It consisted of a general-political, an economic, and a financial part, as well as a preamble which stated that the four commanders in chief "acting jointly," would constitute the Control Council, the supreme organ of control over Germany. The basic objectives were listed in paragraph 4, as follows:

> a. It should be brought home to the Germans that Germany's ruthless warfare and the fanatical Nazi resistance had destroyed

---

46. Hammond (p. 410) offers this comment: "Moreover, the unknowns of the future—the conditions in Germany, the American public temper towards the continuing foreign involvements and the fate of the Big-Three coalition to mention a few—placed a premium on the maintenance of freedom of action for Roosevelt, at least so it appears in retrospect." John L. Snell, in his *Wartime Origins of the East-West Dilemma Over Germany,* p. 102, considered Roosevelt's approach a "policy of postponement."

47. Ibid., p. 403.   48. Ibid., p. 425.

the German economy and made chaos and suffering inevitable and that the Germans cannot escape responsibility for what they have brought upon themselves.

b. Germany will not be occupied for the purpose of liberation but as a defeated enemy nation. Your aim is not oppression but to occupy Germany for the purpose of realizing certain important Allied objectives. In the conduct of your occupation and administration you should be firm and aloof. You will strongly discourage fraternization with the German officials and population.

c. The principal Allied objective is to prevent Germany from ever becoming a threat to the peace of the world. Essential steps in the accomplishment of this objective are the elimination of Nazism and militarism in all their forms, the immediate apprehension of war criminals for punishment, the industrial disarmament and demilitarization of Germany with continuing control over Germany's capacity to make war, and the preparation for an eventual reconstruction of German political life on a democratic basis.

d. Allied objectives are to enforce the program of reparation and restitution to provide relief for the benefit of countries devastated by Nazi aggression and to ensure that prisoners of war and displaced persons of the United Nations are cared for and repatriated.[49]

It is not likely that the drafters of JCS/1067 had much difficulty with this part of the directive, since it reflected frequently announced United States policies directed toward the eradication of Nazism, the punishment of war criminals, disarmament, and demilitarization. While establishing some ground rules for the enforcement of reparations, the directive did not get into specifics, which were left for quadripartite decision. In the same vein, the subject of territorial changes was not touched upon.

The most controversial aspects of JCS/1067 were in the area of economic administration. Paragraph 5, which dealt with economic controls, said that

you will be guided by the principle that controls upon the German economy may be imposed to the extent that such controls may be essential to protect the safety and meet the needs of the occupying forces and ensure the production and maintenance of goods and

49. von Oppen, ed., *Documents on Germany* p. 15.

services required to prevent starvation or such disease and unrest as would endanger these forces. No action will be taken in execution of the reparations program or otherwise which would tend to support basic living conditions in Germany on a higher level than that existing in any of the neighboring countries.

Part II said that the commander in chief would assure that

the German economy is administered and controlled in such a way as to accomplish the basic objectives listed in above-mentioned two paragraphs. Economic controls should be imposed only to the extent necessary to accomplish these objectives, provided that the Commander-in-Chief would impose controls in the full extent necessary to achieve the industrial disarmament of Germany. Except as may be necessary to carry out these objectives, no steps will be taken, *a*) leading toward the economic rehabilitation of Germany or, *b*) designed to maintain or strengthen the German economy.

These harsh terms were somewhat modified by the section dealing with the German standard of living:

You will estimate requirements of supplies necessary to prevent starvation or widespread disease or such civil unrest as would endanger the occupying forces. Such estimates will be based on a program whereby the Germans are made responsible for providing for themselves out of their own work and resources. You will take all practicable economic and police measures to assure that German resources are fully utilized and consumption held to a minimum in order that imports may be strictly limited and that surpluses may be made available for the occupying forces and displaced persons and United Nations prisoners of war and for reparations. You will take no action that would tend to support basic living standards in Germany on a higher level than that existing in any of the neighboring United Nations and you will take appropriate measures to ensure that basic living standards of the German people are not higher than those existing in any of the neighboring United Nations when such measures will contribute to raising the standards of any such nation.

Since the days of the directive's enactment in 1945, practically all comments on JCS/1067 have been unfavorable, if not sharply negative.

Initially, because of the document's fallacious premise of a viable and robust German economy, its most vocal critics were among the Military Government officers who were responsible for its implementation. In later years they were joined by a number of scholars who have made it their task to scrutinize American occupational policies. Their comments ranged from "not a statesmanlike document" [50] "a heavy millstone around the neck of American Military Government," [51] to "modified Morgenthau Plan," [52] "watered-down Morgenthau Plan," [53] and "unjustifiable." [54] As described above, JCS/1067, while drafted by the War Department, was the product of a number of compromises between drastically divergent schools of thought. As any drafting officer who ever had to prepare a paper under such circumstances knows, it is next to impossible to give the final product the clarity and unity of purpose which a "statesmanlike document" would demand. In order to gain the concurrence of War, Navy, State, Treasury, and the White House, JCS/1067 had to satisfy many co-authors, a requirement which is reflected in its text and which critics ought to keep in mind.

As for being a "millstone around the neck of American Military Government," the directive was no obstacle when, from the first days of the occupation, it became necessary to feed the German people through extensive imports at the expense of the American and British taxpayers. It also was no impediment to the early efforts of the American Military Government toward the reconstruction of the German economy, to be described in some of the following chapters. Undoubtedly, the denazification measures initiated by the directive were a handicap in the early reconstruction days; however, at least as the writer sees it, it was a case where whatever the American policy might have been, violent criticism from some quarters would have emerged. As it turned out, in the long run the Germans themselves were often less lenient in these matters than their former enemies.

Regarding the "diluted Morgenthau Plan," we have seen that the proposals advanced by Morgenthau entailed long-range policies directed toward the permanent dismemberment of Germany and the reduction of its people to a mere subsistence level. JCS/1067, by comparison, was not concerned with territorial changes at all. As to the German standard of living, it instructed the military governor to ensure that "it would not

50. Walter L. Dorn, "The Debate Over American Occupational Policy in Germany, 1944–1945," p. 482.
51. Harold Zink, *The United States in Germany,* p. 94.
52. Clay, p. 11.
53. Wallich, p. 345.   54. Zink, p. 357.

be on a higher level than that existing in any of the neighboring United Nations," which of course is quite different from the pastoral Germany which Morgenthau had in mind. (Contrary to the hands-off policy of the original document, the final version authorized some economic controls.)

Most important, JCS/1067 was drafted as an interim directive pertaining only "to the initial post-defeat period." As such it was "not intended to be an ultimate statement of policies of this Government concerning the treatment of Germany in the post-war world."

The preamble continued:

> It is therefore essential that you assure that surveys are constantly maintained of economic, industrial, financial, social, and political conditions within your zone and that the results of such surveys are made available to your Government through the Joint Chiefs of Staff. These surveys should be developed in such a manner as to serve as a basis for determining changes in the measure of control set forth herein as well as for the progressive formulation and development of policies to promote the basic objectives of the United States.

On the other hand, it is a matter of record that Henry Morgenthau exerted considerable influence on the final draft of JCS/1067,[55] a development also confirmed by John J. McCloy, who emphasized that "the influence of the Secretary of the Treasury was reflected in the negative parts of the directive." [56] JCS/1067 nevertheless remained and should be defined as a War Department document. It is true that its economic paragraphs had been greatly hardened on the insistence of the secretary of the treasury, but at the same time it retained a necessary flexibility through the insertion of escape clauses.

As to the comment "unjustifiable," we should remember that there had been general agreement within the cabinet that Germany was to be treated as a defeated nation and that the initial terms of the occupation ought to be punitive. Although there was no causal connection, it also must be said that the directive was completed during the closing months of the war, that is, at a time when some of the worst Nazi-generated atrocities, formerly only rumored, had become confirmed by the hard evidence of visual inspection.

55. Dorn, p. 500.
56. Interview with the writer, 30 Nov. 1967.

Two other comments on JCS/1067 ought to be mentioned because of their source. Henry Stimson, whose department was responsible for the drafting of the directive, considered it in the spring of 1945 "a fairly good paper," but two years later referred to it as "painfully negative." [57] Actually the two statements are less contradictory than they would seem. JCS/1067 can be considered a good document because it avoided the pitfalls of extremism rampant in some Washington quarters during the war, and because its drafters were wise enough to make it an interim directive as well as a flexible instrument. As such it permitted the enactment of occupational practices often quite contrary to those which harsh peace advocates in Washington had originally envisaged. By the same token, its general tone was mainly negative, a factor which will be examined below and which, taking its origin as a wartime document into account, probably was unavoidable.

Much has been made of the fact that, contrary to its preamble, JCS/1067 remained the controlling directive for American occupational policies in Germany for more than two years. Although General Lucius Clay also expressed some misgivings on this point,[58] such criticism fails to withstand closer scrutiny. First, as shown below, Clay's negative comments on JCS/1067 are at variance with his official communications on the same subject in December 1945. And second, as the record indicates, the principal reason for leaving the interim directive unchanged for more than two years was the fact that, while most of the economic principles established in Potsdam paralleled those enunciated in JCS/1067, the conference actually produced several important addenda.

Potsdam established that during the period of occupation Germany was to be treated as an economic unit; furthermore, that measures were to be taken promptly to effect essential repairs of transport, to enlarge coal production, to maximize agricultural output, and to effect emergency repair of housing and essential utilities. Finally, Potsdam expressly stated that the payment of reparations should leave enough resources to enable the German people to subsist without external assistance. "In working out the economic balance of Germany," the Potsdam agreement said, "the necessary means must be provided to pay for imports approved by the Control Council in Germany. The proceeds of exports from current production and stock shall be available in the first place for payment of such imports."

57. Stimson, p. 582.   58. Clay, p. 72.

It must be stressed that, contrary to the views of some sources,[59] it was not up to the deputy military governor to choose between the Potsdam Declaration and JCS/1067 whenever the respective policies differed. This was made clear at an early date by Clay's legal adviser, whose office on August 9, 1946, submitted the following opinion:

SUBJECT: Effect of Tripartite (Potsdam) Agreement of 2 August 1945 on JCS/1067

1. Reference is made to Brigadier Meade's memorandum of 7 August 1945, requesting my opinion on the question whether the Potsdam Agreement supersedes the JCS/1067 Series or whether the provisions of both must be followed in connection with Military Government operations in the United States Zone.

2. The Agreement concluded in Potsdam, August 2, 1945, and approved by the President of the United States, the Chairman of the Council of the People's Commissars of the Union of Soviet Socialistic Republics, and by the Prime Minister of Great Britain, constitutes not only an agreement between these principals on behalf of their respective governments, but also must be considered the policy and instructions for the United States in the United States Zone of occupation and, in matters affecting Germany as a whole, for the representative of the United States on the Control Council. The Agreement supersedes JCS/1067 to the extent that the Agreement covers matters dealt with in JCS/1067; that is to say, the Agreement shall prevail in all respects in which its provisions are in conflict with JCS/1067. Since, however, the latter has not been rescinded by the United States, its provisions remain effective to the extent not in conflict with the Agreement.

3. Doubt might arise as to whether or not in particular respects conflict exists. In such instances the question must be considered in the light of the particular terms of the several documents involved; and may be made the subject of a separate opinion if desired.[60]

At a later date, the Department of State issued a similar interpretation.[61] In other words, *de jure* and *de facto,* JCS/1067 was the exclusive controlling directive for the Military Government only from May 14 until August 2, 1945.

59. Zink, p. 94.
60. Memorandum, Charles Fahy, Legal Adviser, HQ, US Group Control Council (Germany) to Assistant Deputy of Public Services, 9 Aug. 1945 (OMGUS records, 4-35/16).
61. von Oppen, *Documents on Germany,* p. 13.

On December 2, 1945, Brigadier General Bryan L. Milburn, General Clay's chief of staff, circulated a memorandum among all the divisions of the Office of Military Government for Germany, United States (OMGUS), requesting suggestions as to a revision of JCS/1067. As the memorandum indicated, it had been prompted by a query from the War Department [62] to which Clay had sent an interim reply stating that "on the whole, JCS/1067 as modified by Potsdam had proved workable. I don't know how we could have set up our Military Government without JCS/1067." [63] The final answer from OMGUS, dated December 10, 1945, is quoted in part:

> Subject is modfication of JCS/1067. As stated previously we prefer amendment of present paper rather than complete rewriting as latter would necessitate many changes in basic directives and instructions already issued here. We have found JCS/1067 as modified by Potsdam a workable policy with minor exceptions. We prefer that JCS/1067 not incorporate many interpretations of details which have resulted from exchange of cables, such as the details of our restitution policy, as the defining of these interpretations tends to destroy flexibility of directive.
>
> Recently State Department has issued to its field offices an interpretation of Potsdam economic policy. This statement which is fully within Potsdam Protocol is different in tone from previous statements but in full agreement with our own interpretation of Potsdam which we have been applying to our studies here for some weeks. What we need rather than drastic changes in directives, is full support at home to this interpretation of economic policy. Moreover changes in our directives are not so important now as the establishment of central administrative machinery, which is the real stumbling block to further progress.

The proposed changes which followed entailed in essence merely an adaptation of JCS/1067 to the superseding paragraphs of Potsdam.[64]

Since Clay had acknowledged that he could live with JCS/1067 as it was, the War Department finally decided not to attempt a rewriting of

---

62. The War Department query had been prompted by Byron Price's report of 9 Nov. 1945 to President Truman. Price, a wartime director of censorship had visited Germany as the president's personal representative and had returned with a pessimistic appraisal of American occupational policies. Memorandum, Byron Price to the President (OMGUS records, 177-3/3).

63. Memorandum, Milburn to all divisions (OMGUS records, shipment 16). Gimbel regards Clay's reply as "crucial" John Gimbel, *The American Occupation of Germany* p. 5.

64. Clay to Hilldring, 10 Dec. 1945, Cable CC-20130, CAD (OMGUS records, 358-2/5).

the directive at the time. The reasons for this decision can be found in an OMGUS memorandum of February 27, 1946, addressed to General Clay's chief of staff by a staff secretary, Lt. Colonel Walter L. McKee.[65] The relevant paragraphs of the memorandum are quoted in full:

1. During my temporary duty in Washington the matter of revising JCS/1067 in light of the exchange of cables between General Clay and General Hilldring was discussed at length.

2. General Hilldring, others in Civil Affairs Division and the undersigned were agreed that it would be advisable to have a document such as JCS/1067 serve as the basic statement of policy with a possible supplement, the supplement to include those portions of the Potsdam agreement not covered in JCS/1067. Most of those in Washington seem to think that it might be even better to take the Potsdam agreement as the basic document and include in the supplement those portions of JCS/1067 not covered in the Potsdam Agreement.

3. The suggestion made by this Headquarters that JCS/1067 should be revised by incorporating directly in it certain portions of the Potsdam Agreement, was also carefully considered.

4. The discussions in the Civil Affairs Division, and I understand the same view is held by the State Department, resulted in the conclusion that it would be inadvisable at this time to attempt either of the procedures set forth in paragraphs 2 or 3 above. The reasons were:

a. It would be extremely difficult to draft a supplement of either JCS/1067 or the Potsdam Agreement and it would also be difficult to attempt to write a new document which would be a reconciliation of JCS/1067 and the Potsdam Agreement. There are in Washington at this time no personnel who could be conveniently assigned to this task.

b. Both JCS/1067 and the Potsdam Agreement represented a very large amount of work by the State, War, Navy and Treasury Departments at the highest levels with final reference to the President. It is thought that any revision or reconciliation of these documents would have to run the same gamut with consequent delay and possibly dubious results.

65. Memorandum, McKee to Chief of Staff. (OMGUS records, 1067 Correspondence).

    c. Both JCS/1067 and the Potsdam Agreement have been publicized in the newspapers and elsewhere. Any revisions of those documents would also probably get into the Press. It is felt that publicity resulting from such publication would not be advantageous.

    d. General Clay has indicated in his communications to the War Department that it is possible for Military Government in Germany to operate satisfactorily without any revision or reconciliation of the two main policy documents. It is therefore felt that the matter is not of great urgency.

    5. My understanding is that unless further action is taken by this Headquarters vis-a-vis War Department, no revision or reconciliation will be attempted.

This settled the question of revising JCS/1067. Nevertheless, the changing political climate heralded by the Stuttgart speech of the American secretary of state called for the eventual elimination of a basically negative approach to the German problem.[66] Accordingly, JCS/1067 was rescinded in July 1947 and replaced by JCS/1779, a directive which rather than causing a change of policy merely provided the formal confirmation of a *de facto* situation.[67]

66. Cables in OMGUS records: Clay to CAD, 19 July 1946 (177-1/3); CAD to Clay, 13 Aug. 1946 (5-2/1); and Clay to CAD, 16 Aug. 1946 (177-3/3).
67. Hammond, p. 446.

CHAPTER TWO

"TO PREVENT DISEASE AND UNREST"

Under the terms of the Treaty of Versailles, the German Reich lost Alsace-Lorraine, part of Silesia, Danzig, and all its colonies. The Saarland was taken by France temporarily. Germany in this manner had to give up 74.5 percent of its domestic iron ore, 68.1 percent of its zinc ore, 26 percent of its coal production, and 14.6 percent of its arable land. A substantial part of its textile industry was taken by the annexation of Alsace-Lorraine. Also seized were its merchant marine and all its overseas investments, both important sources of foreign exchange. In addition, Germany was forced to surrender one quarter of its fishing fleet, one fifth of its river fleet, 5,000 locomotives, and 150,000 railroad cars.

For several years the Allies were unable to reach an agreement among themselves regarding the sum of Germany's war debts. It is indicative of the prevailing political climate, however, that one of the early proposals suggested annual payments almost equal to Germany's 1913 exports, a plan which would have meant a doubling of its prewar exports while maintaining the prewar import level. In April 1921, at last, the reparation debt was fixed at $30 billion, a sum which, according to a scholarly evaluation by John Maynard Keynes, was three times Germany's maximum capacity to pay.[1]

The reparation plan was presented in the form of an ultimatum which threatened that the Ruhr would be occupied if Germany failed to sign within six days. Thus forced into submission, the vanquished country met the prescribed payment schedule for more than a year. By the summer of 1922, however, economic conditions had deteriorated to such an extent that the German government asked for a moratorium. The request was not granted; instead French and Belgian troops marched into the Ruhr and seized the German mines. Germany's response was a policy of passive resistance financed by the printing presses and leading

1. John Maynard Keynes, *The Economic Consequences of the Peace*, p. 200.

to the complete collapse of the national currency, already seriously weakened by the war.

In April 1921, when the reparation ultimatum was presented, the rate was 62 marks to the dollar (4.20 marks was par). After the French occupation of the Ruhr in January 1923, the value of the mark had dropped to 40,000 to the dollar, and from then on continued to slide with ever-increasing speed. In July it was 200,000; in August, 5 million; and in September, 100 million. By the time the policy of passive resistance came to an end, the exchange rate for one dollar was 4.2 trillion marks. During the last months of the galloping inflation 300 paper mills were busy manufacturing note paper and 2000 printing presses operated day and night.

Since all property invested at fixed money values—deposits in savings banks, government bonds, mortgages, etc.—became worthless, broad strata of the German society, especially the middle classes, were rapidly expropriated. The traumatic experience of this period, when a suitcase of paper money was needed to settle a small debt and the value of the currency fell from hour to hour, left an indelible impression on old and young alike. Twenty-two years later, the vivid recollection of those years was one of the psychological problems with which American occupational authorities had to contend.

In November 1923 a new currency, the Rentenmark, was introduced. Shortly afterwards, a reparations committee under the chairmanship of General Charles C. Dawes, later vice-president of the United States, worked out a provisional reparations plan which gave Germany a breathing spell, greatly reduced its initial payments, and, in addition, provided it with an international loan of $200 million. The fact that an American banking expert, Parker Gilbert, was named general agent of reparations and, together with an international transfer committee, supervised German finances from Berlin, created confidence within international banking circles and to a considerable degree was responsible for the extraordinary inflow of American capital into Germany during the following years. It has been estimated that Germany, from 1924 up to the Hoover moratorium in July 1931, paid 10,821,000,000 marks in reparations as compared with an influx of short-term and long-term foreign loans totaling 20,500,000,000.[2] In other words, foreign resources more than provided for reparations payments. In addition, the influx of foreign capital enabled Germany to modernize and enlarge its

2. Gustav Stolper, *The German Economy, 1870–1940*, p. 179.

factories, to rebuild a merchant fleet, and in spite of its great territorial losses, to exceed its pre-1914 level of exports.

When the foreign loans stopped in 1931, the house of cards promptly collapsed, and one third of the German working population soon found itself without work. In 1933, at the time of Hitler's ascendancy, Germany had six million registered unemployed. The National Socialist regime was able to solve the problem by an extensive rearmament program so that on the eve of World War II only 164,000 persons in Germany were listed as unemployed.

To summarize, Germany prospered after 1923 only because of extraneous economic circumstances, and since it had no healthy civilian economy between the two wars, it was only reasonable to expect that conditions at the end of World War II would be even worse. Also, since most of the capital invested under Hitler had gone into war industries, it was evident that even under the best possible conditions a long period of readjustment would be needed after the war. In addition, the tremendous damage inflicted by several years of saturation bombing had to be considered.

Few if any of the American officers assigned to Military Government were fully prepared for what they had to face. Guided by JCS/1067, which implied the existence of a robust and virile German economy, and still influenced by the persuasive aura of Nazi Germany's military victories, they were in for an agonizing reappraisal of their mission when assuming their posts. The country they faced was an economic wreck.

Central and state governments had ceased to exist, and neither city nor *Land* administrations were able to function. Prominent Nazis who had occupied public office or important private positions had fled. There was no mail service, and the communication as well as the transportation system had been taken over by the occupying armies. In the American Zone there were more than 2.5 million displaced persons waiting to be repatriated to their home countries. And while this was being done, additional millions of refugees poured into West Germany from the eastern parts of Europe. The German cities were in ruins. In Hannover, to cite one example of many, more than three fifths of all dwellings had been destroyed and only five out of a hundred remained untouched. Half of the business houses, 80 percent of the public buildings and 60 percent of the industrial works had been destroyed. Only four out of eighty-seven school buildings were intact. The supply of water, gas, and electricity was nearly nonexistent, and there was no more street lighting.

As an American observer saw it:

> What used to be city blocks looked like unfinished airports, huge piles of rubble, or endless rows of empty, burnt-out structural shells. At night the jagged ruins reached into the sky like twisted fingers of a leprous hand, as a sickening smell rose from the wreckage of the houses that had become the graves of their erstwhile owners. In these fantastic surroundings, the surviving population moved like ghosts—pale, silent, sullen, their spirits broken, their hopes shattered. In daylight their somber faces revealed the long, slow grind of the war, deprivation, the terrors of ceaseless bombings, the horrors of endless devastation, the loss of loved ones, and utter defeat. Their step was leaden, their nerves inert. Their eyes, dead and full of despair, seemed to ask whether the nightmare was finally over, and what further suffering was still in store for them—if the victors would take away from them the few belongings which they had been able to salvage from the ravages of war.[3]

At the end of July, nearly two months after the surrender, less than 10 percent of the industrial plants in the U.S. Zone were operating. About half of these plants were lumber mills supplying military requirements, lumber for housing repairs, and pit props for coal mining operations in the Ruhr. In many cases production for military requirements was accomplished only through the use of communications, transportation facilities, and coal furnished by the army. Most other production was simply the processing of materials and the assembly of parts on hand.[4] The most serious problem facing the occupying authorities was the food situation. Early surveys of available food supplies revealed that only 950 calories per day could be distributed to the average non-self-supplier. Since this also encompassed priority categories such as heavy laborers entitled to larger rations, only 720 calories were available for the so-called "normal consumer." This was less than half the amount which public health advisers of Military Government considered an essential minimum for the maintenance of a working population. Even pessimistic forecasts by agricultural experts had not foreseen such a disastrous emergency.

The powerful German Reich had been deficient in food production from the very first days of its foundation, and prior to 1914 it had

---

3. Hubert Meurer, "U.S. Military Government in Germany," p. 2.
4. *OMGUS, Trade and Commerce*, 20 Aug. 1945.

required an annual import of 12 million tons of foodstuffs. It was essentially this weakness in Germany's economic armor which had hastened the defeat of the Central Powers in World War I. Hence, when Hitler came to power, his government went to great pains to achieve autarky in the agricultural field. Farmers were extensively subsidized, heath and moor land was reclaimed, low land was drained, and natural as well as chemical fertilizers were applied intensively. However, in spite of these vigorous efforts to increase domestic production, self-sufficiency in food came to only 83 percent prior to World War II, as compared to 80 percent at the outbreak of World War I. And even this level of agricultural production was achieved only by the importation of substantial quantities of food and fodder for the livestock population. In balance, the total of Germany's food and fodder imports in the last production year before the war accounted for not less than one third of its total food consumption.[5]

On the eve of World War II, the German leaders, most anxious to avoid the mistakes of their imperial predecessors, promptly organized an extensive food-rationing system which was built around a "normal consumer" ration of approximately 2000 calories per day. It was the same level which five years later public health advisers of OMGUS considered the minimum to avoid "disease and unrest" and to maintain existing standards of health. As long as the victorious German armies were able to live off the land in occupied territories and, in addition, to requisition food to bolster domestic food supplies, rations for the German civilian population were maintained at the prescribed levels. By January 1945, however, Germany's military and economic situation had worsened sufficiently to require a reduction of the "normal-consumer" ration to 1620 calories, and in May, when the war ended, it had dropped to 1000 calories.[6]

Naturally, the agricultural advisers of the American Military Government had been aware of this basic weakness, although they had not foreseen the complete exhaustion of Germany's national economy after five years of war. Nor could they have anticipated the emergency conditions created by the separation of the eastern provinces and the influx of seven million refugees from the East. During the years 1933–37, the area east of the Oder-Neisse line, although it contained only 14 percent of the population, actually produced 25 percent of

5. "History of Military Government: VE Day to June 30, 1946: chap. 8. Economics: pt. 6. Food and Agriculture Branch," p. 55.
6. Ibid., p. 46.

Germany's food output. Approximately one million tons of breadgrains, a little less than one million tons of potatoes and 400,000 tons of sugar annually came from the regions which at the war's end became the Soviet Zone of Germany and the area east of the Oder-Neisse Rivers annexed by Poland. In addition, annual imports from abroad in the American and British Zones had averaged 700,000 tons of breadgrains, 1.2 million tons of food grains, 1.5 million tons of oil seed, and large quantities of fruit, vegetables, rice, chocolate, coffee, etc.[7] In other words, the loss of the breadbasket provinces of East Germany in addition to the increase of the West German population by more than 20 percent created a food crisis of such magnitude that the Western Allies were often hard pressed to cope with it.

The controlling Washington directive for the occupation, read against this background of economic chaos and impending starvation, left key Military Government personnel with a feeling of utter frustration. As we have seen, its general tone and basic approach were essentially negative, and an initial interpretation indicated that it clearly and specifically prohibited Military Government officers from taking any steps directed toward the rehabilitation or maintenance of the German economy.[8] There is probably no more convincing example of the resulting disenchantment and deep concern among the top echelons of the Military Government than General Clay's own account of his reaction and that of his first financial adviser, Lewis Douglas. As the deputy military governor writes, the two men had no misgivings as to the punitive provisions of JCS/1067, such as the dissolution of the Nazi party, the annulment of Nazi laws, the disbandment of the German army, the arrest and trial of war criminals, the automatic arrest of all high-ranking officials of the Third Reich, and Germany's industrial disarmament. They were, however, shocked at the seeming failure of American policy makers to "grasp the realities and economic conditions which confronted Military Government." It appeared obvious to them that Germany would starve unless prompt actions were taken to revive its industrial production. And, as Lucius Clay initially interpreted his instructions, he was "specifically forbidden to take such steps." [9]

Upon his request, Lewis Douglas returned to Washington in order to discuss with John J. McCloy—Douglas's brother-in-law—a possible

---

7. Hoover Report—"Food and Agriculture U.S.–U.K. Zone of Germany," Feb. 1947 p. 9.
8. Clay, *Decision in Germany*, p. 17.   9. Ibid., p. 18.

modification of the economic sections of JCS/1067. When this attempt failed, Douglas resigned. Lucius Clay and his military associates, even had they wanted to, were in no position to follow his example. Faced with two impossible alternatives, namely, the administering of mass starvation under the aegis of the American flag or the open violation of military orders, they were obliged to move in a third direction tradition-ally unfamiliar to the military mind, namely a painstaking legal analysis of their orders. As indicated, Clay had no reservations as far as JCS/1067's military provisions were concerned, and there could be no objections to the basic Allied objective to prevent Germany from be-coming a threat to the world again. Also, in view of the eonomic realities which confronted the Military Government, several key sections of the directive had become of academic significance only. Evidently there was no point in talking about a "support of basic living conditions in Germany on a higher level than that existing in any of the neighboring United Nations." It was somewhat unrealistic to worry about surpluses "which would be made available for the occupying forces and displaced persons," and, as it appeared in 1945, it was rather nonsensical to order "appropriate measures to ensure that basic living standards of the German people are not higher than those existing in any of the neighbor-ing United Nations."

The section which seemed to tie the hands of the Military Govern-ment most completely was contained in paragraph 16 which stated, "you will take no steps a) looking toward the economic rehabilitation of Germany, or b) designed to maintain or strengthen the German econ-omy *except as may be necessary to accomplish the basic objectives set forth in paragraphs 4 and 5*" (author's italics). The same paragraph, furthermore, instructed the military governor "to ensure that the Ger-man economy is administered in such a way as to accomplish these basic objectives." A scrutiny of the objectives as specified in paragraph 4, namely "preventing Germany from becoming again a threat to the world," and "repatriation of prisoners of war and of displaced persons" provided little comfort for the Military Government.

The solution could be found only in paragraph 5, which instructed the Military Government *"to ensure the production and maintenance of goods and services required to prevent starvation or such disease and unrest as would endanger the occupying forces"* (author's italics). Here was the open-sesame—the key to a whole series of future actions. While initially the paragraph may have appeared to some Military Government officials as a not very relevant afterthought, it became step-by-step the escape clause which guided the economic activities of the American Military Government in Germany for more than two years. In conjunction with paragraph 2, specifically ordering an early maximization of agricultural output, the "disease-and-unrest formula," as it was called from then on, enabled the Military Government to disregard certain economic restrictions whenever necessity seemed to demand it. This included the restrictions spelled out in paragraph 32 prohibiting the production of iron, steel, ferrous metals, chemicals, heavy machinery, machine tools, etc. The same escape clause provided the legal justification for the large-scale food imports soon to follow; also, since American taxpayers obviously could not be expected to foot the accruing bills indefinitely, it opened the gates for an early revival of German industry which was now asked "to provide the means to pay for imports." In other words, the most restrictive paragraphs of JCS/1067 pertaining to economics could be temporarily shelved—or at least until German industry was able to produce enough export goods to pay for essential imports.[10]

It stands to reason that the recognition of this line of action did not come from one day to the next.[11] It developed gradually and was greatly facilitated by those paragraphs of the Potsdam Agreement which superseded the directive. As John J. McCloy indicated when questioned on this point: "Clay did precisely what the War Department expected him to do, when he came to grips with concrete occupational problems, that is to whittle away the unworkable clauses of JCS/1067 empirically and piecemeal." [12] The prevention of disease and unrest, or more specifically, the procurement of food for the German population, thus became a priority task of the American Military Government.

The complex and awesome responsibilities which this entailed were

10. A Department of State Press Release of 12 Dec. 1945 said, "It will prove desirable to extend the type and volume of imports into Germany not only because of our interest in avoiding disease and unrest which would endanger our occupying forces but also of our interest in reactivating selected German export industries which would yield a volume of foreign exchange to enable Germany to pay for current essential imports. *U.S. Department of State Bulletin* 13, no. 338 (16 Dec. 1945): 960–965. See also Wallich, *The Mainsprings of the German Revival:* "The Disease and Unrest formula and other loopholes in the top level directives covered these reversals of policy" (p. 347). Also see Hammond, "How stringent would the life of the German people be under this directive? The answer to this question depended upon the military interpretation of 'disease and unrest' " (p. 390).

11. John Gimbel discusses this evolvement of a *de facto* policy. Gimbel, pp. 8–9.

12. Dorn, p. 501. A similar comment citing General Hilldring will be found in Gimbel, p. 8.

shouldered by the small staff of a Food and Agriculture Branch for more than four years.[13] It had the good fortune to be led by two competent Americans: Colonel (later Brigadier General) Hughes B. Hester, an officer in the regular army, and Stanley Andrews, an agricultural specialist from Missouri.[14] Before the administrative apparatus could start to function, however, some bureaucratic underbrush had to be cleared. According to the table of organization established by the European Advisory Commission in London, Germany was to be administered by an Allied Control Council composed of the four commanders in chief. The organizational pattern also provided for a coordinating committee, consisting of the four deputy military governors, with extensive delegated powers. Operating as an executive body, they, among others, were responsible for the supervision of an Allied Secretariat, an Administrative Bureau, and a large number of functional directorates respectively concerned with political affairs, economics, finance, transportation, reparations, restitution, etc.

The American element of the Allied body, the U.S. Group Control Council, had been organized in London in the fall of 1944, but in the early days of the occupation its actual area of responsibility had not yet been clearly defined. According to some views it was to serve prior to the end of hostilities as a planning unit and later as the top-level military headquarters of the United States in Germany, whereas, according to others, the G-5 Section of the U.S. Forces, European Theater (USFET) was supposed to have complete responsibility for military government matters within the American Zone. In the field of food and agriculture, the resulting confusion was reflected by the existence of two independent American offices in Germany, both of which operated under separate though overlapping sets of authority. The conflict dated back to the summer of 1944, when, independent of SHAEF'S Food and Agriculture Section under G-5, the newly established U.S. Group Control Council organized its own Food and Agriculture Branch. The intent was that the former would handle operational matters whereas the latter would take over the functions of the German Ministry of Food and Agriculture in Berlin and assume responsibility for planning and control.

The resulting problem of coordination was aggravated by the physical

13. "Our Food and Agriculture Branch which at its peak never exceeded 100 persons under the inspiring leadership of Hester and Andrews, together with its British associates, re-organized German agriculture and food distribution and saved hundreds of thousands of lives." Clay, *Decision in Germany*, p. 269.
14. Before World War II Colonel Stanley Andrews had been publisher of an American farm magazine. From 1940 to 1943 he had served as General Agent of the Farm Credit Administration of New Orleans.

separation of the two organizations: SHAEF in October 1944 moved to Versailles and eventually settled in Frankfurt am Main, whereas the U.S. Group Control Council remained in London and after a few stops en route established its headquarters in Berlin. By that time it had become clear that the German Ministry of Food and Agriculture no longer existed and that the U.S. Group Control Council was without a German governmental agency to supervise, and that as a result its functions had drastically changed. In the American Zone, on the other hand, the Food and Agriculture Section of G-5 was responsible for the execution and supervision of Allied policies; at the same time, the U.S. Group Control Council, although an integral part of the Control Council, had no authority to direct the implementation of U.S. policies in the field.[15]

As far as Food and Agriculture was concerned, the problem of conflicting authorities was eventually disposed of by the appointment of Colonel Hester as director of the two competing offices; with the assistance of Stanley Andrews and of an able staff, Hester streamlined the two operations until they were merged in Berlin. In a similar fashion the general administrative impasse was solved by General Clay's decision to move the G-5 Section of USFET, with the exception of a small rear echelon, from Frankfurt to Berlin; there it was merged with the U.S. Group Control Council into an Office of Military Government of the United States for Germany (OMGUS), assuming the dual responsibility of representing the United States in the Allied Control Authority and of supervising Military Government activities in the field.

The task of maximizing agricultural production in the American Zone and of supplementing the meager indigenous German rations through food imports from abroad was essentially a unilateral American responsibility. Nevertheless, it is noteworthy that there was better and more effective quadripartite cooperation in matters pertaining to German agriculture than in any other area. It was obviously in everyone's interest to maximize German agricultural production in all four zones, and the quadripartite Food and Agriculture Committee under the Directorate of Economics therefore had few if any controversial issues to contend with. Accordingly, an early Military Government report on this subject could boast that "of 36 papers introduced in 1945, and 78 acted on during the first six months of 1946 not a single one failed of unanimous adoption." [16] The crucial question of treating Germany as an economic unit of course was beyond the competence of the committee; neverthe-

15. "History of Military Government . . . ," p. 5.
16. Ibid., p. 82.

less, it was able to reach agreement on a number of secondary issues such as planting areas for each of the major field crops, plans for the restoration of the German fishing fleet, restoration of livestock numbers, the reactivation of agricultural cooperatives, etc. In short, against a background of increasing dissension and acrimony in the Allied Control Authority, the Food and Agriculture Committee remained one of the few oases where a friendly spirit of inter-Allied cooperation seemed to survive.

While General Clay and his principal advisers were attempting to clarify questions of basic occupational policy and of setting up the administrative machinery, the Military Government detachments in the field were wrestling with the problem of an adequate food distribution under existing conditions. As indicated, the "normal consumer" rations which the Nazi government had been able to maintain at a fairly satisfactory level almost to the end of the war had dropped to 1000 calories in May and to 800 calories in June. By then the German rationing system as directed by the Ministry of Food and Agriculture in Berlin had broken down completely and was supervised—usually in a haphazard fashion—by local authorities. Actually, only in Bavaria was the semblance of *Land* government in being. In the other parts of the American Zone most regional food and agriculture offices had ceased to exist. As far as the larger Nazi food organizations were concerned, none of their staffs remained intact. Many officials had gone into hiding, their offices were closed, and records had been removed or destroyed. Frequently, warehouses, elevators, and food-storage places had been destroyed; the communications system had broken down completely, and it was next to impossible to transport even essential supplies either by vehicle or by rail. Accordingly, the food situation varied with the stocks locally on hand. As it turned out, food offices in the field often were reluctant to follow instructions of a central authority if this entailed the use of food reserves for distribution outside their community. In many cases all the supplies available were quickly distributed in disregard of instructions from above before an outsider could put his hands on them. In the southern dairy regions of the American Zone, for example, special food distributions became the order of the day, while in the north, butter and cheese disappeared from the market.[17]

The precariousness of the situation was accentuated by a growing reluctance of surplus areas to sell their products for the official German currency, the Reichsmark. As American administrators soon discovered,

17. Ibid., p. 27.

the German people were still keenly aware of their disastrous experiences with the runaway inflation after World War I, which had wiped out their savings and left them with grievous financial losses. This time every German endeavored to avoid the mistakes of an earlier generation. As a result, sales against currency were curtailed whenever possible and, concurrently with the gradually diminishing fear of legal restrictions, an extensive barter system developed. Under these chaotic conditions, the complete responsibility for food collection, warehousing, and distribution often fell on the shoulders of Military Government teams, most of whom were short of experienced personnel. The large food reserves of the former German army probably were the only redeeming aspect of these confused days, since they were distributed, by one means or another, among the German population. Many German homes, therefore, had a fairly substantial hidden food stock which helped them over the worst period of ration failure.

By July American Military Government authorities had begun to organize food distribution, and on July 15, 1945, American headquarters established a rationing section for the purpose of coordinating food rationing procedures throughout the American Zone.[18] In addition to the basic ration scale for the normal consumer, temporarily set at 1550 calories and covering about one third of the population, special categories for children, pregnant women, and heavy workers were established. The category for children was subdivided according to age levels, and there were supplementary allowances in calories per day for the labor force as follows: light manual workers, 285 calories; moderately heavy workers, 570; heavy workers, 1145; very heavy workers, 1717; coal miners heavy, 1820; and coal miners very heavy, 2500 calories.

Since most planting for 1945 had been completed before the ending of hostilities, no special program for that year could be initiated. However, early in 1945 OMGUS prepared a crop production plan for 1945/46 and established certain production principles which were generally adhered to during the following years. Pertinent policies were also expressed in a Military Government regulation (February 1, 1946) requiring the German *Land* governments to draft annual agricultural plans which, without changing farm practices too drastically, were supposed to result in "a food output in terms of calories" and result in a diet containing "at least the minimum nutritional requirements." [19] German

18. Ibid., p. 47.
19. Hubert G. Schmidt, *Food and Agriculture Programs in West Germany*, p. 21.

food and agriculture offices at local levels were soon reactivated and reorganized so that they could take over the supervision of collecting, processing, and storing agricultural produce by commodity dealers; the same offices also were made responsible for the distribution among retailers and the inspection of farms as to compliance with production and delivery requirements.

The next step was the re-establishment of a *Land* administrative machinery. Understandably, OMGUS efforts to place operational responsibility in the hands of German officials were considerably slowed down by the denazification process and by the difficulty of finding acceptable personnel. In general, it took about a year until *Land* food and agricultural administrations became fully established and were able to function under Military Government supervision. A newly established Länderrat, composed of the ministerpräsidents of Bavaria, Hesse, Württemberg-Baden, and Bremen, became the main coordinating body and assumed responsibilities such as the allocation of imports, the analysis of *Länder* statistics and reports, the allocation of farm supplies among the *Länder,* and recommendations of ration scales on the basis of available and prospective food supplies.[20] (The subsequent economic fusion of the American and British Zones in 1947 brought food and agriculture and other economic activities under the legislation of the German Bizonal Economic Council and under supervision by the Bizonal Economic Administration, of which the Bizonal Food and Agriculture Administration was one of six divisions. German legislation and administration, however, remained subject to the approval of the Bipartite Control Office [BICO] and of the Bipartite Board.)[21]

From the first days of the occupation the American Military Government used all means at its disposal to increase the agricultural self-sufficiency of the American Zone. Obviously, no policy questions had to be considered, since it was in everyone's interests to develop the domestic agricultural output until an optimum level was reached. In accordance with this basic consideration, the efforts of the Food and Agriculture Branch were directed toward developing a detailed crop-production plan, with a strong emphasis on the production of seed and fertilizers, the reactivation of plants producing farm machinery, and the revival of the German fishing fleet. The four-pronged crop-production plan of OMGUS made a valiant effort to enlarge the area planted to direct-con-

20. A detailed discussion of the role and activities of the Länderrat is beyond the scope of this study. It can be found in Gimbel, pp. 35–51.
21. Schmidt, p. 21.

sumption crops, to increase within this area the proportion of high-yielding crops (mainly potatoes), to reduce livestock slightly by applying the principle of selective culling, and finally, to promote the expansion of home and subsistence gardens. The program for the first year of the occupation provided for the conversion of about 70,000 hectares of meadow and pasture to crop use. At the same time, the area planted to early or late potatoes, Germany's most important single food crops, was increased from 419,000 hectares to 511,000 hectares. Inasmuch as a crop fed to livestock loses 75 to 85 percent of its caloric value in the process of conversion into milk and meat, it was decided to reduce—at least for the first years of the occupation—livestock numbers. The rationale for this measure seemed even more convincing in view of the OMGUS plan to reduce the land planted to food grains and fodder roots, and to limit the area of hay and pasture.[22] As could be expected, however, the livestock adjustment program encountered considerable opposition on the part of the German farmers, who understandably showed little inclination to sell their livestock, one of their most important capital assets, for what they considered worthless Reichsmarks.

A definitely more popular measure of OMGUS was the expansion of a home gardening program by special allocations of seed, fertilizers, and equipment, as well as by appropriate promotional publicity through press and radio. Although there were still shortages of land, fertilizers, and tools, 200,000 new home gardens were established in the U.S. Zone in 1946 and production in the previously existing 1,500,000 was intensified. The Economic Division of OMGUS estimated that in 1946 the home garden program directly assisted 40 percent of the total population in the American Zone and that it provided broad segments of the population more than 100 calories per person per day during the summer months.[23]

Before the war the western zones of Germany had depended heavily on deliveries of seed from other parts of Germany and from abroad. More than 500,000 tons of seed potatoes alone had come from East Germany every year, and commercial vegetable and field seeds had come either from the east or were imported from other parts of Europe. Although it was imperative to increase the self-sufficiency of the western zones, progress was slow because many seeds were biennials and the technical know-how of raising seed had to be developed. In spite of these handicaps, the area in seed-potato production was trebled by

22. "History of Military Government . . . ," p. 62.
23. Ibid., p. 64.

1947, and the acreage under seed-grain cultivation was increased by 50 percent.[24]

Because much of the cultivated soil in Germany is poor and sandy, one of the key factors in obtaining high levels of agricultural production had always been the application of large quantities of fertilizers. As far as nitrates and potash went, domestic production had been adequate, and most of the phosphate needs had been filled from basic-slag, a by-product of Germany's large steel production. Phosphate rock, on the other hand, important for the manufacture of basic-slag, always had to be imported.[25] During the war, these imports were cut off, and most of the domestic nitrogen was diverted into ammunition. As a result, agricultural yields had dropped sharply, and it was estimated that three to four years of extraordinary large fertilizer applications would be needed to make up for the cumulative deficiencies of the war years. Again a good part of West Germany's fertilizer requirements had been covered by deliveries from the Soviet Zone; furthermore, at the beginning of the occupation, world supplies of fertilizers were scarce. Hence, the actual applications of nitrogen during the period 1945/46 were only 17 percent of estimated prewar use; corresponding figures for the applications of potash and phosphate were equally unsatisfactory, 32 and 12 percent, respectively.[26]

OMGUS went all out to raise the West German production of nitrogen and potash and ordered the activation of an idle fertilizer plant in Trostberg, Bavaria, as one of its first actions in the economic field. Even so, only about half of the potash and nitrogen requirements could be met in the following year. In addition, U.S.-financed imports of phosphate rock covered about 35 percent of the phosphate needs of the combined British and American Zones.[27] (Malevolent rumors to the contrary, no fertilizer plants were permitted to be destroyed under the label of "war potential.") During the following years West German production of nitrogen and potash gradually was stepped up through enlargement of manufacturing and mining capacity financed by the Marshall Plan until complete self-sufficiency in these two fertilizers was achieved.

Two additional bottlenecks—the production of farm machinery and the almost complete disintegration of the German fishing fleet—were equally difficult to overcome. As to the former, the production of German farm machinery had declined to such an extent during the war

24. Hoover Report, p. 25.
25. "Food and Agriculture in the Bizonal Area," p. 16.
26. Ibid., p. 17.   27. Ibid., p. 6.

that at the beginning of the occupation practically no replacements were available. Although OMGUS promptly ordered the opening of all plants engaged in the manufacture of farm equipment in the American Zone, shortages of coal, iron, and steel prevented rapid progress. In 1946, for instance, only 100,000 tons of iron and steel could be allocated for the production of agricultural machinery, whereas at least 350,000 tons were needed.[28] To a limited extent the situation was alleviated by the release of tools from military surpluses in the United States.

Since the Bremen enclave was part of the American Zone of occupied Germany, OMGUS became responsible for the supervision of the German fishing ports of Wesermünde, Bremerhaven, and Bremen-Vogelsack. Prior to 1939, the port of Wesermünde had been the largest fresh-fish landing port in Germany, but at the time of the German surrender there were only 24 small, outdated fishing trawlers and some 25 or 30 other fishing boats in port, out of a prewar fleet of 217 trawlers and about 100 other vessels. In Bremen-Vogelsack there was only one herring boat out of a prewar fleet of 66. The first efforts of OMGUS were therefore directed toward locating and returning to home ports all serviceable fishing vessels which had been requisitioned by the German navy for minesweeping, coastal patrols, and other war uses.[29] Again numerous obstacles had to be overcome, and progress was initially slow. Nevertheless, 270,000 tons of fish were brought ashore during the first six months of 1946, as compared to 150,000 tons during the last six months of 1945. When it became clear that the German catch alone was insufficient to meet the fish ration, a program for the importation of fish from Scandinavian countries was promptly developed and implemented with the help of U.S. government funds.[30] (All imported goods were sold in Germany at the same legal prices as domestic products. The proceeds were then credited to a "deferred import account" which was kept in the name of the Military Government.) [31]

The question naturally arises what the practical results of all these complex efforts were. If one takes the extremely low levels of the first postwar year as a basis, one would conclude that Hester and his staff at the Food and Agriculture Branch were quite successful in their efforts to maximize the food production in the American Zone. Starting from a level corresponding to about 74 percent of the prewar production, it was possible to reach 87 percent for the period 1946/47, and 95 percent

28. Ibid., p. 20.
29. "History of Military Government . . . ," p. 77.   30. Ibid., p. 79.
31. Bipartite Control Office. BICO/P(48) 289, 30 Nov. 1948 (OMGUS records).

during the following year. Progress in the British Zone was similar. In the course of two years output rose from 54 percent of prewar production to 69 percent (see Table 2.1). If one considers the complete absence of economic incentives prior to the currency reform, as well as the partly related apathy among the German working population, the results may even be termed remarkable.

TABLE 2.1. Total indigenous calories available
for nonfarm population: trillion calories [32]

Year	U.S. Zone	U.K. Zone
1935–38	6.9	10.6
1945–46	5.1	5.7
1946–47	6.0	6.4
1947–48	6.6	7.3

As will be discussed later in greater detail, the German economy from the early days of the occupation until the currency reform in 1948 was divided into two compartments only tenuously connected with each other. In one, the Reichsmark was recognized as legal tender, and basic wages, salaries, rent, utilities, public transportation, etc., were paid and official rations and allocated products distributed. The second compartment was the so-called gray or black market, where all transactions were based on barter, i.e., the exchange of one commodity against another without the intermediary of printed currency. As a practical example, one ton of wheat would bring the farmer 200 Reichsmarks through legal sales, whereas by trading one pound of butter against clothing, fuel, or farm supplies, etc., he could receive the equivalent of 300 Reichsmarks on the black market.[33] Thus, the German farmer had little incentive to exert himself to grow food for the legal market. Instead there was actually a negative incentive to curtail official deliveries as much as he could get away with. As time went on, therefore, the effective collection of farm products became increasingly difficult, and Germans referred jokingly to farmers "who had Persian rugs spread out in their cow stalls." Had there been an earlier introduction of the currency reform, the availability of food supplies through legal channels would undoubtedly have been much greater and the German dependency on food shipments from abroad would have lessened.

To summarize, if one applied the standard assumption of economic

32. Hoover Report, p. iii.
33. Undated manuscript "Food and Agriculture" (OMGUS records), p. 5.

theory, "everything else being equal," the data of Table 2.1 would have demonstrated a considerable improvement of the food situation. Unfortunately, however, the assumption was not valid, since the increment in the production of indigenous food had been absorbed by a simultaneous growth of the German population in the West by about 25 percent—to a total of 43 million. This compared with a prewar population of 34,160,000 in the American and British Zones, to which were now added 7,000,000 Germans who had come from the eastern provinces and Czechoslovakia as well as the 1,610,000 inhabitants of the American and British sectors in Berlin. The resulting dilemma is drastically demonstrated by Fig. 2.1.[34] Accordingly the per capita availability of

FIGURE 2.1   Total population and relative self-sufficiency in food production in the U.S.–U.K. area of Germany, prewar and 1947/48 [After "Food and Agriculture in the Bizonal Area of Germany."]

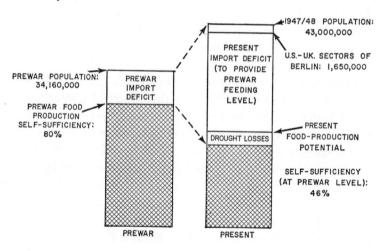

indigenous food for nonfarm consumers in the American Zone, which was 1117 calories in 1945/46, came to only 1091 calories for 1946/47 and to not more than 1203 calories during the following year. The equivalent data for the British Zone were 826, 909, and 1000 calories, respectively (see Table 2.2). In short, there was some progress, but on a per capita basis it was quite small. For all practical purposes, indigenous production could supply no more than about 50 percent of the minimum food requirements needed to maintain a working population.

34. "Food and Agriculture in the Bizonal Area," p. 3.

TABLE 2.2. Per capita availability of indigenous food for nonfarm consumers [35]

Year	U.S. Zone	U.K. Zone	Total
1945/46	1117	826	941
1946/47	1091	909	991
1947/48	1203	1000	1087

It is interesting, and indeed most indicative of the American pragmatic approach to the "negative" policies emanating from the highest Washington quarters, that SHAEF had prepared for the contingency of feeding the Germans and had brought along 600,000 tons of grain in order "to prevent disease and unrest." Half of this amount had to be made available to the British and French Zones, where food supplies were even lower than in the mainly agricultural regions occupied by the U.S. Army. The remaining 320,000 long tons were distributed among the German population in the American Zone. Because of these supplementary supplies it was possible to distribute during the first twelve months of the occupation the consumer rations shown in Table 2.3.

TABLE 2.3. Calories from rationed food distributed to "normal consumers" in the U.S.-U.K. Zones of Germany: calories per capita per day [36]

Month	U.S. Zone	U.K. Zone
July	930	1154
August	980	1154
September	1100	1505
October	1260	1541
November	1540	1526
December	1490	1542
January	1550	1550
February	1540	1555
March	1540	1014
April	1275	1042
May	1280	1050

35. Hoover Report, p. 38.
36. "Food and Agriculture in the Bizonal Area," p. 24; Hoover Report, p. 46. See also Isador Lubin, "Reparations Problems," p. 68. The distribution of food was equally unsatisfactory in other parts of Europe. "Last winter considerable portions of the French industrial population were forced to get along on less than 1550 calories . . . and France is now immeasurably in better shape than many of the other devastated countries of Europe."

While the SHAEF grain reserve was without doubt of decisive importance in helping the German people over the first year of the occupation, the actual ration level maintained was an essential minimum acceptable only because of the emergency and because most German homes still had some hidden food reserves. The question for the American Military Government was, therefore, where to go from here.

Contrary to the views of some American and German critics, there were no problems of policy to be considered. If during the next two years Germans often received less food than they actually needed, the reason was not a lingering policy of revenge, but two bottlenecks of cardinal significance, namely, the question of funding and the existing world food crisis. As to the former, during the period from October 1, 1944, to December 31, 1946, official American economic aid in the form of food was recorded as "Civil Affairs/Military Government Supplies" and totaled approximately 1,300,000 metric tons. This included supplies imported under the "disease-and-unrest" formula which were turned over to the German civilian authorities directly at Bremen Port, in addition to supplies imported by the U.S. Army Services and subsequently issued to the German economy.[37] When it became clear that economic aid would be needed not only at a larger scale but also over many years, a separate food import program had to be set up. Accordingly, the Food and Agriculture Branch of the Economic Division, OMGUS, was given the task of programing food needs on an annual basis and of justifying the resulting program to the deputy military governor. The final approved programs were then included in the OMGUS request to Congress. As of July 1, 1946, U.S. appropriations for aid to the U.S. Zone and the U.S. Sector of Berlin became part of the so-called Government and Relief in Occupied Area (GARIOA) budget. In Washington the responsibility for GARIOA rested with the Department of the Army, or more specifically with the Office of the Food Administrator for Occupied Areas (OFAOA). Although the American Congress was surprisingly sympathetic, it naturally took time to set up the appropriate fiscal apparatus and to overcome the miscellaneous legislative hurdles. Nevertheless, as of July 1, 1946, GARIOA funds became available at an increasing scale and provided the financial means for most of West Germany's imports of food, fertilizers, seeds, and oil products during the following years. Originally, economic assistance in

37. OMGUS, Supply Accounting Branch, Summary for CA/MG Supplies, 10 June 1947 (OMGUS records). *OMGUS Weekly Information Bulletin,* no. 95, 2 June 1947, mentions food shipments of 1,975,500 tons ($290 million) for the period May 1945–30 June 1947 (OMGUS records).

the French and British Zones was the problem of the French and British governments. After the economic fusion of the U.S. and British Zones, the purchases of supplies became a joint responsibility, but the American share, especially after the revision of the fusion agreement in December 1947, became increasingly greater.[38]

While the appropriation of adequate funds by the U.S. Congress was essentially a matter of time, the task of actually procuring the necessary supplies was much more difficult. Before the end of the war, the United States, Canada, and the United Kingdom had set up a Combined Food Board to ensure equitable distribution of food supplies to the Allied Countries. At a later date a large number of countries joined together to form the International Emergency Food Council (IEFC) in Washington, which eventually became the International Emergency Food Committee of UNO's Food and Agriculture Organization. Membership of the IEFC included all important food exporting and importing countries with the exception of the Soviet Union and Argentina. The occupied countries of Germany and Japan were represented on the Committee by the occupation authorities. The IEFC was a voluntary organization regulating the distribution of the exportable surpluses of the world's scarce food commodities such as grain, fats, oil, and nitrogen fertilizers. It is noteworthy that the IEFC had no legal authority over member nations and could not compel them to accept recommendations. In practice, however, the common interest of all countries to work together in overcoming world shortages and in avoiding an excessive inflation of food prices through competitive buying resulted in a general acceptance of and compliance with IEFC recommendations. Exportable surpluses were assessed by the exporting countries and reported to the IEFC which, after a thorough examination, sometimes referred these estimates back for reconsideration. In a similar vein the importing countries submitted their bids on the basis of their needs and their ability to pay. Since demands during the postwar period always exceeded total supply, the IEFC carefully screened the requests against the background of proposed consumption levels, the use made of indigenous resources, and stocks already in the importing country. On the basis of this screening, which often led to substantial cuts in claims, provisional allocations were

38. It would be beyond the scope of this study to discuss other substantial American aid programs such as those privately initiated by the Cooperative of American Remittances for Europe (CARE) and the Council of Relief Agencies Licensed to Operate in Germany (CRALOG), or the child-feeding program of the U.S. Army providing noon meals for 3,500,000 children. Clay, *Decision in Germany*, pp. 268, 276.

made at the beginning of the year and revised as additional information became available. Despite the efforts of the IEFC to equalize the distribution of scarce supplies, this was not always fully accomplished. Within this limitation, however, the IEFC insured on a voluntary basis that each importing country received a reasonable share.

Germany's bids, made on its behalf by the governments of the United States and Great Britain, were considered along with all the other bids. The assumption that Germany received its allocations after other countries had been satisfied was incorrect. With the exception of the Soviet Union, all former enemies of Germany were members of the IEFC. Understandably, these countries, some of which had been devastated by the Germans, were primarily interested in obtaining their share of the world's food supplies. However, at no time were German claims pushed aside to facilitate a more rapid improvement in the standards of consumption of the Allied Countries. Table 2.4 of bids for bread grain and

TABLE 2.4.   Cereals, July 1, 1946 to June 30, 1947 [39]

Claimant	Stated import requirement	Preliminary program estimate
United Kingdom	5,714,000	5,091,000
India	4,400,000	2,300,000
France	1,012,000	450,000
Belgium	1,082,000	634,000
Netherlands	1,147,000	785,000
Rumania	692,000	—
Zones of occupation Germany, British Germany, U.S.	3,438,000	2,837,000
Brazil	1,200,000	800,000
Yugoslavia	1,610,000	—

the corresponding preliminary recommendations of the IEFC for 1946/47 covering the main importing countries evidences the objectivity of this international body.

With the SHAEF grain reserve running out, the March 1946 rations in the British Zone had to be cut back to 1014 calories per day for the "normal consumer." As was to be expected, coal production immediately dropped by 20 percent. The American Zone was obliged to follow

39. OMGUS, Public Information Office Release 3-C-15, 5 March 1948 (OMGUS records, 355-1/5).

with a reduction to 1275 calories, and from April to September the "normal consumer" rations in both zones ranged from 1042 to 1280 calories per day. In this extraordinary emergency—bread grains on the world markets were practically unobtainable—the Office of the Quartermaster General, following General Clay's frantic requests for assistance, stepped into the breach and rounded up all sorts of surplus supplies from army depots throughout the world. Shipments of miscellaneous food items for the U.S. Zone totaled over 135,000 tons from May through August 1946, representing a value of over $90 million.[40] Although low in caloric value, these supplies nevertheless helped to fill German stomachs and made the low ration level of staples more endurable.

With the support of the U.S. Department of Agriculture, grain shipments were also increased in the early summer months. As a result, the U.S. Zone was able not only to improve its own ration level, but also to assist the French and British Zones by diverting U.S. Zone cargoes in emergency situations as loans to these Allies. Total advances to the British Zone came to over 75,000 tons of wheat equivalent, and advances to French account approximated 50,000 tons. As world food conditions improved, all these loans were repaid.[41] Fortunately the 1946 German harvest was a good one, since favorable weather counterbalanced the shortages of fertilizers and seeds and caused some improvements over the preceding year. Accordingly, the basic rations in both zones could again be raised to 1550 calories.

By the fall of 1946 it had become clear that even the full implementation of the 1550 calories for the "normal consumer" would not suffice to keep a working population going and would prevent an early recovery of the German economy. The Byrnes-Bevin agreement which formalized the economic merger of the American and British Zones as of January 1, 1947, therefore established a "normal consumer" ration of 1800 calories as a desirable target to be reached as soon as world conditions would permit.

When Herbert Hoover, upon President Truman's request, made a survey of the critical European food situation in February 1947, he obtained from the U.S.-British Bipartite Food and Agriculture Panel an estimate anticipating annual expenditures of $516,000,000 for food imports into Bizonal Germany to maintain an inexpensive bread and potato diet. The same estimate foresaw an annual expenditure of

40. "Food and Agriculture in the Bizonal Area," p. 6.
41. Ibid., p. 7.

$613,000,000 for a "moderately balanced diet." [42] The Bipartite report
to Former President Hoover also indicated that "normal consumer"
rations had ranged from only 860 to 1550 calories per capita and day
during the first two years of the occupation; in only seven of the first
twenty-one months after VE day had the level in the British and
American Zones been 1550 calories. Although in general the minimum

TABLE 2.5. Minimum daily caloric requirements compared with actual
rations, February 1947: calories per capita per day [43]

	Minimum daily caloric requirements	Actual rations, February 1947	Ration level as percent of requirement
Children			
0–1 year	1000	1120	112
1–3 years	1000	1230	122
3–6 years	1500	1515	101
6–10 years	2000	1760	88
10–12 years	2700	1980	73
Normal consumer	2000	1555	78
Pregnant and lactating women	2700	2560	95
Workers			
Moderately heavy	2700	2060	76
Heavy	3200	2510	78
Very heavy	3700	2855	77
Surface miners	3400	3400	100
Underground miners	4000	4000	100

Note: The rations shown above are for the U.S. Zone, but the rations in the
U.K. Zone were almost identical in total caloric value.

requirements for children under six years of age had been met, and the
special feeding program for coal miners had provided 100 percent of the
prescribed ration, children from six to ten years, as well as pregnant
and lactating women, had received only about 88 to 95 percent of their
respective requirements. The rest of the population, by far the largest
group, had received only 75 to 78 percent of minimum caloric requirements from their ration. Table 2.5, submitted to Hoover in the course of

42. Hoover Report, p. iii.   43. Ibid., p. 46.

his European survey, provides a telling illustration of prevailing conditions.

As was to be expected, the continued undernourishment resulted in lowered body weights and a general deterioration of health among the German population. For example, in August 1946, following a four-month period of rations from 1180 to 1280 calories for the "normal consumer," body weights in the U.S. Zone of Germany as determined by nutritional survey teams were as shown in Table 2.6.

TABLE 2.6. Average body weights in the U.S. Zone compared with standard weights, August 1946 [44]

	Average weight, lb	Deviation from minimum satisfactory weight	
Men			
ages 20–39	133.4	−8.6 lb	−6.0 percent
ages 40–59	130.8	−15.2	−10.4
ages 60+	127.9	−19.1	−13.0
Women			
ages 20–39	119.4	−3.6	−2.9
ages 40–59	118.5	−13.5	−10.2
ages 60+	114.2	−18.8	−14.1

A combined British, French, and American committee of health experts consequently concluded in December 1946 that

> while part of the population of the cities of the three zones of Western Germany is in fairly good nutritional state, a significantly larger proportion is in an unsatisfactory condition, and of these an increasing number show signs of severe under-nutrition. . . . German adults are underweight and, in almost every instance, weights are significantly lower than a year ago. Although children under seven have not been markedly affected by the food shortage, the growth and developments of these between seven and fourteen years is unsatisfactory. Hunger oedema shows an increase and although mild in degree is an indication of the vulnerable groups where it is present. . . . All the evidence obtained compels the committee to conclude that conditions in certain respects are seri-

44. After the Hoover Report, p. 57.

ous. Throughout the last year large numbers of Germans have subsisted on a food consumption that is inadequate for the maintenance of minimum nutrition. The longer this situation continues, the greater becomes the risk of nutritional disaster, should supplies of food be interrupted or ration scales be decreased.[45]

In a simultaneous move, General Clay released an official statement indicating "that existing ration levels would have to be raised to prevent a continuing physical deterioration and permanent damaging of the general health of the German population to a point where realization of the objectives of the occupation would be impossible." [46]

Although the 1946 harvest in Germany had been good, the winter 1946/47 was accompanied by numerous setbacks which affected the food distribution in Germany. Because of a series of strikes in the United States, imports from America did not arrive as expected. Furthermore, there had been an overoptimistic estimate of the indigenous bread grain collection by the inexperienced German agricultural administration, and finally, to make matters worse, Germany was visited by the most severe winter freeze in a generation. Inland waterways were completely blocked for two to three months, electric power failed, and railway locomotives broke down by the hundreds.[47] The cumulative result of these misfortunes was a new food crisis which reached its climax in May 1947, when less than 1100 calories per day could be distributed in the Bizone (see Table 2.7).

Fortunately, however, the end of the food crisis was now in sight. In the course of the following months GARIOA-financed imports rapidly increased and reached an all-time high of 440,000 tons of flour equivalent in June; 409,000 tons in July; 480,000 in August; and 430,000 in September.[48] Slowly the rations could be increased, and in April 1948 the official ration of 1550 calories was again met. A few months later, thanks to a German bumper crop, it was raised to 1990 calories, the level which health experts had recommended all along.

The year 1949 brought about not only another increase in German food production, but also, thanks to the currency reform, a changed attitude of the German farmers regarding the delivery of their produce to the market. As a result, as of December 1949, food rationing for all practical purposes was discontinued—the German food problem was

45. Hoover Report, p. 56.   46. Ibid., p. 1.
47. "Food and Agriculture in the Bizonal Area," p. 8.   48. Ibid., p. 9.

TABLE 2.7. Calories from rationed food distributed to
"normal consumers" in the U.S.-U.K. Zones of Germany, June 1946 to July 1948: calories per capita per
day [49]

Month	U.S. Zone	U.K. Zone
June 1946	1180	1050
July	1235	1052
August	1240	1137
September	1240	1237
October	1550	1550
November	1555	1557
December	1545	1540
January 1947	1545	1540
February	1555	1550
March	1330	1330
April	1180	1180
May	1080	1080
June	1165	1165
July	1260	1260
August	1430	1430
September	1430	1430
October	1425	1339
November	1425	1279
December	1330	1261
January 1948	1426	1405
February	1410	1410
March	1339	1398
April	1563	1564
May	1593	1593
June	1575	1655
July	1980	1995

over.[50] The GARIOA-financed expenditures for food, fertilizers, and
seed shipments to Germany, which had totaled $189 million in the
1946/47 fiscal year, increased to $455 million in 1947/48 and to $487
million in 1948/49 and ended with $385 million in 1949/50. The grand

49. Ibid., p. 25; and *OMGUS, Food and Agriculture,* Monthly Military Government Report, July 1946–August 1949 (OMGUS records, 16-3/5).
50. Clay, p. 270.

total of all GARIOA-financed expenditures in Germany was $1.52 billion.[51]

In July 1947, the "negative" JCS/1067 was replaced by JCS/1779, which instructed the military governor to consider it "his fundamental task to help lay the economic and educational basis of a sound German democracy." The relief measures for occupied Germany described in this chapter had, of course, been conceived, organized, and to a great extent implemented under JCS/1067, which, as we will recall, had instructed the Military Government "to take no steps designed to maintain or strengthen the German economy." JCS/1779 therefore did not entail a drastic change of prevailing policies, but rather the adjustment of theoretical guidelines to Military Government policies which *de facto* had been in existence practically from the start.

The concluding question arises as to why this historically unique aid program in support of a recent enemy was arranged through the back door, namely, the escape clause of the disease-and-unrest formula. The reader may have gathered that the answer will have to be sought in the political climate which prevailed in Washington while the fighting was still in progress. As John J. McCloy confirmed to the writer,

> At the time JCS/1067 was drafted, we were working in a "Vae victis" atmosphere and we had to deal with very strong "enemy" psychology. The atrocities inflicted on the Jews and the concentration camp revelations were most provocative. Morgenthau was quite naturally perhaps the principal exponent of this negative approach, but the President was also thinking along these lines.[52]

Evidently the *Handbook* incident had brought matters to a head. Although the extent of Germany's economic collapse could not have been foreseen at the time, one concludes from the first edition of the *Handbook* that its drafters at SHAEF were quite aware of some of the impending problems. Morgenthau, however, not only disagreed with the pragmatic approach of the *Handbook,* but also stirred up the White House about it.

> We could not follow a soft or even an objective line. In this atmosphere we could not spell out a constructive program. We had to go along with a generally negative approach and "with sweat

51. "Military Governor's Handbook," Budget, 7 June 1949 (OMGUS records, 25-2/5). Ludwig Erhard, *Prosperity Through Competition,* p. 15, arrives at a total of $1.62 billion.
52. Interview with John J. McCloy, New York City, 30 Nov. 1967.

and tears" try to work in some "loopholes" as you put it. It was the only thing we could do. We were in the middle. . . . Morgenthau was of course very unhappy about the fate of the Morgenthau Plan. His influence during the period when JCS/1067 was drafted was considerable. It is reflected in the negative parts of JCS/1067. The influence of the War Department can be found in the escape clauses. Stimson only reluctantly approved JCS/1067. . . . Lew Douglas, subsequently our Ambassador to the United Kingdom— he is my brother-in-law—who was helping Clay at the time in Germany, complained bitterly about the negative aspects of JCS/1067. I told him it was necessary to make the best of it as there was authority to take any steps which would avert disaster. And the fact is that even during that early period, significant rehabilitation steps were carried out. We were not as blind to the facts as JCS/1067 in the light of hindsight made it appear. I think our overall record in regard to the treatment of Germany was constructive if not enlightened.[53]

53. Ibid.

CHAPTER THREE

THE THORNY PROBLEM OF REPARATIONS

Any appraisal of Germany's economic revival under the auspices of the American and British Military Government would be unbalanced and incomplete if it did not include an examination of some of the negative aspects of occupational policy. Accordingly it will be appropriate to mention briefly the American approach to denazification and to discuss in more detail the issue of reparations.

As to the former, it is self-evident that the implementation of the American denazification policy during the first years after the capitulation added to the economic problems of the Military Government. Although the 99 percent support which Hitler enjoyed at the Nazi-controlled polls did not reflect political reality, numerous key positions in industry and in the administrative apparatus were occupied by individuals who had joined the party by necessity or by choice. Their early wholesale removal in accordance with stringent pertinent directives was without question a handicap on the road toward economic recovery; on the other hand, it can be said in support of the American policy that initially very little could have been done by the German side to alleviate the situation anyway, considering the complete collapse of the economy. In other words, if changes in personnel had to be made, this probably was a good time to make them. As indicated before, whatever the denazification policy of the American Military Government might have been, it would have been the object of serious criticism emanating from one quarter or another.[1] Any effort to establish a generally acceptable denazification policy would have meant attempting the impossible. Finally, since the economic consequences of denazification were difficult to

1. "The War Department had as a result of its somewhat indiscriminate use of Nazis in the administration of Aachen . . . come under bitter attack in the press." Hammond, "Directives for the Occupation," p. 402.

measure by any accounting system, we can only acknowledge that, while there were some costs, the total was probably not great.[2]

As to reparations, the policies of the United States naturally were influenced by the experiences of World War I. Sarcastic critics of the unimaginative military mind often quip that the military tend to prepare for the previous war. As far as imagination goes, diplomats hardly deserve a higher score. Whenever faced with a recurring international problem, they seem to reach out for the opposite of the policy that proved unsuccessful last time. In 1918, after the German armies had capitulated on the basis of President Wilson's fourteen points, Germany contended that it had been tricked into surrender and that it had not been defeated on the battlefield. The legend of the stab in the back and the dictate of Versailles complemented this line of reasoning and were to provide the National Socialists with the emotional basis as well as the rationale for a policy of revenge. Inasmuch as the surrender of the German forces on the basis of preset terms had had such disastrous consequences the last time, the opposite solution, namely, the concept of unconditional surrender, emerged in the course of World War II. As we know, there is a school of thought that regards the results of the new approach as equally unfortunate.

The problem of reparations after World War I had haunted not only the peacemakers of Versailles but the whole generation that grew up during the interwar period. It also produced an extensive and learned debate among economic theoreticians who attempted to analyze the repercussions of international monetary transfers in the paying as well as in the receiving countries. While the results of the controversy were inconclusive, they at least had the advantage of acquainting a new generation of college students with the magnitude and complexity of the reparations problem. After the Franco-German war of 1870–71, Bismarck had made the "mistake" of extracting from France an indemnity which, to the surprise of the victors, it was able to pay without difficulty in a short period of time. Since it was the aim of the peacemakers at Versailles to keep Germany in protracted bondage, a new solution

---

2. A public opinion survey among German business executives conducted by the Public Safety Branch of OMGUS in 1947 indicated that "among all the factors having a deterrent effect upon the general economy of the country denazification is a poor last and that in many instances has had the constructive effect of replacing superannuated inefficient management with more youthful, efficient and vigorous direction." Memorandum, Internal Affairs and Communications Division to General Lucius Clay, 9 Oct. 1947: Report on effect of denazification upon industry in U.S. Zone of Occupation, Germany (OMGUS records, 125-1/15).

diametrically opposed to the former had to be sought. In an era of rapid economic development the ultimate capacity of any nation to pay reparations was difficult to appraise. Bismarck evidently had erred by underestimating France's financial capacity and had asked for too little. The victors of World War I, influenced by this example, chose the opposite solution. For several years they tried to force Germany into an open-end obligation which would have required the vanquished to pay an undetermined total over an undetermined number of years. When this policy proved to be unworkable, the peacemakers decided to settle for an amount of $30 billion, a sum which, according to John Maynard Keynes's estimate,[3] was 300 percent of Germany's maximum capacity to pay. The well-known consequences of this policy were mentioned in the preceding chapter and need to be only briefly summarized: first, a short period with Germany meeting its obligations, to be followed by a request for a moratorium; second, an Allied refusal to grant relief and the Franco-Belgian occupation of the Ruhr; third, a German policy of passive resistance accompanied by the rapid collapse of the German currency; fourth, the introduction of a new currency and a greatly reduced reparations program primarily financed by American loans; fifth, a period of artificial prosperity, with inflowing foreign loans exceeding the payment of reparations; and sixth, the crisis of 1930, the final collapse of the German economy, and the end of all reparations payments.

On the academic level, these developments were accompanied by a lively international controversy among leading economists, with Bertil Ohlin[4] in Stockholm and John Maynard Keynes[5] in London as the leading protagonists. The debate not only revealed that there was a considerable lag between facts and theory in the field of large-scale international capital movements, but that there were no ready-made answers for the German reparations problem in an era of international economic interdependence. There was disagreement among the experts regarding the results of changes in the terms of trade between reparations paying and receiving countries, the role of the respective elasticities of demand, and the effects of a transfer of purchasing power from lending to borrowing countries. As far as the theoretical aspects of the reparations problem were concerned, the views of Ohlin and Keynes remained irreconciled. However, in their practical—that is, negative—

3. Keynes, *The Economic Consequences of the Peace,* p. 200.
4. Bertil Ohlin, "The Reparations Problem."
5. Keynes, "The German Transfer Problem."

conclusions the two economists came remarkably close together. Ohlin thought that the simplest and safest way of organizing reparations payments in principle would be a policy of deliveries in kind from Germany to France and to the South American countries, all of which required German commodities. After making this suggestion, however, he was obliged to take it all back by acknowledging that "unfortunately such a policy is outside the range of practical possibilities due to the opposition of powerful American and British export industries." [6] Keynes, on the other hand, summed the problem up in a more general way: "At a given time the economic structure of a country in relation to the economic structures of its neighbors permitted a certain natural level of exports, and arbitrarily to effect a material alteration of this level by deliberate devices is extremely difficult." [7]

The difficulties were only too apparent and for the aftermath of World War II new solutions had to be sought. Since the German reparations debt in 1921 had been expressed in monetary terms, and payments had been effected through proceeds from exports of current production, a new policy could readily be devised. If the German indebtedness this time were to be expressed in quantitative terms, and if reparations from current production were replaced by the removal and delivery of German industrial plants and equipment, the Allied statesmen would have established a new and promising formula, since it was the opposite of the one tried without success the last time. [8]

There is of course nothing in the nature of payments in kind that made them a magic tool to overcome the reparations problem. Regardless of whether the German indebtedness was expressed in monetary terms or in other terms, Germany still had to discharge its obligations by means of exports, the only difference being that the newly suggested method would have obligated the receiving countries to accept German products and thereby would possibly have limited their demands. Only in the case of the Soviet Union, with its never-ending scarcities and no competing domestic market, did reparations payments in kind offer a genuine solution to the problem. [9] Furthermore, as to deliveries of exist-

6. Ohlin, p. 178.
7. Keynes, "The German Transfer Problem," p. 167.
8. Penrose offers the following comment: "The idea that reparations in kind avoided all financial and exchange difficulties seems to have been carelessly adopted without careful consultations with experts who had thoroughly studied the experience of the 1920's. An idea which had strictly limited application was elevated into a dogma." Ernest F. Penrose, *Economic Planning for the Peace,* p. 280.
9. The Soviet economist E. Varga made the same point in an article, "Reparations by Hitler's Germany and Its Accomplices."

ing plants and equipment, it was easy to predict that the loss of a dismantled plant to Germany would usually be far greater than the gain to the recipient; but statesmen rarely concern themselves with such bothersome details.

Regardless of the merits of the new policy, there was general agreement within the American cabinet that in view of the shocking experiences after World War I, this time there should be no reparations from current production and that German plants and equipment should be dismantled and transferred instead. As far as the United States was concerned, no reparation claims were to be made. Accordingly in September 1944 Leo Crowley, the head of the Foreign Economic Administration, was instructed by the president to have his agency prepare a study "of what should be done after the surrender of Germany to control its power and capacity to make war in the future." The instruction also pointed out that the purpose of the study was to prevent Germany from "again becoming a menace to succeeding generations." [10] In compliance with these instructions, FEA set up about thirty technical industrial committees, each of which was composed of representatives of private industry and members of government agencies directly concerned. An effort was also made to add to each group some persons who had had some direct contact with the German economy.[11] The committees were given the mission of studying and recommending disarmament measures in their respective areas of competence, an assignment which they accomplished so effectively that when the recommendations of the individual committees were pieced together the emerging final paper would have reduced the German economy to the pastoral level Morgenthau had had in mind. It appears that this development by no means corresponded to the intentions of the originators of the project, but rather was the unfortunate result of amateurish planning whereby each committee was encouraged to proceed independently and without the necessary coordination with the other groups. When the products of the individual committees were finally put together, everyone realized the impossibility of establishing a viable economy on this basis.[12] Obviously, the job had to be done over; but much valuable time had been lost, and when in March 1946 the final FEA plan arrived at last in Berlin, the quadripartite staff responsible for the drafting of a reparations plan had

10. *Technical Industrial Disarmament Committees,* Enemy Branch, Foreign Economic Administration (Washington: U.S. Gov. Printing Office, 1945), 1:1.
11. Ratchford and Ross, *Berlin Reparations Assignment,* p. 48.
12. Clay to McCloy, 3 Sept. 1945, pp. 2–3 (OMGUS records, 410-2/3).

already completed its own work.[13] Two basic policies recommended by the FEA group, i.e., the complete dismantling of all war plants and the limitation of Germany's heavy industry to peacetime requirements, are also found in the Potsdam Agreement, but since these recommendations merely reflect the oft-stated war aims of the three signatories, any claim to authorship on the part of FEA would rest on tenuous ground.

In Great Britain the drafting of a reparations policy did not progress any faster. At an early date, an interdepartmental committee, headed by Sir William Malkin, a prominent civil servant, had begun to work on the reparations problem and had reached the conclusion that reparations in kind this time should replace reparations expressed in monetary terms.[14] The committee also had come up with the more original idea of reparations for the purpose of collective security, so that German money payments would be used to support future Allied military expenditures.[15] These studies, however, took place on a relatively low governmental level and efforts to bring them to the attention of the British cabinet failed. Sir William Malkin himself was killed in an airplane disaster on the way to Yalta.[16]

The problematic nature of the reparations issue is stressed by an anecdote which the American economist E. F. Penrose tells in his *Economic Planning for the Peace*. Penrose, who served during the war as economic adviser to Ambassador John Winant in London, maintained friendly personal relations with Lord Keynes. Greatly concerned about the lack of adequate plans for the postwar treatment of Germany, he attempted to impress on Keynes the need for initiative in the preparation of reasonable plans for reparations, a suggestion which evidently evoked little interest. As Penrose describes it, "Keynes' attitude was defeatist, and while admitting that there was a muddle, he spoke as if there was a hopeless muddle and as if nothing could be done about it." [17] In the light of Keynes's concluding comments in the "German Transfer Problem" which were cited above, his reluctance to become involved in this troublesome issue will be readily appreciated.

Neither the United States nor Great Britain therefore had any definite plans for reparations when Roosevelt, Churchill, and Stalin met at Yalta in February 1945. During the first tripartite discussions of the problem, it became quite clear that the general label of "reparations" actually related to at least three policy aims of the Allied powers: demilitariza-

13. Ratchford and Ross, p. 36.
15. Ibid., p. 219.
17. Ibid.

14. Penrose, p. 217.
16. Ibid., p. 275.

tion, deindustrialization, and the extraction of indemnities. While these concepts often overlapped, they were, of course, by no means identical. As to war plants there was a quick and general agreement that they should be destroyed or, whenever appropriate, they should be dismantled and ownership transferred in partial payment of reparations claims. The policy of deindustrialization, on the other hand, was much more difficult to agree upon, since, among other things, it entailed the intricate question of where to draw the line between a war potential and a peaceful industry; it also involved the determination of a desirable future level for German industry, a most difficult task which tormented the unfortunate economists taxed with providing an answer.

As to the extraction of indemnities, it was to be expected that the Soviet would present the highest claims. As far as devastation was concerned, there was no comparison between Russian sufferings and the damages incurred by the Western nations. While the physical destruction in the Soviet Union was much more severe in absolute terms, the gap became even greater if related to the recuperating powers of the respective countries. The Russians actually were faced with the task of rebuilding their country from scratch. Viewed against this background, the magnitude of Soviet reparations claims hardly seems excessive.[18] As James F. Byrnes, who participated in the conference at Roosevelt's specific request, writes, the subject of reparations was foremost in the minds of the Soviet delegates when the question of Germany came up.[19] I. M. Maisky, then a deputy commissar for foreign affairs, suggested two categories of reparations, namely, "withdrawals" of factories, machinery, machine tools, rolling stock of railways, investments in foreign enterprises, etc., and second, payments in kind from current production over a period of ten years. As to the first category, he explained that 80 percent of Germany's heavy industry should be confiscated and taken away physically. Aviation plants, facilities for the production of synthetic oil, and all other war plants should be eliminated entirely. According to Soviet views, 20 percent of Germany's heavy industry would suffice to maintain its peacetime economy. All reparations were to be completed within ten years but the removal of factories and equipment should be terminated within two years. Maisky added that the total of German reparations should be fixed at $20 billion and that half of this amount would have to go to the Soviet Union.

18. Ibid., p. 282. Penrose, however, without substantiating his comment, considers the Russian demands "exorbitant."
19. Byrnes, p. 26.

In reply Churchill questioned the feasibility of extracting from Germany such a large amount. Since he also brought up Great Britain's unsatisfactory experiences with reparations after the last war, Stalin in turn had an opportunity to offer his views on the breakdown of reparations payment in the twenties and early thirties. As he saw it, the crises would have been avoided had there been payments in kind, in place of monetary transfers, an understandable oversimplification, since Stalin was not familiar with the intricacies of a free-market economy. Roosevelt remarked that the United States did not want any of Germany's factories, machinery, or tools. The German assets in America which had been seized and would be held for reparations represented a relatively insignificant sum of only $150 million. He and Churchill both stated that the American and British people wanted the Germans to live, although their living standard should not be higher than that of other European countries.[20]

The three statesmen finally agreed to set up a tripartite Reparations Commission to convene in Moscow at an early date in order to work out a detailed reparations plan. The decision was incorporated in a document, the text of which is cited in full:

PROTOCOL

On the Talks between the Heads of Three Governments at the Crimean Conference on the German Reparations in Kind.

(1) Germany must pay in kind for the losses caused by her to the Allied nations in the course of the war. Reparations are to be received in the first instance by those countries which have borne the main burden of the war, have suffered the heaviest losses and have organized victory over the enemy.

(2) Reparations in kind is to be exacted from Germany in three following forms:

a) Removals within two years from the surrender of Germany or the cessations of organized resistance from the national wealth of Germany located on the territory of Germany herself as well as outside her territory (equipment, machine tools, ships, rolling stock, German investments abroad, shares of industrial transport and other enterprises in Germany, etc.), these removals to be carried out chiefly for destroying the war potential of Germany.

20. *Foreign Relations . . . Malta and Yalta*, p. 622.

    b) Annual deliveries of goods from current production or a
       period to be fixed.

    c) Use of German labor.

(3) For the working out on the above principles of a detailed plan for exaction of reparations from Germany an Allied Reparations Commission will be set up in Moscow. It will consist of three representatives—one from the Union of Soviet Socialist Republics, one from the United Kingdom and one from the United States of America.

(4) With regard to the fixing of the total sum of the reparation as well as the distribution of it among the countries which suffered from the German aggression, the Soviet and American delegation agreed as follows:

"The Moscow Reparation Commission should take in its initial studies as a basis for discussion the suggestion of the Soviet Government that the total sum of the reparation in accordance with the points (a) and (b) of the paragraph 2 should be $20,000,000,000, and that 50 percent of it should go to the Union of Soviet Socialist Republics."

The British delegation was of the opinion that, pending consideration of the reparation question by the Moscow Reparation Commission, no figures of reparation should be mentioned.

The above Soviet-American proposal has been passed to the Moscow Reparation Commission as one of the proposals to be considered by the Commission.[21]

As one can see, the protocol acknowledged explicitly the principle of reparations from current production notwithstanding that this was quite contrary to the original position of the American government. Unfortunately the language of the protocol was less lucid with its reference to the sum of $20 billion. While the amount was properly identified as a Soviet suggestion and the British objection also was duly recorded, the final sentence which mentioned a "Soviet-American proposal" was hazy enough to permit an intentional misinterpretation, an opportunity which Soviet diplomats, when it appeared convenient, did not fail to utilize.

The Reparations Commission created by the Crimean agreement met in Moscow in June 1945. Edwin W. Pauley, an American businessman who had made a fortune in oil and who had been given the rank of ambassador as President Truman's personal representative, headed the

21. Ibid., pp. 982–83.

United States delegation. This choice was in accordance with the tradition of presidential appointments, which more often than not rest on the incumbents' personal contacts rather than their professionalism. It also reflected a cherished American dogma whereby a man with the mythical distinction of having met large payrolls is able to tackle almost any governmental task entrusted to him. Unfortunately Pauley himself not only seemed imbued with this doctrine, but according to some sources he also handled his important assignment in a somewhat nonchalant fashion reminiscent of similar cavalier performances by aristocratic emissaries in Europe's diplomatic history.[22]

At the Moscow meeting, the Reparations Commission attempted for more than a month to clarify the question of the size and distribution of German reparations, as well as the problem of payments from current production, without arriving at any tangible result. Presumably Pauley began to realize by then that there was quite a difference between business negotiations with his peers in the West and the inimitable negotiation techniques applied by his diplomatic counterparts from the Kremlin. Although he cabled some optimistic reports to the State Department in Washington, no agreement had been reached by the middle of July when the commission, in order to attend the Potsdam Conference, had to transfer its activities to Berlin.

On the agenda at Potsdam, reparations continued to hold a place as one of the most troublesome issues. The Soviets promptly brought up the $20 billion figure, and Molotov remarked that the United States, by not accepting this figure, was trying to reverse a decision reached at Yalta.[23] The American reply that the acceptance of this amount as a basis for discussion did not mean a commitment naturally failed to impress Soviet diplomats, who recognize logic only when it is to Mother Russia's advantage. The American delegation finally concluded that the only way to solve the problem was for each country to satisfy reparations claims out of its own zone.[24] According to some calculations the value of industrial equipment considered unnecessary for Germany's peacetime economy located in the Soviet Zone was 40 percent of the whole. James F. Byrnes, who in the meantime had become secretary of state, therefore proposed to give the Russians an additional 10 percent from the western zones, and if more plants and equipment from the west were desired, to approve an exchange for food and coal from the east. The Soviets

22. Penrose, pp. 282, 283, 285.
23. *Foreign Relations of the United States; Conference of Berlin* (Potsdam), 2:428–39.   24. Ibid., 2:275.

responded first by trying to put a price tag of $2 billion on reparations deliveries from the west, and when this attempt failed, they accepted Byrnes's proposal.[25] Because of its significance, the Potsdam Reparations Agreement (Part IV) is quoted herewith in full.

In accordance with the Crimean decision that Germany be compelled to compensate to the greatest possible extent for the loss and suffering that she has caused to the United Nations and for which the German people cannot escape responsibility, the following agreement on reparations was reached:

1. Reparations claims of the USSR shall be met by removals from the Zone of Germany occupied by the USSR and from appropriate German external assets.

2. The USSR undertakes to settle the reparations claims of Poland from its own share of reparations.

3. The reparations claims of the United States, the United Kingdom and other countries entitled to reparations shall be met from the Western Zones and from appropriate German external assets.

4. In addition to the reparations to be taken by the USSR from its own Zone of occupation, the USSR shall receive additionally from the Western Zones:

(a) 15 percent of such usable and complete industrial capital equipment, in the first place from the metallurgical, chemical, and machine manufacturing industries, as is unnecessary for the German peace economy and should be removed from the Western Zones of Germany, in exchange for an equivalent value of food, coal, potash, zinc, timber, clay products, petroleum products, and such other commodities as may be agreed upon.

(b) 10 percent of such industrial capital equipment as is unnecessary for the German peace economy and should be removed from the Western Zones, to be transferred to the Soviet Government on reparations account without payment or exchange of any kind in return. Removals of equipment as provided in (a) and (b) shall be made simultaneously.

5. The amount of equipment to be removed from the Western

25. Ibid., 2:512, 539.

Zones on account of reparations must be determined within six months from now at latest.

6. Removals of industrial capital equipment shall begin as soon as possible and shall be completed within two years from the determination specified in paragraph 5. The delivery of products covered by 4(a) above shall begin as soon as possible and shall be made by the USSR in agreed installments within five years of the date hereof. The determination of the amount and character of the industrial capital equipment unnecessary for the German peace economy and therefore available for reparations shall be made by the Control Council under policies fixed by the Allied Commission on Reparations, with the participation of France, subject to the final approval of the Zone Commander in the Zone from which the equipment is removed.

7. Prior to the fixing of the total amount of equipment subject to removal, advance deliveries shall be made in respect of such equipment as will be determined to be eligible for delivery in accordance with the procedure set forth in the last sentence of paragraph 6.

8. The Soviet Government renounces all claims in respect of reparations to shares of German enterprises which are located in the Western Zones of occupation in Germany as well as to German foreign assets in all countries except those specified in paragraph 9 below.

9. The Government of the United Kingdom and the United States of America renounce their claims in respect of reparations to shares of German enterprises which are located in the Eastern Zone of occupation in Germany, as well as to German foreign assets in Bulgaria, Finland, Hungary, Rumania and Eastern Austria.

10. The Soviet Government makes no claims to gold captured by the Allied troops in Germany.[26]

In addition, several of the "economic principles" of the Potsdam Agreement (Part III B) also affected the reparations issue. The production of arms, ammunition, implements of war, aircraft, and sea-going ships was prohibited "in order to eliminate Germany's war potential." For the same reason, the production of metals, chemicals, and machinery was to be strictly controlled and "production capacity not needed for

26. Ibid., 2:1505–6.

permitted production was to be removed" (paragraph 11). Germany was to be treated as a single economic unit, and to this end common policies were to be established in regard to foreign trade programs for Germany as a whole, reparations, industrial production, etc. (paragraph 14). Allied controls should be imposed to implement industrial disarmament and reparations, as well as to assure "the production and maintenance of goods and services . . . essential to maintaining in Germany average living standards not exceeding the average of the standard of living of European countries. (European countries means all European countries excluding the United Kingdom and the Soviet Union)" (paragraph 15). The last of the "Economic Principles" (paragraph 19) finally stipulated that payment of reparations should leave enough resources to enable the German people to subsist without external assistance. The proceeds of exports from current production and from stocks were to be available in the first place for payment of imports.[27]

The most important provision pertaining to reparations was contained in paragraph 15, since it established—in very general and nonprofessional terms—the basis for determining reparations. In addition, the preamble to the Potsdam Reparations Agreement deserves attention, since the wording "in accordance with the Crimean Decision" seems to reflect implementation of the Yalta Agreement rather than an intent to supersede it. The same applies to the introduction to Part III (Germany), which specifically stated "the purpose of this agreement is to carry out the Crimea Declaration on Germany." The quoted text is of course of pivotal significance because of the official United States position that Potsdam superseded Yalta. Byrnes felt very strongly about this because, as he later emphasized, "nowhere in the Potsdam Protocol is there any provision for the payment of reparations from current production. All prior discussions were superseded by the formal reparations agreement at Potsdam. The Soviet Union's renewal one year later of its demand for $10 billion of reparations from current production and its continued use of German labor is inexcusable." [28]

There can be no doubt that the American delegation regarded Potsdam as the final agreement superseding Yalta, and Byrnes's annoyance therefore will be appreciated. On the other hand, one cannot help wondering why, contrary to all legal practice, it was nowhere stipulated that the new agreement superseded prior tripartite documents which dealt with identical topics. Furthermore, as far as deliveries from current

27. Ibid., 2 : 1505.   28. Byrnes, p. 85.

production were concerned (a principle accepted by the three powers at Yalta), there are at least three references under Potsdam which seem to confirm rather than to negate their validity: first, paragraph 19 (Part III) which states that "proceeds of exports from current production and stocks shall be available *in the first place* [author's italics] to the payment of imports" and thereby acknowledges the possibility of a "second place" use; second, paragraph 4(a) (Part IV) which by implication provides for an exchange of items of *current production* from the Soviet Zone for industrial equipment from the Western Zones; and third, paragraph 8 (Part IV), whereby "the Soviet Government renounces all claims in respect of reparation to shares of German enterprises in the Western Zones" without offering an identical disclaimer with regard to proceeds from current production.[29]

There was indeed no reference in the Potsdam Agreement to the Soviet proposal regarding a reparations total of $10 billion for the Russian account. However, the sum had been recorded in the Yalta Protocol as a Soviet demand, and the principle of reparations by German labor had even been accepted by the three powers. If one subscribes to the premise that Potsdam implemented rather than superseded Yalta, it would seem that Byrnes's scorn was not fully warranted and that the Soviets were by no means out of bounds in again presenting their monetary claim and in actually using German labor. Naturally they were aware of the underlying aim of the three powers at Potsdam to settle pending matters, but since it was to their advantage, they simply took whatever Potsdam gave them and later reopened the issues which, as they interpreted them, had not been closed.

Although Potsdam provided only an imprecise formula and some very general "principles" for the determination of reparations, Pauley claimed that "reparations policies were now clearly defined and complete." He admitted that these policies were "of a very general character,"[30] but nevertheless decided that his job was ended and returned to the States with all the members of his staff. There he issued an optimistic statement indicating that the reparations plan was thoroughly workable since it embraced all the basic policies required for active administration. "For this administration the responsibility rests solely with the occupying authorities," he said.[31]

---

29. Penrose arrives at a similar conclusion: "At Potsdam the discussion on the subject was inconclusive, but annual deliveries were not ruled out" (p. 299).
30. Ratchford and Ross, pp. 47–48.
31. *U.S. Department of State Bulletin* 13, no. 323 (2 Sept. 1945): 308–9.

What Pauley did not mention was that not a single representative of his delegation to the Moscow Reparations Commission remained in Berlin to provide continuity in the work. Only a few documents were left and "it was only with the greatest difficulty that Mr. Pauley was prevailed upon to dictate a statement which would give some information and guidance to those who would have to take over his task." [32] Whereas the United Kingdom and the Soviet Union had retained teams of specialists who had come to grips with the reparations problem in Moscow and Berlin, a new American group without experience and without the benefit of records had to take over on behalf of the United States. As to the "clearly defined" reparations policy, it will be recognized that Potsdam did not give any guidance at all as to how the average European living standard was to be determined.[33] The resulting difficulties were outlined by Benjamin Ratchford. Were consumer goods and services alone to be considered or did the standard of living encompass all the elements of a country's economy? Was it to be expressed in monetary or in physical terms? The United Kingdom and the Soviet Union had been specifically excluded, but was Germany proper to be included in the computation of economic data? What period of the past was to be used as a basis? Was the average to be considered an upper limit and any level below it an acceptable goal? Did the average as a limitation pertain to each industry and, if affirmative, was there to be no compensation for industries where the lack of natural resources or the control of the war potential provided for little or no German production? Furthermore, should excess equipment in peaceful domestic industries be made available for reparations? Should the controlled production of machinery, metals, and chemicals with their military potential be enlarged to include goods for exports or not? These were just a few of the questions which the Potsdam reparations agreement had failed to answer, leaving it up to the Control Council to come up with the appropriate solutions.[34]

On August 10, 1945, as a first step toward the implementation of the reparations part of the Potsdam Agreement, General Clay appointed a German Standard of Living Board under the chairmanship of Dr. Calvin B. Hoover from Duke University, then an economic adviser to General Draper. In accordance with the Potsdam formula, the board was in-

32. Ratchford and Ross, pp. 47–48.
33. "It would be difficult to find in the recorded history of international relations a more intellectually disreputable and administratively unworkable formula for determining the economic fate of a nation." Penrose, p. 284.
34. Ratchford and Ross, pp. 67–68.

structed to recommend within thirty days the general standard of living for the German peacetime economy, to specify the broad categories of end items required to maintain such a standard, to provide an estimate of the necessary exports and imports, and to recommend the production volume of basic industries that would be needed to maintain a German peacetime economy. While the heads of some key departments of the Military Government served as members of the board, their function was mainly advisory, and most of the actual research was performed by Dr. Hoover, Dr. Don D. Humphrey from Duke University, and Dr. Edgar M. Hoover, Jr., from the University of Michigan.

The period 1930–1938 was selected as a basis for determining the European average standard of living as referred to by Potsdam. During those years the German standard of living had been about one third above the European average and the board therefore concluded that a 26 percent reduction of the German standard of living would have to be made in order to implement the Potsdam formula. Since by coincidence this contemplated future level corresponded to the actual German standard of 1932, the production and consumption of that year—with some exceptions—was taken as a guide.

The resulting calculations of the board—performed on a factual and professional basis "reflecting neither a hard peace nor soft peace bias" [35] —provided, among other things, for an additional steel output of 7.8 million ingot tons, an installed electric generating power capacity of 11 million kilowatts, and an annual production of 100,000 passenger cars, of 408 million RM worth of machinery, 138 million RM of precision and optical instruments, 420 million RM of chemicals, 453 million RM of textiles, etc. (all at 1938 prices).[36] Exports and imports were estimated to be in the vicinity of 4 billion RM as compared with an actual total of 4,619,000,000 RM in 1936.

These figures as well as the other detailed recommendations of the Board were included in a "Hoover Report," [37] copies of which somehow reached the American press. With few exceptions the reactions of the news media were hostile, and there was vociferous criticism of alleged Military Government plans for a "soft peace." Since Morgenthau by that time had been out of office for more than six months and his influence on the conduct of foreign affairs was nil, the public outcry only confirmed that there was a substantial body of opinion in the United States

35. Ibid., p. 75.   36. Ibid., p. 81.
37. There is no connection between this report and the Hoover Report mentioned in the bibliography and the notes to Chapter 2.

which, influenced by the hard evidence of Nazi atrocities, favored a stern peace for Germany.

The organization set up by the Control Council to work on reparations was the Level of Industry Committee, a quadripartite planning group which functioned as a subordinate part of the Economic Directorate. The first American delegate at the committee was Dr. Calvin Hoover, with Dr. Benjamin U. Ratchford from Duke University as alternate. Members of the committee conducted the major part of the negotiations, and only when an agreement could not be reached were matters referred to the Economic Directorate and from there to the Coordinating Committee. The Control Council composed of the four zone commanders also had to intervene in the case of a few issues of cardinal significance, such as the one pertaining to the permissible level of German steel production. At its first meeting on September 18, 1945, the Level of Industry Committee accepted the "Hoover Report" as a basis for discussion and then proceeded with its difficult assignment.[38]

In view of widespread misrepresentations and misunderstandings, a brief appraisal of the nature of the Level of Industry Committee's work seems appropriate. In essence the committee was an economic planning group which, under the terms of reference established by Potsdam, was given the responsibility of determining production and consumption ceilings for a German economy to become effective at an undetermined date. This date, however, was far away. As a practical example, the committee argued whether the German steel production should be limited to five, seven, or nine million tons annually, while actual steel production was in the vicinity of one million tons. According to the best available estimates, four or more years would elapse before the ceiling could be reached.[39] In the same vein, while a future annual level of 3 billion RM of German exports was being discussed, actual exports for 1946 totaled 600 million RM at best. In other words, the committee's extensive research and arduous work actually represented a theoretical exercise. A possible exception arose from the fact that the committee was supposed to set an upper limit on the number of plants and equipment selected for reparations. As we shall see, even this practical objective was soon discarded.

Of equal significance is the fact that the theoretical level of industry which the committee attempted to establish was not meant to set a

38. Ratchford and Ross, pp. 86–88.
39. Clay to Frank Keefe, 9 Feb. 1947 (OMGUS records, 149-3/3). See also Gimbel, p. 58.

permanent limitation on the German economy. While the terms of Potsdam in this respect were somewhat vague, an early policy statement by the U.S. Department of State (December 12, 1945) was very explicit:

> The present determination (of a level of industry) however, is not designed to impose permanent limitations on the German economy. The volume of permitted industrial production of a peacetime character will be subject to constant review after February 2, 1946. . . . The United States intends, ultimately, in cooperation with its Allies, to permit the German people under a peaceful democratic government of their own choice to develop their own resources and to work toward a higher standard of living subject only to such restrictions designed to prevent production of armaments as may be laid down in the peace settlement. . . . In the view of the Department of State the Berlin Declaration is not intended to force a reduction in German living standards except as such reduction is required to meet her reparations payments. In effect, the Berlin Declaration merely provides that Germany's obligation to make reparation for the war damage which her aggression caused to other countries should not be reduced in order to enable Germany to maintain a standard of living above the European average. The Department of State further interprets the standard-of-living criterion to refer to the year immediately following the two-year period of reparations removals.[40]

A supporting statement issued on the same day by the secretary of state reiterated that as soon as the German people regained control over their economy, "they would be subject only to such residual limitations which will be determined by agreement among the occupying powers. In the opinon of this Government, these limitations should be designed solely to prevent German rearmament and not to restrict or reduce the German standard of living." [41] It is worthy of note that these official statements of the United States government were made eight months after the German capitulation and even before a plan for reparations had been drawn up.

40. Published in the *U.S. Department of State Bulletin* 13, no. 338 (16 Dec. 1945): 960–65.
41. General Hilldring considered Byrnes's statement "a useful reaffirmation of the principles underlying the Potsdam Agreement," adding that "CAD not only propounded the questions but also prepared Mr. Byrnes' statement." Memorandum, Hilldring to Assistant Secretary of War, 13 Feb. 1946 (Record Group 165, National Archives).

On March 28, 1946, after seven months of intensive efforts, the work of the Level of Industry Committee, with the active assistance of the Economic Directorate and the Coordinating Committee, was brought to a successful end. The final product of its labor, the "Plan of the Allied Control Council for Reparations and the Level of Post-War German Economy," as it was called, constituted a compromise between four independent draft plans submitted by the representatives of the United States, the Soviet Union, Great Britain, and France. As a rule the levels of industry proposed by the USSR were the lowest and extensive haggling was occasionally required to arrive at a compromise. Judging from the reported fervor and intensity of the disputes, one must assume that the participants were not aware of the futility of their task. The Plan reduced the original American figure of 7.8 million tons of steel to 5.8 million; instead of 100,000 passenger cars only 80,000 were authorized; a capacity of 11 million kilowatts of electricity was reduced to 9 million kilowatts; the annual production of copper was reduced from 160,000 tons to 140,000, of lead from 130,000 tons to 120,000 tons, etc.[42]

It has been charged that General Clay as well as General Draper had been "too anxious to reach decisions thereby letting the Soviets outwait and outwit us."[43] While such criticism possibly was not unfounded, there were very good reasons for an American accommodating attitude. Since the fall of 1945, General Clay's primary concern had been the establishment of unified administrative machinery which among other tasks was to implement a quadripartite export-import plan.[44] The Soviets had consistently refused to move ahead, indicating that these issues could only be broached after the question of reparations had been settled. General Clay and General Draper were obviously aware that, except for its relevance to the dismantling process, any level-of-industry plan drafted at that time would have little practical significance. Under the best of circumstances three or four years of continuous economic progress would be needed until the limitations established by the Plan would become effective, and in the light of the cited State Department statement even this eventuality was somewhat nebulous. It was also more than likely that in the meantime political changes would occur affecting in one way or another the theoretical assumptions on which the Plan was based. Under these conditions was it wise to fight too long about figures which soon might become meaningless? Furthermore, was the Soviet position, namely that the question of reparations had to be

42. Ratchford and Ross, p. 145.   43. Ibid., p. 170.
44. Clay to Hilldring, 10 Dec. 1945, Cable CC-20130 (OMGUS records, 358-2/5).

disposed of before the implementation of economic unity could begin, not simply a delaying tactic? If "progress toward completing the Plan overshadowed all other considerations in the eyes of General Draper and General Clay," as was charged,[45] there was indeed a valid rationale for such an approach.

As indicated, the practical consequence of the Plan was the establishment of a basis for the dismantling of plants and equipment, but even this selection-out process turned out to be in the main a paper activity. On the basis of the Plan, 1546 plants were earmarked as surplus and available for reparations. According to General Clay, they represented a total value of $600 million—probably too low an estimate.[46] This included 336 war plants such as airplane factories and plants for the production of high explosives, war chemicals, shells, cartridge cases, etc., which would have been available for reparations under Potsdam even without a quadripartite Level-of-Industry Plan. (A "war plant" according to Control Council Directive No. 39 was a plant or a part of a plant specially constructed for the production of certain specified munitions. The criterion was that it actually was built for the purpose.) In other words, the starting figure for the discussion of deindustrialization, not including the war plants, was 1210 plants. As of May 1946, only 24 of these plants had been allocated as "advance reparations" in the U.S. Zone; and their dismantling had actually begun.

In this connection, it is necessary to mention that the term "plant" with regard to reparations was used to identify a particular group of equipment within one company which had been designated for reparations. Such earmarked equipment varied from a single small piece of machinery to the entire equipment of an operating company, and it is important to know that the term "plant" as used in this respect did not include the buildings, drawings, patterns, jigs, dies, tools, etc.[47]

In November 1945—that is, at a time when the Level of Industry Committee was still engaged in drawing up the quadripartite reparations plan—representatives of Albania, the United States, Australia, Belgium, Canada, Denmark, Egypt, France, the United Kingdom, Greece, India, Luxembourg, Norway, New Zealand, the Netherlands, Czechoslovakia, the Union of South Africa, and Yugoslavia met in Paris in order to decide how the reparations from Germany should actually be distributed. As the result of their deliberations the so-called Paris Agreement

45. Ratchford and Ross, p. 170.   46. Clay, *Decision in Germany*, p. 324.
47. "Report on Selected List of Plants Scheduled for Removal as Reparations from the Three Western Zones of Germany to ECA Advisory Committee," Jan. 1949, p. 2 (OMGUS records).

was signed. It established an Inter Allied Reparations Agency (IARA) as of January 24, 1946, which was scheduled to complete its task within five years. The principal responsibility of the Agency was to determine the percentage each Member Government was entitled to on the basis of material damage suffered, the loss of human life incurred, and the contribution of the respective government to the war effort; to establish reparations accounts for each of the signatories; and to distribute the receipts accordingly. The IARA established two main categories of reparations, one for "industrial and other equipment removed from Germany, merchant ships, and inland water transport," the second for all other forms of German reparations—German external assets, patents, trademarks, artistic and literary property rights, etc. As envisaged, the work of the Inter Allied Reparations Agency was to be completed in 1951.[48]

Almost immediately after the signing of the "Plan for Reparations and the Level of Post-War German Economy," from here on referred to as the First Level of Industry Plan, General Clay increased the pressure for the acceptance and implementation of a quadripartite export-import plan, a development discussed later in greater detail. When several attempts of the American representatives at the Control Council failed to activate the administering of Germany as an economic entity, Clay on May 4, 1946, ordered a stop to all further dismantling in the U.S. Zone with the exception of the twenty-four plants mentioned above and several war plants, the dismantling of which had been in progress for some time. A few weeks later in a summary report to Washington on the German situation Clay suggested among other things the economic merger of the American and British Zones.[49] In other words, thirty-seven days after its promulgation, the quadripartite Level of Industry Plan lost

48. The proportionate shares of industrial equipment were to be allocated as follows:

COUNTRY	PERCENT ALLOCATED	COUNTRY	PERCENT ALLOCATED
Albania	0.35	India/Pakistan	2.90
Australia	0.95	Luxembourg	0.40
Belgium	4.5	Netherlands	5.60
Canada	1.5	New Zealand	0.60
Czechoslovakia	4.30	Norway	1.90
Denmark	0.35	Union of South Africa	10.0
Egypt	0.20	United Kingdom	27.80
France	22.80	United States	11.0
Greece	4.35	Yugoslavia	9.60

After "Three Years of Reparations," Special Report of Military Government, Nov. 1948, Table I (OMGUS records).
49. Clay to Hilldring, 26 May 1946, Cable CC-5797 (OMGUS records).

whatever practical significance it ever had. It is equally noteworthy that
the proposal to combine the two zones emerged so quickly. Against the
background of this timetable, one must assume that when Clay and
Draper became "too anxious to reach decisions" in the final phase of
quadripartite negotiations, the alternative solution of a bizonal merger
already had been considered.[50]

After Clay's dramatic gesture, his announced policy was somewhat
modified when, as of June 28, 1946, all war plants were made available
for destruction or dismantling.[51] The total so classified in the U.S. Zone
at the time was 98 plants, of which 69 had been completely or partly
dismantled. The very slow implementation of the reparations program
was also evidenced by an official American statement presented almost a
year later (March 1947) indicating that in the American Zone not more
than 80 war plants had been dismantled or destroyed and that the total
number of plants allocated for reparations was 174 as of that date.[52]

It stands to reason that as a consequence of the bizonal merger in
January 1947, a complete re-evaluation of the reparations program had
to be made. The economic calculations on which the quadripartite plan
rested presupposed the existence of an economically unified Germany.
Since this assumption could not be considered valid any longer, new
research studies had to be made. The resulting *Revised Plan for Level of
Industry in the US/UK Zones of Germany* was published on August 29,
1947, and although it observed the same objectives as the original plan,
it drastically changed the production levels originally computed. The
much disputed level of steel production was raised from the earlier
limitation of 5.8 million to 10.7 million ingot tons; the capacity of the
automotive industry was increased from 40,000 passenger cars and
38,000 commercial vehicles to 160,000 and 61,500, respectively; instead of a fabricating capacity of 140,000 tons of copper, 215,000 tons
was now envisaged; all limitations on electric power and several export
industries were removed; etc.[53]

Whereas the effect of the old plan would have been to limit total
industrial capacity to 70 or 75 percent of German production in 1936,
the revised plan was expected to retain sufficient capacity in the bizonal

50. Clay mentioned the possibility of bi- or tripartite arrangements in a letter to
McCloy of 29 June 1945 (OMGUS records, 410-2/3).
51. "A Year of Potsdam: The German Economy Since the Surrender"
(OMGUS records).
52. Statement on reparations by Secretary Marshall at the Moscow Conference,
17 March 1947, *Department of State Bulletin* 16, no. 404 (30 March 1947):
563–64.
53. *Revised Plan for Level of Industry*, pp. 6–9.

area "to approximate the level of industry prevailing in Germany in 1936, a year that was not characterized by either boom or depressed conditions." [54] However, since the bizonal area in 1946 already had a population 6 million persons larger than in 1936 and was expected to have a population of 42 to 44 million by 1952, the per capita productive capacity envisaged by the new plan was expected to be about 75 percent of 1936. Again the theoretical aspects of this exercise in economic analysis have to be stressed, because at a time when a steel production of 10.7 million ingot tons was being discussed, the actual steel production in the bizone was about 2 million tons; and when $2 billion of bizonal exports were being planned, actual annual exports (1947) totaled $350 million, with only moderate increases for the immediate future in sight.

Of considerable practical significance, however, was the effect of the revised plan on the contemplated extent of reparations, because of the 1210 plants (nonwar) earmarked under the original plan for reparations, 687 could now be removed from the reparations list, thereby reducing the former grand total of 1546 to 859. (The last two figures include 336 war plants.) [55] By this time, United States policy guidances and official public statements had fallen in line with the constructive efforts of the Military Government, which had been in evidence in the economic field from the beginning of the occupation. Of symbolic significance in this connection was the withdrawal of JCS/1067 and its replacement, as of July 11, 1947, by a new directive JCS/1779. One will recall some of the major economic provisions of JCS/1067 had been superseded by the Potsdam Agreement. Since the originating War Department had neither the authority nor the intent to alter the provisions of Potsdam, the main purpose of the change was to dovetail the text of the new directive with the language of the tripartite agreement and to eliminate outdated negative statements whenever warranted. JCS/1779 still demanded the punishment of war criminals, as well as denazification and demilitarization of Germany. Also in compliance with Potsdam, all war industries were to be dismantled or destroyed and reparations were to be exacted in order to compensate for the losses suffered as a result of German aggression.

On the other hand, the level of industry agreed upon as the basis for reparations "should not permanently limit Germany's industrial capac-

54. Ibid., p. 4.
55. "It stands to reason that the reduction in reparation payments caused emphatic and repeated protests on the part of the Inter Allied Reparations Agency." Reparations Report to the Military Governor, Sept. 1945–June 1949 (OMGUS records).

ity." The last sentence corresponded with the previously mentioned policy statement of the Department of State of December 12, 1945, and clarified the less explicit language of the Potsdam Agreement. The new directive reiterated the basic American interest in a just and lasting peace throughout the world and stated that "such peace can only be achieved if conditions of public order and prosperity are created in Europe as a whole." Since this required "the economic contributions of a stable and productive Germany," the U.S. government intended to "create those political and economic, and moral conditions in Germany which will contribute most effectively to a stable and prosperous Europe." The main objective of the U.S. government, according to the new directive, was to establish "a form of political organization and a manner of political life which, resting on a substantial basis of economic welfare, will lead to tranquillity within Germany and will contribute to the spirit of peace among nations." In order to realize this objective the commanding general was directed to consider it his fundamental task to help lay the economic and educational basis for a sound German democracy. JCS/1779 also said that while the economic rehabilitation of Germany was primarily a responsibility of the German people, "Military Government should provide the general policy guidance and assist in the development of a balanced trade." In this connection the U.S. military governor was directed to support the removal of existing trade barriers, to encourage the return of foreign trade to normal channels, and to prepare the reorganization of German finances on a sound basis. Although from the standpoint of practical policy implementation JCS/1779 provided for no changes, it did away with the punitive tone of JCS/1067 and offered instead a constructive approach. Also, most pleasing to General Clay's orderly mind, now at last he had his instructions in a single document.[56]

The initial thaw was followed by a rapid change in the general political climate. On June 5, 1947, in a speech at Harvard University, Secretary of State George C. Marshall offered the financial assistance of the United States to the European Nations in their efforts toward economic reconstruction, and in the following April the Foreign Assistance Act of 1948 established the necessary legislation for the European Recovery Program. Since it appeared contradictory to extract reparations from Germany while simultaneously providing funds for its reconstruction, the Act stipulated that "the Administrator (of ECA) will

56. *U.S. Department of State Bulletin* 17, no. 421 (27 July 1947): 186–93; Clay, *Decision in Germany*, p. 238.

request the Secretary of State to obtain the agreement of those countries concerned that such capital equipment as is scheduled for removal as reparations from the three Western Zones of Germany be retained in Germany if such retention will most effectively serve the purposes of the European Recovery Program." [57]

The ECA Industrial Advisory Committee under George M. Humphrey (later secretary of the treasury) was therefore directed to conduct a study of the capital equipment in 381 nonwar plants in Germany earmarked for reparations. The committee was broken up into two groups, one responsible for the inspection of chemical, nonferrous metal, and mechanical engineering factories, the other charged with the survey of the German steel industry. The former worked with the assistance of four prominent American engineering firms,[58] whereas the latter enlisted the help of the president of the U.S. Steel Export Corporation, George Wolf. It is noteworthy that in December 1948 when the committee went to work, out of 523 plants allocated for reparations, only 187 had actually been dismantled. The professional and objective approach of the Humphrey Committee was reflected in the letter covering its voluminous report to the administrator (Paul Hoffman) stating that, "although we recognized the danger to world peace from future German aggression which is greatly feared by some of the Western countries, we also were impressed with the menace to future peace that could follow from projecting the German economy at too low a level. That could result in even greater insecurity for the Western world." [59] In the report the committee recommended that out of 381 plants inspected 167 would be "better able to contribute to European recovery if retained there than if released for reparations and moved elsewhere." The committee furthermore suggested that while the current production of steel in the Bizone was limited to 10.7 million ingot tons per year and the occupying powers had decided upon a 13.02 million tons of ingot steel capacity, a 13.5 million ton capacity should be retained, entailing a suggested increase of 4 percent. The 167 plants recommended for retention encompassed 37 steel plants, 35 chemical plants, 7 nonferrous metal plants, and 88 plants in the general mechanical engineering category.[60]

The negotiations with Britain and France for the acceptance of the

---

57. Price, *The Marshall Plan and Its Meaning*, pp. 25–26; Foreign Assistance Act of 1948 (80th Cong., 2d sess., vol. 62, pt. 1, p. 150), sec. 115(F).

58. Coverdale and Colpitts; F. H. McGraw and Company; Sanderson and Porter; Stone and Webster Engineering Corporation.

59. Report of Industrial Advisory Committee to ECA Administrator, p. 1 (OMGUS records).

60. Ibid., p. 4.

proposals of the Humphrey Committee were conducted in London by Ambassador Lewis Douglas and produced a tripartite agreement of April 13, 1949, whereby 159 plants were removed from the reparations list. As of spring 1949, the list of plants for reparations had been reduced to 364, to which figure of course the original 336 war plants had to be added. However, this was still not the last word on the reparations issue. As time went on, German resentment of reparations had increased, and the critical views of the German people were expressed more vocally. In addition to the fact that most people resent paying for damages caused to others, in Germany there also had been the shocking experiences of the twenties, with mass unemployment, a runaway inflation, starvation, and a breakdown of public morals. Superimposed on this historical background was the Goebbels propaganda that so effectively exploited the Morgenthau Plan in order to condition the German mind. Other occupation policies such as denazification and demilitarization also were unpopular, but German feelings in this respect were divided, whereas the reparations issue was a perfect instrument for arousing a national opposition. As seen with German eyes, the new Allied policy of reparations by the removal of plants and equipment in place of deliveries from current production only made matters worse.

Economic facts, statistical data, and rational thoughts naturally counted very little in such an atmosphere. Official factual information was not believed and rumors flourished. Indicative of this state of affairs was former President Herbert Hoover's angry criticism of Allied occupational policies in Germany when he returned from his mission to Europe in the spring of 1947. Hoover charged that Allied forces were dismantling German fertilizer plants and, following a closed meeting with the Senate's Foreign Relations Committee, he told reporters that "American, British and Russian forces are busy as bees destroying fertilizer plants while all of Europe is gasping for fertilizers needed for food production." [61] Evidently, Hoover's comments were prompted by information supplied to his staff in the course of their visit to Europe. The rebuttal of these charges came in the form of an OMGUS cable, excerpts of which read as follows:

There had been no destruction of phosphate fertilizer plants in Germany, and none of the existing plants have [been] or will be declared for reparations. . . . In the U.S. Zone posphate fertilizer

61. Noce to Clay, 20 April 1947, Cable WX-96474 (OMGUS records, 205-2/11).

capacity is being expanded. Recently . . . [OMGUS has] authorized construction of new plant with capacity 16,500 tons per year.
. . . There had been no destruction of synthetic ammonia plants
or auxiliary fertilizer conversion plants by the Western Zones.
Synthetic ammonia is a prohibited industry; however, Control
Council had authorized production of synthetic ammonia for Germany's peacetime requirements until such time as exports can pay
for all imports. Germany has sufficient nitrogen plant capacity to
meet her nitrogen fertilizer requirements. Germany has sufficient
potash mine and plant capacity to meet her potash fertilizer requirements. Present fertilizer deficiencies of nitrogen are due
chiefly to shortages of coal and power. Every effort being made to
bring potash production up to maximum.[62]

Naturally as always happens in such cases, the original sensational
charges made headlines in the American press, whereas the sober facts
supplied by OMGUS attracted little public attention.[63]

While the destruction of war plants still could be explained to the
German people, the rationale for the dismantling of other production
facilities was not accepted and the rumored explanation that "reparations aimed at reducing German industrial capacity in order to make it
practically impossible for Germany to compete on the world markets" [64]
was widely believed. The German demand for an end of the dismantling process was presented repeatedly and insistently, not only through
the German elected representatives,[65] but whenever an opportunity presented itself in German-American channels, as for instance through the
German American Republican League. Rational explanations by the
American military governor—to the effect that "it will require the greatest efforts of the German people to achieve within five years the level
that has been agreed," [66] that it "was futile to retain more capacity in
individual fields than the area's general resources can support" or that
"it was an entirely sound policy to make reparations in form of plants
which are surplus to the needs of the future German economy and for
whose present operation raw material and other resources are not avail-

62. Clay to Noce, 20 April 1947, Cable CC-8865 (OMGUS records, 205-2/11).
63. Gimbel, p. 59.
64. Speech by Bürgermeister Brauer of Hamburg at the Minister Präsidents'
Conference, Wiesbaden, 22 Oct. 1947, as cited in a letter of the American Consul
General, Hamburg, to Secretary of State, 3 Nov. 1947 (OMGUS records, 24-
2/7).
65. For other German official reactions, see Gimbel, pp. 178–80.
66. Clay to Chairman, German American League, Nov. 1947 (OMGUS
records, 149-3/3).

able" [67]—failed to convince anybody in Germany of the correctness of the American and British reparations policy.

Not all the criticism of this policy, however, was based on emotion and misinformation. The German Verwaltungsamt für Wirtschaft for instance in a report entitled *The Effect of Envisaged Dismantling on Germany's Economic Situation and Its Role in European Reconstruction* pointed out that the drafters of the Second Level of Industry Plan, when calculating available industrial capacities, had taken as a basis maximum output which had been achieved only temporarily during the war. The report contended that gross capacity which unavoidably entailed some double counting had been used. It also said that the excessive strain on production facilities during the war and the failure to make vital repairs had helped to distort calculations. Among other points, it was stressed that "a dismantled plant in the iron producing industry will yield no more than 20 to 25 percent of usable production facilities. The rest is scrap because a dismantled blast furnace or dismantled melting and annealing furnaces cannot be recreated." [68] While such criticism was presumably well founded, it failed to recognize the temporary nature of the two Level of Industry Plans, assigning them a practical significance for Germany's economy which they did not have.

The mounting German opposition nevertheless had the effect of enlisting the support of the newly elected German government under Konrad Adenauer, which, although new in office, began to negotiate for a further curtailment of the dismantling process. As a result, the Petersberg Agreement of November 22, 1949, provided for a removal of additional 17 plants [69] from the reparations list, thereby reducing the final grand total to 683 plants.

As to the value of all plants and equipment removed from the three western zones as reparations, there are three sets of figures at our disposal. General Clay mentions 912 million RM as an estimated reparations value and by applying a 30 percent conversion factor arrives at a total of $270 million.[70] The Bremen senator, C. W. Harmssen, in his detailed study *Am Abend der Demontage* covering six years of reparations, arrives at a total of 1.3 to 1.4 billion DM. Using a 1.8 factor to establish current values, he arrives at a total of 2.5 billion DM or about

67. Clay to Congressman Frank B. Keefe, 9 Feb. 1948 (OMGUS records, 149-3/3).
68. Verwaltungsamt für Wirtschaft, *The Effect of Envisaged Dismantling on Germany's Economic Situation and Its Role in European Reconstruction* (Frankfurt am Main, 1948; OMGUS records).
69. Harmssen, *Am Abend der Demontage*, p. 176.
70. Clay, *Decision in Germany*, p. 325.

$625 million.[71] Finally, Dr. Henry C. Wallich of Yale University starts out with an amount of 708,500,000 DM as established by the Inter Allied Reparations Commission at 1938 prices. Allowing for "a near doubling of prices since 1938, for an especially severe depreciation schedule applied by the Allies plus the loss of some buildings and installations," he concludes with an estimate of 2 billion DM or $500 million.[72]

A summary of the rapid and radical changes in the American reparations policy probably should begin with the abortive Morgenthau Plan which, although not an instrument of American official policy, was aimed at creating a pastoral Germany and the reduction of the German people to a mere subsistence level. Already at Yalta a different language was used when Roosevelt envisaged a future German standard of living "not higher than that of other countries such as the Soviet Republic." JCS/1067, appearing in May 1945, gave a similar definition since it stipulated that the German standard of living should not be on a higher level than that existing in any of the neighboring United Nations. A few months later, Potsdam brought about the first important change by establishing the principle of a German standard of living "not higher than the average of other European countries excluding the United Kingdom and the Soviet Union." Considering the low standard of living of the latter, this of course meant a less severe policy than discussed at Yalta. The next step came with the statement of the U.S. Department of State indicating that the level of German industry to be established under Potsdam would only be used to determine surplus plants and equipment but not to limit a future German industrial expansion. Then followed the publications of the First and Second Level of Industry Plans, the former arriving at an industrial level about 25 percent below the one reached in 1936, and the latter taking the level of 1936 itself as a basis. This and later developments reduces the original number of 1210 reparations plants (excluding 336 war plants) by more than two thirds to the final figure of 347.

The actual effects of the dismantling process on the German economy are difficult to appraise. Its relative lack of impact, however, becomes quite apparent if one relates the high German estimate of 2.5 billion DM for the total value of dismantled plants to the West German investment figure of 19.3 billion DM for the first year after reparations had come to an end. As far as the economic theoreticians are concerned, the

71. Harmssen, p. 26.   72. Wallich, p. 370.

history of German reparations after World War II provided no answer to their dispute. The problem of reparations after World War I obviously was caused by the magnitude of the sums involved; it was one thing to envisage an international transfer of $30 billion and quite another to plan for 1 or 2 percent of this amount. Inasmuch as reparations after World War II totaled only about $500 million, a policy of deliveries from current production following the destruction of war plants probably would have been more advantageous for everyone concerned.

Chapter Four

Starting from Scratch

The student of economic history who examines the state of the German economy in the fall of 1945 when the first export-import program was launched in the American Zone may find it difficult to suppress a feeling of bewildered disbelief. The term "chaotic" is simply a superficial and inadequate euphemism for the political and economic conditions that prevailed, and only traditional American optimism can explain why an export-import program was launched at such an early date. When we survey the obstacles which OMGUS had to overcome to get German exports started, we can begin by concentrating on the catastrophic situation in the coal mines, or we can discuss the transportation problem with more than 60 percent of all locomotives and more than 40 percent of all freight cars out of action, or we can refer to a host of additional and equally obstructive factors. However, all these barriers, although difficult enough to overcome, were dwarfed by one cardinal problem of the Military Government: it had been given responsibility for a country without a currency.[1]

Generally the word "inflation" is used to describe the financial and economic crisis which gripped Germany after the war. While the term is appropriate to some degree, it should be remembered that the situation in Germany not only differed from the classical example of a runaway inflation after World War I, but actually produced an economic phenomenon of its own, probably without precedent in economic history. In 1923 the German mark had been traded against other currencies on

---

1. The Verwaltungsamt für Wirtschaft considered the removal of excess money in circulation "the decisive condition for a restoration of the general readiness to work." "History of Economic Planning," p. 9. Kenneth Dayton regarded the lack of purchasing value of the currency as "the greatest single obstacle to effective economic recovery." Dayton to Director OMGB on problems of policy in effectuating the export-import program, 2 April 1947, p. 3 (OMGUS records, AG.091–31).

international and German markets, and although the dollar eventually was quoted at 4.2 trillion marks, it was always possible to establish an international price for the mark. In 1945, after the collapse of the Third Reich, on the other hand, there were no quotations for the Reichsmark on the international market and all trading of Reichsmarks against foreign currencies had ceased.

From 1935 to 1945 German currency in circulation had increased from approximately 5 billion to 50 billion RM and bank deposits had grown from 30 billion to 150 billion RM. At the same time, the government debt, without taking war damage and other war-connected claims of 350 billion RM into consideration, had climbed from 15 billion to 400 billion RM. On the other side of the ledger, it was estimated that Germany's national real wealth had decreased by one third by 1945 and that for the first postwar years its capacity to produce had been reduced to about 50 percent of the prewar level.[2] Indeed, it did not require a financial wizard to figure out that a monetary reform was an essential step toward the economic recovery of the country, that such action should be taken as quickly as possible, and that without it no effective program for the reconstruction of Germany could be undertaken. Had any additional evidence been needed it could be found in the liberated countries of Europe. All of them had hastened to establish a new and firm accounting basis for their respective economies; among others, France, Belgium, the Netherlands, Austria, and Czechoslovakia had introduced currency reforms.

Accordingly, one of the early actions of the military governor was the appointment of a committee of financial experts, who were given the responsibility of preparing a comprehensive program for the reorganization of Germany's currency and finance. The committee, consisting of Joseph M. Dodge (General Clay's adviser), Gerhard Colm, Raymond Goldsmith, and a staff of five American economists,[3] went to work in March 1946, at a time when the economic unity of the four zones was still considered a valid premise. Six weeks later the committee's report, marked "secret," was submitted to General Clay under the title "A Plan for the Liquidation of War Finance and the Financial Rehabilitation of Germany." As defined by the authors, its general objective was "to provide means of adjusting the financial aftermath of the war and to clear the way for the interzonal financing necessary for the peacetime

2. Colm-Dodge-Goldsmith Report, p. 1.
3. Horst Mendershausen, Robert Eisenberg, Lloyd Metzler, Jerome Jacobson, and Gerald Matchett.

reconstruction permitted under the terms of the Potsdam Agreement and the decisions of the Allied Control Council." [4]

Members of the committee, after consulting with the American, French, British, and Russian staffs of the Finance Directorate, had visited the four zones and had talked to German bankers, industrialists, and tax experts. In the American Zone they had also attended a meeting of the Länderrat and had spoken with some of the *Land* ministers of finance. As a last step, they had studied the financial reforms of some of the liberated countries. The Colm-Dodge-Goldsmith Report, as it was to be called, recognized that a financial reform could not be expected to eliminate all the obstacles preventing a rapid increase of German industrial and agricultural production; on the other hand, it proposed removing the confusing and demoralizing "veil of money" to establish a firm accounting basis for the German economy. As the authors of the report saw it, a monetary reform was a first, highly important step toward the ultimate Allied goal for Germany, namely, an economy that would permit the Germans to obtain a standard of living equal to the continental European average. The committee's proposals, submitted with this basic consideration in mind, suggested a three-pronged approach to the problem. First it mentioned the creation of a new currency, the Deutsche Mark, and the reduction of all monetary claims and obligations at the ratio of 1 DM for 10 RM. The reduction was to pertain to currency, bank deposits, mortgages, and public and private debts, but not to the debt of the German Reich which was to be invalidated. Banks, insurance companies, and charitable organizations were to receive sufficient amounts of a new German governmental debt so that they would be able to meet their reduced obligations. Prices, wages, salaries, rents, and taxes would be the same as in the old currency.

As a second step, the committee suggested a 50 percent mortgage on all real estate, plant, equipment, and inventories in order to reduce the disparity in sacrifice imposed on holders of monetary claims and owners of real assets. The third recommended step was a progressive capital levy on individuals' net worth in order to extract greater contributions from the more affluent Germans, in accordance with their respective financial capacities. The committee envisaged a levy ranging from 10 to 90 percent to be paid in installments over a period of ten years. In addition, the committee recommended a limitation on occupation costs and reparations; the organization of a German central bank which would

4. Letter of transmission to General Clay, 20 May 1946, Colm-Dodge-Goldsmith Report.

issue and control the currency; provisions for transitory business credits; a small increase in prices for industrial products; and a slight reduction in the prevailing rates of direct taxes. As to the value of the new currency, a rate of approximately twenty-five cents for the new Deutsche Mark was suggested "in order to enable Germany to compete in the world markets without giving her an undue advantage over her competitors."[5] The first step of the plan was to be implemented in the fall of 1946, the second step one year later, and the third step two years later. By 1949 the currency reform was to be completed.

The committee also examined an alternative approach, namely, to delay financial reform until there was an increase in production. While it was recognized that there were some advantages in such a timetable, Dodge and his associates felt that the risk of a continued erosion of confidence in the Reichsmark accompanied by further deterioration of workers' and business morale should outweigh all other considerations. For the same reason they advised against a postponement until the government budget could be balanced or a German central administration could be created. In conclusion, quoting extensively from the protocols of Potsdam, they emphasized that financial reform was necessary for the attainment of the political and economic goals of the occupation of Germany as established by the Potsdam Agreement.[6]

It is significant that the proposals submitted to General Clay by the American experts contained the key provisions for a German currency reform which, in spite of the glaring urgency, was to be promulgated only after two trying years had elapsed. The "Plan for the Liquidation of War Finance and the Financial Rehabilitation of Germany" was promptly dispatched to Washington, where it was scrutinized by the Departments of War, State, and Treasury.[7] Simultaneously copies were sent to the Allied members of the Control Council, who began discussing the plan at the meetings of the Finance Directorate.[8] Although Washington's approval came through by August 1946, French and Soviet opposition made it impossible to reach a quadripartite agreement. Only in March 1948, after the breaking up of the Allied Control Council, did the three Western powers decide to proceed with the West German currency reform, and on June 20, 1948, it finally was put into effect.[9]

5. Colm-Dodge-Goldsmith Report, p. iii.
6. Ibid., p. 5.
7. Clay, *Decision in Germany*, p. 210.
8. Major General Draper to K. I. Koval, Deputy for Economics to Soviet Commander in Chief, 17 June 1946 (OMGUS records, 148-3/3).
9. Clay, *Decision in Germany*, p. 213.

Since the reconstruction of the German economy lagged during the first three years of the occupation, and the appalling conditions in occupied Germany were only too apparent, many writers tended to place the blame for the slow progress on the doorstep of the American and British military administrators. Critics, in accordance with their respective political views, offered as the alleged causes for the impasse the influence of Morgenthau, the effects of JCS/1067, the spirit of revenge, reparations, the First Level of Industry Plan, the idea of a "pastoral" state, the lack of competent Allied personnel, and denazification. While there was a kernel of truth in most of these critical observations, it is this writer's belief that the obstructive effects of all these factors combined were less damaging by far than the two-year delay in the establishment of a new German currency. At the same time, it will have to be recognized that political considerations made a postponement in all likelihood unavoidable and that even with the wisdom of hindsight it would not be easy to suggest a reasonable alternate course of action.[10] Because it was clear from the outset that a unilateral introduction of a new German currency would complete the break-up of Germany into two political parts, it was the intent of American foreign policy to postpone this irrevocable step as long as possible. The Western Allies therefore proceeded with the currency reform only after the East-West split had become an acomplished fact and only when the situation in Germany as well as economic repercussions in western Europe made a further postponement too hazardous.

If inflation is described as a situation where too much money is chasing too few goods, economic conditions in postwar Germany would clearly meet this definition. On the other hand, if the traditional example of a spiral were given whereby an increase in wages leads to a price rise which in turn causes further increases in wages and so on, it would not apply to the German phenomenon. Since the days of the German runaway inflation of 1925, most governments had mastered the techniques of monetary controls, and Dr. Hjalmar Schacht had perfected the art to a very fine degree. Although there had been a tenfold increase of currency in circulation since 1930 and an estimated concurrent growth of the public debt from 15 to 700 billion RM,[11] prices and wages in Nazi Germany had remained stable. On one hand, this had been accomplished by rigid controls, and on the other by the rationing

10. For example, Penrose, chaps. 15, 16, 17; Balabkins, passim. Schwarz acknowledges "the devastating effect which a breaking up of the war-time alliance would have had on world public opinion." *Vom Reich zur Bundesrepublik*, p. 73.
11. Colm-Dodge-Goldsmith Report, p. i.

of all essentials at an adequate level, a policy that could be fully implemented as long as Germany held most of Europe in bondage. The draconic enforcement of economic laws by the Gestapo also played an important role. In short, there was little inclination to acquire additional supplies illegally, especially since the risks incurred by anyone involved in black-market transactions were extraordinarily high. When the American Military Government took over in Germany, it found an elaborate and carefully composed set of regulations which governed food collection, marketing, rationing, and pricing. Furthermore, in the words of one astute observer, the Allied administrators inherited "the deeply rooted discipline of the German masses and their fear of authority into which twelve years of Nazi terror had bludgeoned them." [12]

In the next three years, however, two interrelated developments advancing concurrently brought about a gradual erosion of the wartime economic pattern and thereby produced a progressive economic paralysis. On one hand, the American and British Military Governments were unable to maintain or implement the ration levels of the Nazi economy, and on the other, as the Germans became acquainted with the ways and means of their democratic conquerors, their fear of authority gradually lessened until it came close to the vanishing point. Generated by steadily decreasing inhibitions and growing temptations, a new economic pattern developed for which there was no historical precedent. The German market became divided into two sectors, one in which entirely insufficient quantities of rationed goods were sold at official prices against the payment of Reichsmarks, and the other in which most products were available provided that items of equal scarcity could be offered in exchange. In the second sector the Reichsmark had been eliminated as a currency, although it was often used as a means of camouflage in order to give barter deals the appearance of legal transactions. In place of the Reichsmark, cigarettes frequently assumed the role of money, since they fulfilled some of the prerequisites of a currency, namely, durability, divisibility into small "denominations," transportability, and wide acceptance not only in Germany but also abroad.

After the collapse of the Third Reich, the German population became increasingly aware that something would have to be done by the authorities to eliminate the monetary "overhang." Although official discussions on the subject were kept secret, there were continuous rumors among the population indicating that 90 percent of the currency would soon be declared worthless. Every German businessman had learned from per-

12. Stolper, *German Realities*, p. 96.

sonal experience or, if he was of the younger generation, from the reported trials and tribulations of his parents, that under the threat of a runaway inflation the first rule was to sell as little as possible against payment in the threatened currency and then seek protection in the acquisition of gold, foreign currencies, and real property. The possibility of taking refuge in gold or foreign currencies had been blocked by Nazi legislation which made the clandestine possession of such assets a criminal offense punishable in extreme cases by death. There remained as the only way out the acquisition of real goods by barter, or "compensation trading," as it was officially called, a process that was subsequently to assume incredible and even grotesque proportions.

Under the Third Reich, compensation transactions had been forbidden by a War Economic Ordinance of March 25, 1942.[13] This was enforced with relative ease as long as there were adequate supplies. After the German surrender, however, as distrust in the currency grew, the manufacturer who needed raw materials for his factory, the farmer who required equipment and essential supplies for his land, and the white- or blue-collar worker who wanted food for his family had little choice but to resort to barter when official allocations became inadequate or unavailable. In other words, compensation trading developed as the inescapable result of unsatisfactory commodity flows and of a widespread rejection of the Reichsmark as a means of payment.

The following example of a manufacturer of chinaware in Selb who needed steel for the repair of one of his factory buildings will provide a useful illustration. Since it was impossible for him to obtain an allocation of steel under existing conditions, he dispatched an emissary to Düsseldorf, where contact was established with a dealer owning a small stock of the urgently required material. The dealer, who had no use for chinaware, needed typewriters, as well as a supply of electric light blubs for his office. After an extensive search, the china manufacturer's legman discovered a manufacturer of typewriters in Nürnberg and a Frankfurt firm producing light bulbs. Both companies had initiated a policy whereby they served a midday meal to their workers in order to keep them on the job. Since tableware was needed for their newly established canteens, the triangle could be closed. The chinaware was shipped to Nürnberg and Frankfurt, the typewriters and the light bulbs to Düsseldorf, and the steel to Selb. No currency was exchanged, although the transactions were recorded on the books of the four firms at the prevailing official prices. The reader will not fail to take note of the

13. *Reichsgesetzblatt*, pt. 1, 26 March 1942.

involved, costly, and time-consuming logistics of such transactions, made even more complicated by an inadequate postal and telephone service and the prevailing censorship. Accordingly, all the details of the deals had to be worked out through personal contact. It is difficult to appraise the volume of compensation trading, but a Düsseldorf Chamber of Commerce estimate serves as a guide. It indicated that about one half of all transactions in 1947 took place outside regular channels.[14] Taxes obviously could be easily evaded through the barter system, and government attempts toward meaningful planning were rendered futile.

From the outset, the policies of the American Military Government regarding compensation trading were contradictory, and the implementation of these policies by German administrators was often quite perfunctory. Actually there were continuous attempts to draw a line between "legal" and "illegal" barter, the latter pertaining especially to illicit trade in rationed food.[15] As an example of legal trading, one sees the "Barter Ring" in Stuttgart, opened with the concurrence of the American Military Government in July 1945. It consisted of a group of retailers, each firm specializing in its own field of consumer goods. Purchases were made at an appraised value based on official prices with an allowance for depreciation. The seller received the appraised price in cash and—most important—a barter certificate for the same amount which entitled the holder to purchase barter articles up to the face value of the certificate in any one of the member stores.[16] The cost of the services rendered by the member firms and their profits were covered by a 10 percent appraisal fee and a 15 percent surcharge based on a percentage of the appraised value. Food, beverages, tobacco, and fuel were excluded by the Barter Ring, and inferior merchandise was not accepted. The existence of the Stuttgart Barter Ring and its advantages were advertised by newspapers and radio so that the system was soon imitated in other towns. According to the Military Government report, "The Barter Ring at Stuttgart was among the most successful barter organizations in the U.S. Zone. By the end of February, it had closed one transaction for every six persons of the 366,000 people in Stuttgart." In essence, the Military Government was faced with a situation it was unable to cope with as long as the problem of the German currency and

14. Stolper, p. 98.
15. *OMGUS Trade and Commerce,* Jan. 1946, p. 3, expresses the view that "the practice of barter in all areas of commerce paradoxically contributes to price stability. Even though it is a reflection of a basically dangerous economic situation, barter tends to neutralize much of the monetary inflationary pressure."
16. Ibid., Feb. 1946, p. 10.

inadequate commodity supplies could not be solved. An attempt to legislate in this matter in March 1947 remained largely ineffective.[17] The dilemma was neatly summed up in a memorandum to the director of the Economic Division by the American economist Horst Mendershausen, who served on General Draper's staff:

> Until the causes of compensation trading are attacked effectively, it can be legalized only at the expense of the remnants of economic controls and monetary economy; it can be suppressed only at the expense of production and deliveries. Military Government has little to gain from the proclamation of hard and fast rules legalizing certain types of compensation transactions or prohibiting others.[18]

It is not surprising then that in view of the existing legal twilight, the scope of compensation trading varied from region to region, from industry to industry, and from plant to plant. In the same vein, the official German attitude toward it changed from prosecution in Nord-rhein-Westfalen to tacit toleration in Schleswing-Holstein, to official approval in Württemberg-Baden and even to partial legalization in Hesse.[19] While barter was a matter of necessity in the case of the German business community, it was even more pressing for white- and blue-collar workers and their families. Their wages generally only suf-ficed to pay for official food rations, rent, utilities, transportation, and taxes. There was no purpose in asking for higher wages, because even when an increase was authorized, additional money was almost mean-ingless. Instead, industries began to supplement the money income of their employees by additional payments in kind. As a rule these con-sisted of merchandise manufactured in the respective factories. On weekends—which lasted longer as time went on—the workers took off to the countryside where their own wares were traded for eggs, butter, milk, or whatever food items were available to supplement their inade-quate official rations. Many of the workers maintained regular jobs only in order to be entitled to ration cards and the social benefits which depended on regular employment. They spent most of their time black-marketing, and it was this activity that often provided the bulk of their incomes. As an American observer described it:

> The crowds in the devastated towns were perpetually on the move. Never before did Germans travel so much, never before were

17. Military Government Law No. 50, May 1947 (OMGUS records).
18. Undated memorandum, Horst Mendershausen to General Draper (OMGUS records).
19. Ibid.

German trains so shockingly over-crowded. Dark, unheated passenger cars with broken windows carry as much freight in bundles and trunks and baskets as persons—a nation spending a large part of its life in searching for means of survival rather than working.[20]

The story of a Ruhr miner which appeared in the U.S. *Congressional Record* exemplifies the situation.[21] The miner whose weekly wages totaled 60 RM also owned a hen which laid five eggs in a week. He usually ate one egg and bartered the remaining four for twenty cigarettes; each of the cigarettes brought 8 RM on the black market—for a total of 160 RM. In other words, the hen earned nearly three times as much as the miner did for his six days' work in the coal mine.

Conditions on the German farms generally paralleled those in the factories. Since only minimal quantities of farm machinery and spare parts could be made available through official channels in the first postwar years, the farmers often were compelled to divert some of their products to barter purposes rather than to fulfilling official delivery quotas. During the second year of the occupation, according to a German agricultural journal, definite exchange rates for barter transactions developed. Sixty nails, for instance, brought 1 pound of lard; one sack of twine was traded for 12 pounds of bacon; 100 kilograms of fertilizers, for 200 kilograms of potatoes, and so on.[22]

One of the most detrimental consequences of the absence of a meaningful currency was the creeping paralysis which affected all economic endeavors and the resulting disintegration into a series of localized economies. The writer in this connection recalls his days with the Military Government in Munich when, in an atmosphere of general indifference, he and his colleagues toiled many long hours to get exports from Bavaria started. During the summer whenever he passed by the Isar River, its banks were crowded with healthy-looking Germans who baked all day in the sun. The writer clearly remembers his feeling of disgusted annoyance, but in retrospect he has arrived at a more objective appraisal. Why indeed should these men and women have spent their days at work when their reward would only have been some almost useless pieces of paper money?

It is appropriate to keep this state of affairs in mind when one examines the sustained efforts on the part of the American and British

20. Stolper, p. 97.
21. *Congressional Record*, 80th Cong., 1st sess., Senate Committee on Appropriations. European interim aid and GARIOA hearings, Nov. 1947, p. 532.
22. Rheinischer Landwirtschaftsverband, *Landwirtschaftliche Zeitung* 115, no. 1 (1948): 13.

Military Governments in their mission to repair a broken-down communication system, to restore transportation, to increase coal production, to rebuild industry, to maximize agricultural production, and to promote exports. To start out, the revival of the German government-operated communication system was expedited by the loan of American Army equipment and the work of a small group of American professionals,[23] with the result that three months after the surrender post offices in the American and British Zones were functioning normally. At that time telephone service remained available to only 115,000 subscribers, and there were about 900,000 calls per month.[24]

By the fall of 1945 the Allied Control Council authorized the resumption of mail service between the four zones, and by February 1946 interzonal telephone and telegraph service was again in operation. To the chagrin of American officials responsible for the promotion of exports, however, German businessmen were unable to communicate with their business contacts abroad during the first year of the occupation; only after April 1946 was international mail service restored, and even then, because of the necessities of a military occupation, it had to be restricted to the transmission of nontransactional communications. A year later, when international telephone and telegraph service was resumed, there were more than 600,000 telephones in service to handle more than 11 million calls per month. Also, as General Clay reports, a million and a half relief parcels were received from the United States and distributed through the German postal system in May 1947 alone.[25] By that time communications within the Bizone were again normal and traffic greatly exceeded the prewar volume. Since postal, telephone, and telegraph charges were payable in an almost useless currency, this increase was not surprising; once the new currency was introduced traffic returned to a normal level.

A more difficult endeavor of the Military Government was the restoration of transport facilities, with which the war had wrought havoc. Railroad bridges, marshaling yards, railroad stations, and tunnels had been priority targets for Allied bombers, and in the closing months of the war the scorched-earth tactics of the Nazi High Command had aimed to destroy whatever the bombs had left intact. In the Bizone alone 2340 bridges, 3400 kilometers of tracks, 12,800 switches, and 4600 signals had been destroyed.[26] Although a relatively large part of the rolling stock was still on hand, only a fraction of it was serviceable, and

23. Clay, *Decision in Germany*, p. 187.   24. Ibid., p. 186.
25. Ibid., p. 187.   26. Stolper, p. 84.

for a long time repairs could not keep up with the continued break-downs. In addition the North German harbors were filled with sunken ships and the Rhine was closed to navigation because of destroyed locks and bridges.

By as early as July 1945 more than three fourths of the railroad tracks in the American Zone had been restored, but railroad facilities were limited by single-track bridges and had to be used primarily for military traffic, as well as for the return of millions of displaced persons to their homelands.[27] In order to increase the available rolling stock, 25,000 railway cars brought into Germany by the American Army were turned over to the German railroad administration, which was given increasing responsibilities at an early date. In addition, 12,500 U.S. Army trucks were made available in the spring of 1946 to the German economy through sale on a deferred-payment basis.[28] By April 1946 the Rhine was opened to navigation throughout its entire length and considerable progress had been made in repairing the ports. Since railroad freight services remained inadequate for some time, the distribution of essential food and fuel had to be accomplished by the use of waterborne transport. In addition, in the fall of 1946, thirty U.S. Army truck companies were actually required to assist in moving grain and potatoes from farms to warehouses.[29] One major complication arose from the fact that the former German High Command had treated the railroads of the occupied European countries as one entity throughout the war. Accordingly, when the war ended German locomotives and freight cars were scattered all over Europe, while about half of the freight cars in Germany were foreign. Subsequently, tens of thousands of German cars that crossed the borders with export or transit freight were retained abroad, and vigorous American-British protests were in vain.[30] Nevertheless, in spite of all the difficulties there was continuous progress in the reconstruction of the German transport system. By the time of the currency reform, General Clay was able to describe it in these terms: "Although still not fully back to normal it was able to take care of the requirements of a revitalized German economy." [31]

The reconstruction of the German coal industry was another cumbersome task for the Military Government. Prior to the war, the German output had been 158 million tons of hard coal and 162 million tons of brown coal, with the former mainly concentrated in the British and the

27. Clay, *Decision in Germany,* p. 188.
28. Ibid., p. 189.   29. Ibid.
30. Ibid., p. 191.   31. Ibid., p. 190.

latter in the Soviet Zone.[32] West German production of 384,000 tons of
hard coal a day in 1936 had been increased to 440,000 tons during the
war, but had come to an almost complete standstill by the time of the
German capitulation.[33] On the other hand, according to an American
estimate, there were more than 5 million tons of coal stocks in the Ruhr
when the Allies occupied the area. From the outset, in view of the
critical importance of the Ruhr coal for Germany and for the rest of
Europe, the American and British Military Governments gave first
priority in their food ration schemes to coal miners, with the result that
their daily ration of 3600 calories was usually met. Nevertheless, the
daily production of hard coal in 1946 never exceeded 200,000 tons, or
52 percent of the prewar level.[34] At the beginning of 1946 a daily output
of 180,000 tons was reached, but the subsequent lower food rations
caused an almost instantaneous 10 percent drop. Although a period of
steady progress followed, the daily production in June 1947 was still
only 219,000 tons, reaching a peak of 280,000 tons in the late fall when
an extra distribution of army K and C rations, as well as some surplus
clothing, provided an extraordinary incentive for the miners. Once the
distribution had been made, however, the daily production again
dropped to less than 260,000 tons.[35] As was to be expected, the currency
reform in the summer of 1948 drastically accelerated the recovery, and
in March 1949 there was a production of 330,000 tons per day—still 14
percent short of the 1936 average.[36]

Several factors were jointly responsible for this slow recovery. During
the first three years of the occupation, the general food situation was at
the root of the evil; although food rations for the miners themselves were
generally adequate, the "normal consumer" rations of 1000–1500 calories which their women and children received were obviously insufficient. Another negative element was the need for a complete overhaul
and renovation of the mining equipment, which, like everything else, had
suffered through the war. In particular, a shortage of pit-props hampered mining operations; traditionally the bulk of them had come from
the Soviet Zone; with this source cut off, pit-prop supplies were sought
in the American Zone but for a long time they were inadequate to meet
the requirements.[37] Finally there was a general aging of the Ruhr miners,
a process which was only slowly alleviated by the return of soldiers from
the war. In 1945, some 65 percent of the workers in the Ruhr mines

32. Stolper, p. 85.　　　　33. Ibid., p. 87.
34. Ibid.　　　　35. Clay, *Decision in Germany,* p. 195.
36. Ibid.
37. F. S. V. Dennison, *Civil Affairs and Military Government,* pp. 410–11.

were forty years of age or older, as compared with 25 percent in 1913! [38]

The delays in the reconstruction of the transportation system complicated the distribution of coal in West Germany, as well as in the European countries dependent on German deliveries. As to the latter, the American and British Military Governments were in the unfortunate situation where any of their actions was bound to evoke criticism, where it was impossible to satisfy all the parties concerned, and where a concession to one side invariably led to a protest by the other. Understandably, the liberated countries of Europe often took the position that they were entitled to priority coal allocations. Since the output of English coal also was far below normal, West European requirements not satisfied by deliveries from the Ruhr had to be met by extensive imports from the United States, with the American taxpayer footing the bill. It was clearly a case of being damned whether you did or you didn't. Accordingly, at the Paris Conference of the Council of Foreign Ministers in the fall of 1946, the U.S. representative, Major General William Draper, declared, "Immediate exports of more coal from the Ruhr would mean less coal for exports in the long run. If additional coal was exported reducing the supply already inadequate for minimum internal needs, there could result only further debilitation of the German economy which would drag the coal output down with it." [39] German statistical data for the period indicate that, as compared with 1936 when 18.6 percent of the coal output of the British Zone had been exported, the relevant figures for the first postwar years were: 22.3 percent for 1946; 15.2 percent for 1947; and 20.9 percent for 1948,[40] giving an arithmetic average of 19.5 percent for the three postwar years. Judging from this record and contrary to the vocal complaints expressed by some German quarters at that time,[41] it appears that the American and British Military Governments performed a difficult task with considerable objectivity.

38. Stolper, p. 87.
39. Clay, *Decision in Germany,* pp. 193–94. In a similar vein, Clay offered the following comment to the War Department: "We cannot overlook the fact also that coal applied to those industries which could provide exports from Germany would produce several times the value of exports in the form of coal and would therefore reduce the need for financing of food imports into Germany by the United States and consequently assist in making Germany and particularly the U.S. Zone self-supporting." Clay to Echols, 16 July 1946 (OMGUS records, 177-1/3).
40. Deutsche Kohlenbergbau Leitung, Zahlen zur Kohlenwirtschaft, Nov. 1951, 1936 Statistisches Reichsamt, *Statistisches Jahrbuch für das Deutsche Reich* (1937), pp. 145, 253. Balabkins (p. 123) cites slightly different figures: 1936, 18 percent; 1946, 20.4 percent; 1947, 14.6 percent; 1948, 21 percent.
41. J. Semler, speech on 4 Jan. 1948 at Erlangen (OMGUS records, 150-3/3).

If one considers the problems encountered in some of the key sectors of the economy, it is hardly surprising that the revival of German industrial production during the first years of the occupation was very slow. From June to December 1945 most of the efforts of industry had to be directed toward house cleaning and repair. As a first step, the rubble and the debris resulting from the bombing had to be removed. Later when the opening of nonwar plants was authorized, damaged machines were repaired, buildings were roofed over, and whenever possible, usable equipment was moved into undamaged factory shops. Fortunately many manufacturers, in expectation of the unavoidable collapse, had retained considerable amounts of cash, which enabled them to meet the largely unproductive payrolls during the first months when most banks remained closed.[42] Indicative of the slow progress is an American Military Government report which carefully lists such modest accomplishments as the opening of a paper mill producing newsprint, of a steel rolling mill facilitating the manufacture of stoves, and of a window-glass factory in Bavaria "which was critically needed by the Army for the displaced persons program and for high priority German civilian requirements." [43] During the period August–December 1945 coal loadings for the U.S. Zone from the Ruhr rose from 517,000 tons to 658,000 tons, and in September for the first time all the essential electric power requirements could be met. As a result, the very important nitrogen fertilizer plant in Trostberg was reopened. All in all, the visible results of American reconstruction efforts by the end of 1945 were very meager. Industrial production in the U.S. Zone increased from about 5 percent of the 1936 level in June to not more than 20 percent by the end of the year. The average of the first eight months of occupation was still below 10 percent. The most disturbing element was the dwindling stockpiles of raw materials and of semifabricates which had kept some manufacturing going during the fall; there was little new output for a replacement of the used-up supplies.[44] It stands to reason that a good part of the rehabilitation efforts of 1945 began to bear results only during the following year. In the spring of 1946 several pig-iron furnaces were activated, and by the end of the year a monthly output of more than 27,000 tons was reached.[45]

The following data on specific degrees of progress in various segments of the German industry during the first 20 months of the occupation are

42. "Review of Industry, May 1945–Sept. 1947," p. 3. Manuscript, OMGUS records.   43. Ibid., p. 3.
44. Ibid., p. 4.   45. Ibid., p. 6.

estimates. More than average progress was made by the mining industry and in the production of electric power. Steel production in the U.S. Zone rose to 45 percent of the 1936 level, while the output of machinery and optics as well as of chemicals and building materials was close to the general average. Glass production was even above the 1936 level of output, while lumber was just below that level. The light consumer goods industries, especially encouraged by the Military Government, did not come up to expectations because of a lack of raw materials and shortages of coal. For instance, the amount of textile yarn produced during the last half of 1946 was only about one fourth of the 1936 rate.[46] By November, production in the U.S. Zone reached a temporary high of 47 percent of the 1936 level but the general outlook was still grim. No substantial improvement was in sight, and the paralyzing effects of the absence of a meaningful currency became more and more noticeable.

The list of formidable obstacles encountered in the reconstruction of the West German economy would be incomplete without some reference to the psychological barrier separating victors and vanquished after the war. As mentioned previously, from September 1944 to the end of April 1945, the Nazi propaganda machine was able to tell the German people without ever being challenged of the allegedly official American plan to destroy their industry and to transform the country into an economically insignificant agricultural state. Even after the beginning of the occupation, the population was not told differently, and only Secretary Byrnes's speech in the fall of 1946—the first full formulation of U.S. policy after the end of the war, to be discussed in Chapter 5—seemed to herald a new American approach. In the meantime, there had been the Potsdam Declaration with its emphasis on reparations and a reduced level of German industrial production. Furthermore, since there was considerable uncertainty regarding the scope and practical implications of the Allied policy, the German public at large quite naturally expected the worst. This trend was intensified by the news media, which reported mostly the negative aspects of American occupational policy, while paying scant attention to the practical actions which were usually positive and constructive. The ambivalence of American policies naturally also impeded an effective handling of public relations by OMGUS, a deficiency causing harsh comments on the part of another observer:

> There was little attempt made to build up good public relations between the German people and the bizonal administration. The

46. Meurer, p. 141.

application of some of the principles of psychological warfare should not have ended with the surrender. The German people were never shown the honest attempts that were being made to alleviate and better the lot of the average German. . . . A more skillfully executed information program to show the Germans that the bizonal agencies were concerned with their food, fuel, and shelter problems, and showing in understandable terms the vast quantities of supplies the Allies were sending to them, would have brought more whole-hearted public cooperation and support.[47]

German suspicions, on the other hand, had their counterpart in the feelings of many American officials who not only found it difficult to distinguish between "good" and "bad" Germans, but often were incensed by the widespread inertia. The rational explanation for the German behavior, namely, the aftereffects of incessant Allied bombing, the shock of the complete collapse, and most important, the absence of incentives, rarely came through in this atmosphere of mutual distrust.

The promotion of German exports was originally in the hands of a small staff of military officers who had been transferred from their assignments with the army and navy during the closing days of the war to the Economic Division of the American Military Government in Berlin. Selected on the basis of professional skills, the export-import staff included some officers with economic training, as well as others with banking and foreign trade experience. As everywhere in the Military Government, there was a rapid turnover of personnel because individuals with long wartime service were gradually being discharged while others with shorter service took their places. Eventually the military staff was "civilianized," as the term went, as officers who chose to stay on acquired the status of War Department civilians and new arrivals from the United States with a similar status filled their ranks. By the end of 1946, that is, prior to the establishment of a combined American-British export-import agency, the Export-Import Section of OMGUS had a staff of about fifty, including twenty German commercial specialists.

It seems indicative of the initially limited capabilities of German foreign trade that the table of organization of OMGUS assigned responsibility for export-import matters to one of three sections of a Trade and Commerce Branch, which in turn was a component of an Economic

47. Robert Slover, *The Bizonal Economic Administration,* p. 247.

Division. (The other two sections respectively took care of price control and internal trade.) The division was headed by Brigadier General (later Major General) William Draper, a New York investment banker by profession and a reserve officer by inclination. The Trade and Commerce Branch in turn was supervised by Frederick Winant, a career civil servant and a brother of the American ambassador at the Court of St. James's. Dr. Roy J. Bullock, who headed the Export-Import Section, had been director of the School of Business of the Johns Hopkins University in Baltimore, and during the war had served with the Board of Economic Warfare and the Foreign Economic Administration.

As one will recall, the Potsdam Agreement stipulated that "during the period of occupation Germany shall be treated as a single economic unit. To this end common economic policies shall be established in regard to import and export programs for Germany as a whole." Accordingly, it was expected that a central German department for foreign trade would soon be established, and on August 15, 1945, as a preliminary step toward this goal, a quadripartite Export-Import Subcommittee was set up. With due speed it drafted an interim arrangement to govern the export-import activity of the four zones while the adoption of an export-import plan for all of Germany was still pending. As approved by the Control Council on September 15, the interim plan stated that:

a. Proceeds from exports should be credited to a special account of the Control Council and shall be used for payment of imports of each respective zone. Payment for imports into one Zone for the account of exports from another may be made only by the decision of the Control Council, or may be agreed between any Zone Commanders.

b. In the preparation of the export-import plan, the exports and imports of each Zone made before the time of completion of the final plan, will be taken into consideration. If the final plan has not been approved as of 31 October 1945, the interim arrangement will be reviewed.

c. Provisional prices of exports of goods, raw materials and merchandise shall be fixed by the Commander of each Zone pending condition of final settlement. Payment should be made at the rate of not less than 80 percent of provisional prices. Provisional prices to be fixed by the Zone Commander are to be applied in the first place to all deliveries from 1 August 1945.[48]

48. *OMGUS Trade and Commerce*, Aug. 1945.

It was understood that the provisions of the Potsdam Agreement whereby imports in Germany should be restricted to goods necessary for minimum standards of consumption and production would apply. Payments for exports and essential imports were to be made in U.S. dollars or other foreign currency acceptable to the Allied Control Council. The implementation of the interim export-import arrangement was left to the respective zone commander.[49]

During the following months, when each of the four powers was due to submit proposals regarding a final export-import plan, no progress was made and it became increasingly clear that their views on the course of action to be followed differed greatly. The Soviets originally took the position that they were unable to submit an export-import plan until reparations were agreed upon, "because of the tie-up on their side between reparations and the exchange of commodities from the East."[50]

The United States pressed most energetically for some early joint action and submitted its draft on December 21, 1946, to the Export-Import Subcommittee with the purpose of "bridging the gap between the Zonal interim export-import plan and the final central German administrative agency for foreign trade."[51] The American paper envisaged the establishment of an Allied export-import bureau which would operate under direction of the Export-Import Subcommittee. The bureau's major positions were to be filled by representatives of the four occupying powers, while Germans would occupy the subordinate ones. The draft contemplated a gradual subordination of zonal operations to operations for Germany as a whole by a central agency; a gradual increase in the use of German personnel in administration and ultimately in policy-making positions; and finally a gradual transition from export-import trade on a government-to-government basis to a system of governmental regulation of export-import transactions carried out by commercial firms. The control of foreign exchange, however, was to be retained by the Allied Control Authority.[52] According to the thinking of the American drafters, the export-import bureau was to carry out policy directives of the Allied Control Authority and to perform "designated export-import operations for Germany as a whole." It was not to serve as a

49. Hutton and Robbins, "Postwar German Trade," p. 1.
50. William Draper to Clay, on current status of exports-imports, 19 Nov. 1945 (Omgus records 5-1/1).
51. Statement of U.S. Proposal for Export Import Bureau of Germany, submitted to Trade and Commerce Committee ACA, 11 Feb. 1946 (OMGUS records, 123-2/3).
52. Ibid.

coordinating agency for zonal operations but all of its activities would be assigned to it by the Allied Control Authority.[53]

It appears that the American proposals were too progressive even for the British Allies, who felt that economic progress in the four zones was still so incomplete as to make the functioning of a large-scale centralized organization impossible; they thought that "the American plan was too far advanced for dealing with present day realities."[54] Although the French expressed similar reservations, the primary opposition came from the Soviet Union. Its representative at the Economic Directorate in a final clarification of the Russian position on April 5, 1946, declared, "We will adhere to the principal of Zonal foreign trade and individual responsibilities of the countries for the results of the occupation of their Zone and substitute this for the collective responsibility of all the powers. In accordance with this the Soviet Delegation cannot accept any other position than that of a Zonal principle."[55]

An excerpt from the minutes of the forty-ninth meeting of the Allied Control Authority Coordinating Committee held three days later reflects the growing impatience of the American Military Government:

215. U.S. Position on Import-Export Plan

General Clay informed his colleagues that during the discussion in the Economic Directorate of an export-import paper, the view had been expressed that this was a Zonal problem and could not be resolved until Germany had a favorable trade balance or until the Reparations Plan had been consummated. Recognizing the responsibility of each Zone to meet its deficits after all German resources for its internal needs and for export had been exhausted, the Potsdam Agreement provides for a common export-import plan. The Level of Industry Plan was based on a balanced import-export plan, and if such a plan was not to be established, then the Reparations Plan had no validity. Since reparations deliveries were still in an early stage, there was time to consider this problem, but if a common import-export plan could not be agreed [upon], then at a suitable time in the not too distant future, the U.S. Delegation would invoke the above-cited basic assumption of the Level of Industry Plan and would accordingly require revision of the Reparations Plan.[56]

53. Ibid.
54. Memorandum, Dr. Roy Bullock to Fred Winant, 3 Jan. 1946 (OMGUS records, 123-2/3).
55. Statement by K. I. Koval at ACA, 5 April 1946 (OMGUS records, 5-1/1).
56. OMGUS records, F. W.'s Export Import Folder.

If the Soviets entertained any doubts as to the seriousness of Clay's warning, it was dispelled at a quadripartite meeting on May 3, 1946. Its proceedings were summarized in an OMGUS cable quoted here in full because of its significance:

Subject: Import-Export Program

At last meeting of Coordinating Committee, British, French and American supported a paper which provided for the pooling of indigenous resources based on a uniform standard of consumption and utilization of proceeds from all exports to provide funds for essential imports. Soviet representatives opposed the paper, taking the position that for the present, imports-exports must be conducted on a Zonal basis with only surpluses available for export and for the common pool. When Soviet representatives were advised that their position was inconsistent with Potsdam, their reply was a query to the French if the French were ready to establish central administrative machinery. Of course the French answer was their usual statement that they favored treatment of Germany as a single economic entity but still opposed central administrative machinery.

The American position was reiterated strongly. We stated that a common import-export program pooling all indigenous resources and the proceeds from all exports was an essential part of Potsdam. We regard Potsdam as a whole and can not accept its parts unless the whole is to be executed. The reparations program is based on a common import-export program and without the latter, the U.S. Zone would not provide reparations. We further stated that a common import-export program definitely required central administrative machinery to be effective. Therefore we regarded reparations, the import-export program and the establishment of central machinery as subjects which had to be decided concurrently in view of their effect on each other. We also stated that in the absence of a decision by the Allied Control Council to develop a common import-export program we would necessarily have to cease further dismantling of reparations plants and deliveries.

This was not intended as a bluff and in fact we have ordered any further dismantling of reparations plants in the U.S. Zone to be discontinued except for the 24 plants which have been allocated for advance deliveries. We feel strongly that there is considerable question as to the advisability of removing even these 24 plants if there is to be no common treatment of Germany as an economic unit. However, in view of commitment to IARA for 20 of these plants, we felt it inadvisable to discontinue their dismantling.

While we are prepared to continue the paper allocation of plants for reparations, we do not propose to take any further physical efforts to carry out the reparations program until major overall questions are resolved and we know what area is to compose Germany and whether or not that area will be treated as an economic unit. Until this is resolved, any further action on our part would create an additional financial liability for the U.S. to support its Zone in Germany.[57]

While American efforts towards the origination of a quadripartite export-import plan slowly but surely came to naught, Roy Bullock and his staff concentrated on their mission to revive exports in the U.S. Zone. The first step, namely the instruction to Military Government detachments in the field to locate and freeze all "exportable surpluses" in the respective districts, presented hardly any problems. But from there on the obstacles became staggering. As indicated earlier, for a long time there was no international mail service nor was it possible for Germans to communicate with foreign countries by telegraph or telephone. Military security considerations, as well as the lack of foreign exchange, precluded German travel abroad, and the absence of adequate housing in addition to the food problem prevented the admission of foreign buyers. These impediments were reinforced by the Trading with the Enemy legislation prohibiting direct contact between German and foreign business firms. In addition, the general stage of economic affairs as outlined in the first part of this chapter played a retarding role. (General Draper listed the following: "Primary Difficulties in Developing German Exports: Lack of a foreign exchange rate; need for transactional mail; need for Germans to travel abroad; and need for a German export agency which would have the authority to hold foreign funds.") [58]

It seems odd and even ironic that because of these conditions, an agency of the United States Government was obliged to assume the role of a Soviet-type Ministry of Foreign Trade with complete operational responsibility during the first postwar years for all aspects of exports and imports, including the arbitrary determination of export prices. In a

57. OMGUS to AGWAR for WARCAD, 3 May 1946, Cable CC-4277 (OMGUS records, 427-2/3).
58. Memorandum for General Hilldring, 6 Sept. 1946 (OMGUS records, 148-3/3).

communist-controlled economy, market forces actually have little or no effect on prevailing price patterns, and the establishment of the cost factor becomes an object of governmental decisions. In a similar fashion, prior to the currency reform OMGUS was obliged to determine its export prices unilaterally, as there was no definite relation between controlled domestic Reischsmark prices and those obtainable in foreign exchange on the world markets.

As to the former, most prices dated back to November 1936, when at the beginning of the Second Four Year Plan, a price-stop decree by the price commissioner of the Nazi government had frozen all prices for goods and services.[59] Subsequent price changes, as well as the establishment of prices for new products, were subject to careful scrutiny by the supervising price offices and required the concurrence of the price commissioner. Violations of price laws were regarded as economic crimes against the state and violators were severely punished, in extreme cases even by the death penalty. In view of the tight controls and because of adequate supplies, German prices during the war had remained relatively stable; actually during the long period from 1936 to 1944 the index of German wholesale prices rose by only 13 percent and the cost-of-living index went up by 14 percent.[60]

After the German surrender, Allied policies aimed at the maintenance of existing price levels [61] and the Allied Control Council in May 1946 assumed jurisdiction for the prices of thirteen basic commodities, among which steel, coal, iron, chemicals, foodstuffs, and electric power were the most important. The responsibility for price adjustments of other commodities was turned over to the German authorities, who, of course, operated under the guidance and supervision of the Military Government.[62] However, since the two main factors of wartime price stability, i.e., adequate supplies and domestic controls, no longer existed, a gradual thaw of the frozen prices set in, with the result that prices for consumer goods during the period May 1945 to July 1947 rose by 97 percent, while the price increase for industrial raw materials was held to 22 percent.[63]

The isolation of German prices from the influence of world markets over a period of years, of course, had been brought about not only by

59. "Verordnung über das Verbot von Preiserhöhungen," *Reichsgesetzblatt* 1936, p. 955.
60. Klein, *Germany's Economic Preparations*, p. 154.
61. *OMGUS, Trade and Commerce*, March 1946, p. 12 (OMGUS records, 17-1/5).
62. Ibid., May 1946, p. 9.   63. Ibid., Aug.–Sept. 1947, pp. 7–8.

price policies but also by extensive governmental subsidies and a very complex system of foreign-exchange controls. Accordingly, OMGUS was faced with the dual problem of establishing sales prices in foreign currency abroad and of deciding on the Reichsmark prices to be paid to the German exporter.

As to the latter, namely, the determination of a "maximum legal price" for export, the question arose whether the current internal German selling price or any special export price which might have existed under German law before the defeat should be used.[64] Under the Nazi policy of utilizing exports as a means of economic warfare, various approaches to encourage exports had been taken. The Reichsmark export price had been higher than that for internal sales whenever this was deemed beneficial to German politics or to the German economy and when the goods could be sold abroad at the higher price. In other cases the Reichsmark export price was fixed lower than the internal price in order to assist German producers in meeting foreign competition. Often some sort of subsidy payment made up the difference. Sometimes losses from export sales were compensated for by allowing higher than normal profit margins on internal sales. In practice this was, of course, the equivalent of a subsidy.

After scrutinizing the former pattern of German export prices at a time when the objectives of German export policy under the Third Reich no longer applied, OMGUS decided that all future Reichsmark payments to German exporters would be based on the controlled internal price. The problem of fixing the export prices in foreign currency for buyers abroad was infinitely more difficult to solve. From the outset, it was the aim of the American Military Government to sell at the highest possible export prices in order to reduce the burden on the American taxpayer. In the same vein the Finance Division of OMGUS stated in unequivocal terms that it was "unwilling to support any policy which undertook to sell German products at less than the competitive market could stand or less than the real cost of producing these goods, taking into account that food for the workers and raw materials for the product must be bought on world markets at world prices." [65] However, to state such a policy and to implement it were two different matters.

The relation of German internal and world market prices varied from product to product, and the determination of world market prices, as

64. Ibid., May 1946, p. 8.
65. OMGUS to AGWAR for WDSCA, 19 Nov. 1946, Cable CC-7006 (OMGUS records).

well as the establishment of a meaningful exchange rate, therefore became one of the major causes of concern for Roy Bullock's export-import staff. In theory, the resources of the United States Foreign Service were at their disposal. In practice, however, the data supplied were often quite inadequate, since the requests for market information entailed hundreds of diverse items, including raw materials from hops to lumber, industrial products from locomotives to spinning machines, and consumer goods from chinaware to toys. Although the initial reluctance of some commercial attachés to cooperate in such an extraneous venture was overcome by the issuance of State Department directives to the field, the task of researching markets for a multitude of products with countless specifications was usually beyond the physical and organizational capacity of our embassies and consulates.

As far as the establishment of export prices to the United States was concerned, OMGUS turned to the government-owned U.S. Commercial Company, a wartime subsidiary of the U.S. Commodity Credit Corporation, for advice in the summer of 1946. A few months later, the writer accompanied Louis Marx, a leading American manufacturer of toys, who had come to Germany at General Eisenhower's request, on a survey trip of the toy industries located in or near Nürnberg, Bavaria. When it turned out that the prices quoted by Marx were far higher than those offered by the U.S. Commercial Company, it was decided to seek the advice of American firms in the case of other products as well.[66] Subsequently, representatives of Montgomery Ward, R. H. Macy, and other American importers were invited to Germany, and export prices for a number of consumer goods were established with their assistance.

The intramural debate at OMGUS regarding an appropriate exchange rate for exports lasted for more than a year and resulted in a variety of recommendations and several suggested rates, ranging from a proposed mark worth 10 cents to one worth 40 cents. The complexity of the problem may be judged from the following data excerpted from an OMGUS document, "The Problem of the German Exchange Rate," dated December 12, 1946.[67] The paper demonstrated that by relating fixed legal Reichsmark prices to the highest dollar selling prices of certain exportable raw materials the following divergent exchange rates would evolve:

66. OMGUS to AGWAR, 10 Oct. 1946, Cable CC-5253 (OMGUS records, 427-2/3).
67. OMGUS records.

Coal per ton: German price: 15 RM; world price $9;
                   exchange rate 1 RM = 60 cents
Hops per ton: German price: 700 RM; world price $182 to $276;
                   exchange rate 1 RM = 26 to 39 cents
Salt per ton: German price: 34 RM; world price $4.80
                   exchange rate 1 RM = 14 cents

The study also indicated that German exports from the U.S. Zone from the beginning of the occupation up to September 22, 1946, had amounted to 17,282,000 RM, or $6,122,000, with an average rate of 35.4 cents. As the paper pointed out, "The use of a fixed exchange rate of 1 RM = 35 cents would have cut the dollar proceeds of these exports from $6.1 million to $4 million. Transactions up to $1.5 million would have been unprofitable and therefore not concluded, and the proceeds of the remaining transactions would have decreased by $600,000." Recognizing that the "price situation in Germany as well as conditions in the world markets will for some time make it impossible and hazardous to expose German prices with a fixed rate of exchange to uncontrolled adjustment," the paper suggested an interim exchange rate of 30 cents for the Reichsmark to provide an orderly procedure for adjustment of internal prices and to eliminate losses in dollar proceeds, as well as the need for drastic revisions of the domestic price level. In addition, the use of internal price adjusting factors was recommended.

Based on the examination of 32 export transactions since the start of the occupation, the study then produced a list of "adjusting factors" as examplified by the excerpted data in Table 4.1.

The study concluded that the application of internal adjustment factors would have given the German manufacturers 20,400,000 RM as export proceeds instead of the above-mentioned sum of 17,282,000 RM. At the same time "the dollar selling prices which in all cases were the highest obtainable" would have remained intact.

The principle of internal adjustment factors, however, was not adopted by OMGUS, and eventually a system of multiple exchange rates was introduced instead.[68] Generally the rates ranged from 25 to 40 cents for the controlled internal Reichsmark price, depending on the product and in some cases the market conditions in the importing country. The initial promotional efforts of OMGUS favored products with the higher

68. The establishment of an interim exchange rate and the simultaneous application of internal adjustment factors was considered "unnecessarily complex," Wilkinson to Szymcak, 27 Dec. 1946 (OMGUS records, 148-3/3).

TABLE 4.1. "Adjusting factors" for export transactions

Selected Transactions	Total proceeds expressed in internal German prices (1,000 RM)	Proposed adjusting factor	Total proceeds expressed in adjusted export prices (1,000 RM)	Total export proceeds in $1,000, using exchange rate 1 RM = 30 cents
Salt	291	.47	137	41
Hops	4981	.86	4284	1285
Hops	3501	1.31	4586	1376
Potash	553	2.02	1117	335
Bicycle wheels	168	1.35	227	68
Printing mach.	5	1.65	8	2
Roller bearings	21	2.06	43	13
Photo. gelatine	265	1.41	374	112
Printing ink	11	1.25	13	4
Potato diggers	66	1.13	75	22
Soda ash	9	1.04	9	3
Cement	77	1.22	94	28

exchange rates and were directed toward industries with a high labor quotient, promising maximum export yields with a minimum of import outlays.

Whereas the issue of exchange rates was essentially a matter of continuous and often quite difficult market research, the selection of the best suitable export currency became an object of high-level economic policy. From the start it was the decision of OMGUS to sell only in dollars, and Dr. Bullock, when questioned on this point, indicated that this had been the established policy, "possibly on the U.S. Treasury's advice," when he assumed responsibility for exports from the American Zone in October 1945.[69]

Actually, since all essential imports of food and petroleum products into Germany had to be paid for in dollars, and since American dollars and Swiss francs were the principal freely convertible currencies for several postwar years, the decision to demand dollar payments seemed sensible and basically sound. However, it disregarded the postwar dollar shortage, which hampered Germany's traditional European trading partners, with the exception of Switzerland and possibly Sweden. Their

69. Interview with Dr. Roy Bullock, 14 March 1968.

resulting resentment was enhanced by the fact that many of these countries had been the recent victims of Nazi aggression and therefore thought that their purchases of German products should be charged to the respective reparations accounts. As an alternative solution, bilateral settlements through the delivery of surplus products to Germany on a quota basis were often suggested. In fact, those proposals could be presented quite convincingly since the precedent of bilateral quotas, customary in Europe in the thirties and applied by Dr. Schacht as a tool of German economic conquest, had become an accepted way of European economic life. From the standpoint of OMGUS, both policies seemed unacceptable. Reparations from current production were contrary to Potsdam, as interpreted by the United States, and irreconcilable with some of the basic tenets of American-British occupational policy. Bilateral quotas, on the other hand, were anathema in view of America's established policy of international free trade through the application of a multilateral most-favored-nation clause.

During the first months after the German capitulation, that is, prior to the assumption of a centralized economic control by OMGUS, a few small barter transactions had been consummated with some of Germany's neighbors, and in the area of the U.S. Third Army a barter board had even been constituted for the purpose of screening and approving barter transactions. OMGUS, however, put an early stop to this by instructing the field in October 1945 that "barter transactions should be discouraged because of their tendency to distort and restrict commerce" and that all transactions negotiated by the barter board were to be forwarded to Berlin for approval before becoming valid.[70] As it developed, none of the requested approvals was ever granted.

The evolving foreign-trade policy of OMGUS continued to require dollar payments for German exports; at the same time under the disease-and-unrest formula, it provided for the importation at the American taxpayers' expense of essential food items, fertilizers, seeds, and petroleum products, all of which were classified as "category A imports." As to other imports, the policy excluded nonessentials but encouraged the importation of raw materials for the manufacture of exportable products; this second group, "category B imports," had to be paid by dollar proceeds from German exports. Contrary to an erroneous interpretation,[71] there was never a general "import embargo" imposed by the

70. OMGUS to USFET Director OMG, 23 Oct. 1945, CABLE CC-17917 (OMGUS records, 5-1/1).
71. Balabkins, p. 151.

American Military Government but rather a priority system in logical recognition of the fact that the German economy was bankrupt and that American taxpayers could not be expected, in addition to feeding the vanquished enemy, to start paying promptly for the restoration of the German economy.

On the other hand, it does not seem surprising that the American export-import policies were highly unpopular in the European countries, where large segments of the economies depended almost entirely on the German markets.[72] As General Clay commented:

> The European countries did not want to sell to Germany products which could be sold elsewhere for dollars and they did not want to pay in dollars for German products. . . . Italy wanted to sell us fruit in exchange for products which had dollar value. The Dutch government in 1947 resorted to every possible means to force us to purchase surplus vegetables. Food was badly needed in the Zone. Fruit and vegetables would have added desirable variety if we could have afforded it, but they represented no measurable increase in the food supply, whereas the several million dollars they would have cost brought in new raw materials to keep factories in production for essential needs in Germany or for exports. We could buy raw materials only for dollars.[73]

It appears that the Finance Division strongly supported the dollar policy. The Economic Division, on the other hand, expressed doubt whether "the stimulus to the economic recovery of Germany . . . through a revival of foreign trade even . . . on an inconvertible money basis would not in the next two years do more to reduce Germany's deficit and as a consequence the burden on the United States taxpayer . . . than rigid adherence to our present policy of dollar payment." [74]

OMGUS frequently explained that any major change in its basic export-import policy would mean expenditures for secondary requirements from resources needed to procure primary necessities. The argument failed to convince governments of surrounding countries, which naturally sought to protect the interests of large groups of their citizens directly concerned with the export industries.[75] The American policy of "dollar sales only" was strictly enforced for more than a year, although it became increasingly evident that it was not in harmony with the eco-

72. Clay, *Decision in Germany,* p. 196.
73. Ibid.
74. Memorandum, Draper to Clay, 25 March 1946 (OMGUS records).
75. Tennenbaum, "Why Do We Trade for Dollars?" p. 17.

nomic conditions of the European countries and actually tended to retard their recovery. During the next two years several significant changes were therefore made; these will be discussed in the following chapters.

As to the logistics of exports from and imports into the U.S. Zone of Germany, detailed instructions were issued within the framework of Title 13, part 3, of U.S. Military Government Regulations.[76] Similar to the organizational pattern of OMGUS headquarters in Berlin, Export-Import Sections were also established in the Military Government Offices of each of the three *Länder*—that is, in Munich, Stuttgart, and Wiesbaden. Berlin, however, remained responsible for the negotiation of imports and the determination and approval of all exports. The basic foreign-trade policy of American Military Government was defined as follows:

> Exports from the U.S. Zone of Germany will be stimulated in every way consistent with internal economic objectives to provide sufficient funds to meet the obligations arising from imports of food, merchandise, raw materials and supplies currently required for minimum subsistence. The Office of Military Government for each *Land* will instruct the *Minister-praesident* that the importation of food, merchandise, raw materials, and supplies in order to raise the living standard of the German people above the level of minimum subsistence will depend entirely on exports being made in sufficient volume to provide the necessary foreign exchange to pay for such imports [13–302. Policy].

While within OMGUS the Economic Division was charged with the responsibility for approving imports and exports, the Finance Division was required to satisfy itself that "all disbursements made out of accounts under its direct control both for financing exports out of Germany and imports into Germany are in accordance with the financial provisions of the interim export-import program approved by the Control Council." The Finance Division was also responsible for "the carrying out of such accounting as may be necessary to implement the purely financial aspects of this plan (13–305–1. Organization for exports and imports). As to the development of programs for exports, Title 13 provided that

> The *Ministerpraesident* of each *Land* will be required to propose a program for the export of commodities that are immediately avail-

76. OMGUS records.

able, and a program for the production of commodities for export. The *Ministerpraesident* will be directed to coordinate the programs with the *Ministerpraesidenten* of the other *Laender* and to submit to a report thereon to the Office of Military Government for the *Land*. The Office of Military Government for the *Land* will forward the programs to the Economic Division, Office of Military Government for Germany (US), through functional channels.

Accordingly in December 1945, three German Aussenhandelskontore (Foreign Trade Bureaus) were established to act as agencies of the respective *Land* economic ministry in each of the three *Länder* in the U.S. Zone. These Aussenhandelskontore served as connecting links between German exporters and the Export-Import Sections of OMGUS. They collected information on goods available for export, processed inquiries from abroad regarding exports and assisted in the actual movement of goods under export contracts. The Export-Import Sections at the *Land* level supervised and promoted export sales and deliveries. Export transactions in the U.S. Zone were initiated either by a request for a specific item from abroad or by offers from German suppliers who indicated that goods were available for export. Prices and other terms were agreed and contracts concluded between representatives of the country concerned and OMGUS. Once export agreements had been made, a numbered release was submitted through the appropriate *Land* military government to the *Land* economic ministry, which in turn instructed the German exporter to prepare goods for export shipment.[77]

Title 13 further stated:

The proceeds from exports in the form of promises to pay on demand U.S. dollars or other foreign currency acceptable to the Allied Control Authority will be held by the Finance Division of the Office for Military Government for Germany (US) and will be available for the purchase of, or payment of approved imports [13–307. Handling of proceeds from exports].

The German supplier, on the other hand, received the controlled Reichsmark price of the goods on presentation of an invoice and an export payment certificate to the *Land* economic ministry. Accordingly, the Finance Division, OMGUS, was to set up a Reichsmark checking account at the German Reichsbank Branch in Frankfurt am Main "to be used for compensating the *Land* governments or other persons for sums provided by them to pay for exports from Germany" (Title 13. 13–312. 1).

77. Hutton and Robbins, p. 2.

As to German imports, the Economic Division, OMGUS, decided on the basis of requirements submitted by the Länderrat which commodities were to be imported. OMGUS further negotiated or authorized the negotiation with foreign suppliers for the goods to be imported into the U.S. Zone.[78] With regard to the settlement of payments for imports, the German *Land* governments were instructed to pay into the above mentioned account at the German Reichsbank Branch in Frankfurt am Main the Reichsmark proceeds of sale of imported Military Goverment supplies or of supplies imported through commercial channels "as an installment payment pending the final settlement of Reichsmark values" (Title 13. 13–312. 1f).

As one will have gathered from above, Title 13, which governed all foreign trade transactions of the U.S. Zone during the initial phase of the occupation, entrusted the entire decision-making machinery in this sphere to a small group of American officials at OMGUS. This highly centralized procedure provided for obligatory functional channels necessitating the transmission of each piece of correspondence from exporter to German Foreign Trade Bureau (Aussenhandelskontor), to U.S. Export-Import Section at *Land* level, to Export-Import Section, Berlin, to U.S. Embassy (or pertinent governmental bureau) in the importing country, and finally to the eventual client. Communications going in the opposite direction had to observe the same route.

The following excerpts from a protocol on a "Conference on Trade between the Swiss Delegation and Representatives of the Office of Military Government for Germany (US)" which took place in Berlin on October 7 and 8, 1946, casts additional light on the complicated mechanics:

Procedure regarding exports to Switzerland

a. OMGUS is at present the exclusive exporter of goods from the U.S. Zone of Occupation. Therefore, Swiss importers of such goods must contact the Trade and Commerce Branch of OMGUS through official channels for inquiry and for negotiation of contracts. If and when business correspondence by mail of a nontransactional character is permitted between Swiss and German firms, preliminary negotiations may be carried on directly. The final conclusion of contracts will in any case be negotiated by OMGUS.

78. Ibid.

b. If and when an agreement is reached, OMGUS will request the Swiss importer to open an irrevocable bank credit in favor of OMGUS providing for payment to the credit of the account of OMGUS with the Swiss National Bank in U.S. dollars. The bank issuing the credit will transmit to OMGUS through official channels confirmation of the opening of the credit. At the same time, the Swiss importer will be requested to produce a certificate stating that the Division of Commerce in Berne approves of the transaction. The statement of certification will be forwarded by the Division of Commerce in Berne to OMGUS through channels. As soon as OMGUS is in possession of the aforementioned two documents, OMGUS will conclude the contract with the Swiss importer and take necessary steps for delivery of goods according to the terms of the contract.

c. The same procedure will apply in the case of processing of raw materials or semi-manufactured products supplied by Swiss firms.

Procedure regarding imports from Switzerland

OMGUS is at present the exclusive importer of goods into the U.S. Zone of Occupation. Therefore, OMGUS will keep the Division of Commerce in Berne informed of the kinds and quantities of goods which it desires to import from Switzerland. The Swiss authorities will contact possible Swiss exporters who will make direct offers to OMGUS through official channels. If and when an agreement is reached between OMGUS and the Swiss exporter, the Swiss exporter will request an export license from the Swiss authorities, and a license from the Swiss National Bank covering the exchange of dollars into Swiss francs to pay for the export. If both are granted, copies of both licenses will be forwarded by the Swiss exporter through channels to OMGUS. Upon receipt, OMGUS will conclude the contract with the Swiss exporter and will make payment by issuing a payment order in Swiss francs in favor of the Swiss exporter, drawn on the Swiss National Bank. This payment order will be honored by the Swiss National Bank to the debit of the account of OMGUS with the Swiss National Bank in U.S. dollars, within the amount of the available balance at the day's buying rate for U.S. dollars, on the strength of the license as issued.[79]

79. OMGUS records, 150-3/3.

Hamstrung by a nonconvertible German currency, the lack of raw materials and the absence of economic incentives for export sales, the export staff in Berlin, in addition to bureaucratic procedure, also had to contend with highly inadequate means of communication. As one of its memoranda to the chief of staff indicated, "in some instances, telephone calls were placed with booking operators in the morning and the numbers were not reached until late that afternoon, or for two or three days, while in other instances members of the Section have spent from one to two hours on the telephone trying to reach a number. And often when the numbers are reached, interruptions, cut-offs and poor connections have placed an almost unsurmountable handicap on the interested parties." [80] Under these circumstances it seems less surprising that progress was slow than that any export transactions were actually completed at all.

Export sales from the U.S. Zone in the calendar year 1946 were in the vicinity of $28 million and included $24.5 million of raw materials and semifabricates, but only $3.4 million of finished goods, Germany's primary exports before the war. In the first category, the major items were hops, lumber, salt, and potash, whereas the finished goods consisted of shipments of chinaware, cameras, printing machines, and a multitude of small items. It is noteworthy that the $28 million represented only 5 percent of the exports shipped from the geographic area of the U.S. Zone of Occupation prior to the war. Even if related to the theoretical limitations established by the Allied planners, the 1946 export figure was only 7 percent of permissible exports as specified under the quadripartite Level of Industry Plan.

The main recipients of German exports, in declining order, were the United Kingdom, Holland, Belgium, and the United States. Dwarfing the export figure in magnitude was that of the imports into the U.S. Zone, which for the period August 1, 1945, to December 31, 1946, grossed about $335 million—almost 90 percent of it imports of food, seeds, and chemical fertilizers. The 1946 balance of trade for the U.K. Zone showed a similar deficit, although coal exports from the Ruhr lessened the disparity between receipts and disbursements.[81]

General Clay in his memoirs acknowledges that American foreign trade policy was an effort to pull the German economy up by its own boot straps and that General Draper had expressed serious doubts late in

80. Memorandum, Fredrick Winant to Chief of Staff, 16 April 1946 (OMGUS records, 123-2/3).
81. Hutton and Robbins, p. 3.

FIGURE 4.1   Exports compared with imports for the U.S. Zone of Germany, August 1, 1945 to December 31, 1946. [After *OMGUS, Trade and Commerce, Monthly Report*, Dec. 1946–Jan. 1947.]

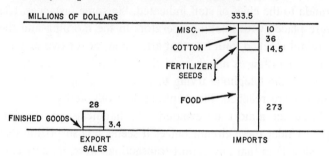

1945 and early 1946 as to its practicability.[82] On the other hand, Draper's suggestion to ask Washington for "one billion dollars in order to finance essential imports other than food" was still beyond the realm of political feasibility in 1946, and much more modest approaches, such as the experiment of "self-liquidating imports," had to be taken at that time.

Under this type of program, the steamship *Velma Lykes*, which cleared Houston, Texas, on July 20, 1946, carried a cargo including some 350 tons of raw cotton for the U.S. Zone of Germany. It was the first shipment against a contract that OMGUS had negotiated with the U.S. Commodity Credit Corporation whereby 50,000 tons of cotton valued at approximately $30 million were to be sent to Germany. It was Germany's biggest foreign-trade transaction since the end of the war. The 50,000 tons of raw cotton were to be paid for by the proceeds from the export of finished cotton textiles. It was expected that after all the costs of the cotton had been paid, at least 20,000 tons of the finished textiles would remain in the U.S. Zone for the German economy.[83] On October 25, a similar agreement between OMGUS and the U.S. Commercial Company provided for an interim advance of $7,750,000 by Commodity Credit Corporation for the procurement of raw materials for export production under five separate programs, namely:

Ceramics	$1,000,000
Light machinery and optics	1,750,000

82. Clay, *Decision in Germany*, p. 196.
83. *OMGUS, Trade and Commerce*, July 1946, p. 9.

Basic chemicals	3,500,000
Building industry	1,000,000
Miscellaneous	500,000

As in the cotton transaction, the U.S. Commercial Company was to be repaid from the proceeds of the resulting exports.[84]

All this, of course, was only a modest beginning, and the American export staff still had a long and difficult road ahead. Nevertheless, some of the underbrush had been cleared, and since the merger of the American and British Zones was imminent, the economic signs seemed to point up. Some American and German publications describing the first years of the American occupation have been quite critical of the policies of the American Military Government, as indicated by headings such as "the do-nothing period"[85] or "muddling through."[86] The writer, who during these critical years served as a member of OMGUS's export-import staff, believes that "starting from scratch" would be a more appropriate label!

While it has to be left to the individual critics whether they wish to look at the doughnut or the hole, a more serious view must be taken of the all-too-frequent appraisal that accuses the American Military Government of repressing the German economy during the first years of the occupation under the influence of a Morgenthau-inspired JCS/1067. Since the opposite was actually the case, such evaluations should be relegated to the realm of historical myth. It is, of course, quite true that some American planners were busily engaged in drawing up theoretical levels beyond which the German economy was not supposed to develop, and that the elements of OMGUS concerned with reparations carried out their respective responsibilities as described in a preceding chapter. At the same time, however, most of the OMGUS staff was actively engaged in the reconstruction of the German economy from a starting point close to zero and had neither the time nor the desire to focus on theoretical limitations which one day—three to four years hence by expert estimate—might or might not take effect.

Divergent appraisals not only disregard demonstrable and clearly recognizable facts but also seem to reveal an inadequate appreciation of the workings of American government which rarely implement top-level policy guidances mechanically, but rather reflect the multitude of contradictions so inherent in the American society.

84. Draper to Mr. DeWitt Schieck, President USCC, on a general understanding and agreement between OMGUS and U.S. Commercial Company, 25 Oct. 1946 (OMGUS records, 123-1/3).
85. Meurer, p. 146.   86. Balabkins, pp. 3–33.

CHAPTER FIVE

THE JOINT EXPORT IMPORT AGENCY (US/UK)

It is understandable that Secretary of State Byrnes's speech in Stuttgart on September 6, 1946, has often been referred to as a turning point in American occupational policy. Prior to that date a German who wanted to learn about American plans for the postwar treatment of his country had only a few guideposts to go by: the Morgenthau Plan which had been leaked to the press in September 1944 and whose validity as an instrument of U.S. policy had never been officially acknowledged or denied; the Potsdam Agreement of August 1945; the Joint Chief of Staff Directive No. 1067, which was released for publication several months later without making it clear that some of its key provisions had already been superseded by the earlier Declaration of the Three Powers; and finally the quadripartite Level of Industry Plan of March 1946. While all these documents stressed the restrictive aspects of American policies toward Germany, they contained no reference to the laborious and costly reconstruction of the economy in progress in the American Zone since the occupation began.

By contrast, Soviet authorities, with their traditional flair for seizing opportunities for propaganda, had covered the Russian Zone with posters quoting Stalin's statements to the effect that the German state could never be destroyed and that the German nation would survive the Nazi regime. At the same time, notwithstanding these official pronouncements, Soviet authorities were engaged in a policy of indiscriminate spoilage in their area.[1]

There is some unintended irony in Secretary Byrnes's description of the circumstances which led to his Stuttgart appearance. One would have thought that the United States Government at last had decided to clarify the American position in a belated recognition of the prevailing general confusion regarding its plans for Germany and that such action

1. Friedmann, *The Allied Military Government in Germany*, p. 25.

had been taken spontaneously. According to Byrnes's memoirs, however, this was by no means the case, and the speech at the Stuttgart Opera House was in essence a reaction to and prompted by Molotov's propagandistic statements at the Paris Foreign Ministers Conference in July 1946.[2]

The Russian representatives on that occasion had played on the understandable German fears about their future by declaring that it would be a mistake to contemplate Germany's annihilation as a state or to plan its agrarianization and the destruction of its principal industries. The aim of the Soviet government was not to destroy Germany, he said, "but to transform it into a democratic and peace-loving state which besides its agriculture will have its own industry and foreign trade." A policy directed toward the creation of a pastoral state and the elimination of its principal industries, would only result in making Germany an incubator for dangerous sentiments of revenge; such a policy without doubt would play right into the hands of German reactionaries and would endanger Europe's future tranquillity and peace. As to the discussions about a possible separation of the Ruhr from Germany, Molotov remarked that, since it was self-evident that Germany could not exist as an independent and viable state without the Ruhr, such concepts simply complemented the plans for destruction and agrarianization of Germany. He added that the Allies should put no obstacles in the way of an increase in the German output of steel, coal, and manufactured products of a peaceful nature. But he failed to mention that at recent quadripartite meetings about the future level of German industry it was the Soviet representatives who had voted for the lowest figure and that a higher level was established only at the insistence of the United States and Great Britain.

Prodded into action by Molotov's misleading and propagandistic statements and the similar misrepresentations in the Soviet-controlled East German press that followed, the secretary of state consulted with General Clay and decided to go to Germany to deliver a major public address which would clarify the views of the United States government about the future of Germany before the world.

If one scrutinizes the substance of the speech, one cannot fail to conclude that it hardly differed from the declaration to which Great Britain, the Soviet Union, and the United States had subscribed thirteen months earlier.

2. Byrnes, p. 187.

With regard to the basic Allied goal of German demilitarization and reparations, Byrnes simply reiterated that the Potsdam Agreement should be carried out so that Germany's war potential would be reduced by the elimination of its war industries and by the reduction and the removal of industrial plants not needed for its peacetime economy. He added more positively that Germany should be freed from militarism and the German people should be given an opportunity to apply their great energies and abilities to the works of peace so that "in time they could take an honorable place among the members of the United Nations." In a further reference to reparations, Byrnes restated the original American principle whereby there would be no reparations from current production. Such reparations, he said, directing his words mainly to Moscow, would be wholly inconsistent with the level of industry now established under the Potsdam Agreement. "This level has been set by the four Allies with the explicit aim of permitting Germany to maintain average European living standards without assistance from other countries." Again clearly addressing himself to the Soviet Union, he added that in many important aspects the Control Council unfortunately was neither governing Germany nor allowing Germany to govern itself. The United States regarded a common financial policy as essential for the successful rehabilitation of Germany and considered it almost certain that a runaway inflation accompanied by economic paralysis would develop unless the German house could be put in order through such a common financial policy.

As to the political sphere, the secretary indicated that the American government would support the French claim to the Saar and that it was also prepared to recognize the annexation of some territory in East Germany by Poland as compensation for the area east of the Curzon Line ceded to Russia. The extent of the area to be annexed, however, should be determined when the final settlement would be made. More pleasing for German ears were Byrnes's comments about the Ruhr and the Rhineland, which, he said, the United States considered indisputably German. It therefore would not support any encroachment on this territory nor any division not genuinely desired by the people concerned. On the other hand, however, since the resources of these regions should never again be used for destructive purposes, the United States government was in favor of controls necessary for security purposes, while excluding measures that "would subject the Ruhr and the Rhineland to the political domination or manipulation of outside powers." In a positive vein Byrnes also remarked that Germany must be given a chance to export goods in order to import enough to make its economy self-sustaining. Germany was a part of Europe, he said, and recovery in Europe and particularly in the states adjoining Germany would be very slow if Germany with its great resources of iron and coal were to be turned into a poorhouse.

The secretary of state summed up his speech by declaring that the United States could not relieve Germany from the hardships inflicted upon it by the war which the National Socialistic regime had started, but that it would attempt to give the German people "an opportunity to work their way out of these hardships so long as they respected human freedom and clung to the path of peace." [3]

Although the speech contained no change in substance when compared with previous American policy statements, there was a very considerable difference in tone; furthermore, while the *de facto* reconstruction of the German economy had been under way in the American Zone for more than a year, it now had received official recognition as a major policy aim of the United States.[4] The public appearance of the American secretary of state had been carefully staged with an impressive display of elite units of the American army in the streets, an array of American and German dignitaries at the Stuttgart Opera House, and a simultaneous broadcast to the German people. The intentional misrepresentation of American plans for Germany had thus been officially and dramatically corrected.

America's innate lack of patience, which often works to the detriment of United States foreign policy, proved to be rather beneficial when it came to deciding which course of action the United States should follow in Germany. America had gone to Potsdam in the expectation that the wartime alliance with the Soviet Union would be continued and that a common postwar policy, the broad outline of which had been established prior to the surrender, would be effectively implemented. In the course of the following year, there was some progress as far as the Allied goal of a maximizing of German agricultural production was concerned; but otherwise it was mainly the negative provisions of Potsdam such as demilitarization, denazification, and reparations that were implemented on a quadripartite basis. The cardinal decision of Potsdam, namely, economic unity and the creation of a central administration, not only

3. Ibid., p. 191.
4. Schwarz, p. 116, arrives at a similar appraisal.

had not been carried out but there were many indications that the Soviet Union had no intention of living up to these commitments in a foreseeable future.

In the meantime, Germany remained broken up into four hermetically separated areas with severe restrictions on interzonal travel and an almost complete freeze on the exchange of goods. For the time being, none of the four areas was self-supporting, although the economies of the British and Soviet Zones could be expected eventually to take care of themselves. The U.S. Zone was a source of only few raw materials and evidently would remain dependent on American support for an unlimited period of time.

On the positive side, the first year of occupation had helped to clarify the concepts of American policy makers. As reflected at Stuttgart, the United States Government had reached the conclusion that while the Saar could be detached from Germany without major damage to its economy, the Ruhr and the Rhineland clearly could not. Furthermore it had not been recognized that the re-establishment of economic unity was the crux of the German problem and that, unless this key provision of Potsdam was soon implemented, the quadripartite Level of Industry Plan and the related decisions on reparations would lose all practical meaning. According to the economic plans drafted by the four powers, the German economy was to be restricted to a level roughly corresponding to 75 percent of its industrial output in 1936. Inasmuch as Germany's actual production in 1946 had not even come halfway towards this bench mark and, in the opinion of American experts, would take another three to five years [5] to reach the agreed level, there was clearly no point in reflecting on a limitation which could be of only academic significance for several years to come.

At the same time, however, conditions were such that some decisive action toward the economic amalgamation of the four zones seemed essential, and that as long as a complete unification was politically not feasible, a partial solution had to be sought. This theoretical consideration was, of course, influenced by the special conditions respectively affecting the economies of the British and American Zones. While the former had the industrial potential to make the area self-supporting eventually, it was weak in agricultural production. Moreover, the financial situation of the occupying power made it highly questionable whether the dollar subsidies required for an interim period of several years actually would be made available. The American Zone, on the

5. Byrnes, p. 180.

other hand, had more agriculture but much less industry, and the prospect of a deficit in its balance of trade for many years to come. The financial resources of the responsible government, of course, was such that—Congress willing—the combined trade deficits of both zones could be covered. There had been some informal and tentative pooling of bizonal export proceeds and import costs since the fall of 1945.[6] While an economic merger of the two zones could not be regarded as a panacea, it seemed a logical step in order to move things off dead center and to implement at least in part the economic unity which Potsdam had prescribed.

The proposal to merge the economies of the two zones was submitted to Washington in May 1946 in the form of a lengthy cable which also included General Clay's recommendations regarding the composition of a future German state, the drafting of a German constitution, and the establishment of a quadripartite Ruhr Control Authority for the German coal and steel industry. As Clay pointed out, his proposal should be acceptable in principle to the Soviet Union, France, and Great Britain. However, if agreement on a quadripartite basis could not be reached, at least the economies of the British and the American Zones ought to be merged. The bizonal area "could within a few years become self-supporting although food would have to be provided during the period until industry could be rehabilitated sufficiently to provide requisite exports to support food imports. Recognizing fully the political implications of such a merger, it is our belief here that even those implications would not be as serious as the continuation of the present air-tight Zones." [7]

In Washington the projected bizonal merger had been discussed before, and since it had become increasingly clear that the Soviet Union had no intention of treating Germany as an economic unit, it was decided to go ahead with the plan. Accordingly, at the Foreign Ministers Conference in Paris the American secretary of state again asked for an early establishment of a central German administration to secure Germany's economic unity and then announced that while this matter was still pending the United States was prepared to join with any other occupying government for treating their zones as an economic unit. The current situation, which tended to promote inflation and economic paralysis, should not be permitted to continue, he said, because on one hand it imposed unnecessary sufferings on the German people, and on the other it increased the financial burden on the occupying powers. The United States was not prepared to wait any longer and considered it its

6. Clay, *Decision in Germany*, p. 74.   7. Ibid., p. 78.

duty to press for the establishment of a unified economic administration in Germany at the earliest possible moment.[8] As could be anticipated under the circumstances, the Soviet Union and France remained non-committal, whereas the British representative, Ernest Bevin, promptly declared that his government would go along with the American proposal in principle.

The negotiations regarding the implementation of the contemplated fusion were conducted on a Military Government level by General Clay and his British counterpart, Lt. General Sir Brian Robertson, with the result that the economic merger of the two zones was made effective as of January 1, 1947. The Byrnes-Bevin Agreement of December 4, 1946, formalizing the move, provided for a pooling of all domestic resources and imports in order to achieve a common standard of living. It also stipulated that for economic purposes the two zones were to be treated as a single area. The economic unification was to be supervised by German administrative agencies scheduled to operate under the joint control of the American and British commanders in chief. While working out the details of the merger, the two military governors were under instructions to avoid the appearance of a bipartite political action that might tend to reduce the chances for the desired unification of all of Germany.[9] Accordingly, the Soviet Union and France not only were repeatedly invited to participate in the bilateral venture but also were kept informed as to American-British plans for the bizonal economic organization. For the same reason and at the expense of efficiency, the military governors decided not to establish one West German administrative center where American-British and German offices would be located, but rather to put the newly established bureaus into four different West German towns. The administration for food and agriculture therefore was set up in Stuttgart, for transportation in Bielefeld, for economics in Minden, and for communications, civil service, and finance in Frankfurt.[10] On the Military Government side, bizonal administration consisted of a Bipartite Board encompassing a secretariat and six bipartite panels for policy guidance. Furthermore, there were six bipartite

8. Actually the bizonal merger was considered the first step toward the economic unification of Germany. In this connection see also General Draper's speech before the Executive Committee for Economics in Minden, 11 Oct. 1946 (OMGUS records, 1-1/4).

9. Byrnes, p. 196.

10. The authority and responsibilities of these German agencies were not clearly defined. A discussion of the resulting American-German misunderstandings and increasingly acrimonious debate is beyond the scope of this study. It will be found in Gimbel, pp. 94–100.

control groups located in the same four cities as the corresponding German administrative offices.

The establishment of a quadripartite foreign-trade agency with the responsibilities for buying, collecting, storing, transporting, and selling abroad the goods Germany would export had been the subject of intramural discussions at OMGUS headquarters since November 1945. It was envisaged that the same agency would take the responsibility for "collecting within foreign countries the proceeds of all exported goods and for the utilization of these proceeds by purchasing goods for import into Germany. Furthermore, the agency would be responsible for transporting the imports to the German border and for selling these goods within Germany." [11]

It will be recalled that in December 1945 the United States Representative at the Allied Control Council's Export Import Sub-Committee had submitted a paper outlining the organization of a quadripartite foreign-trade agency with the ultimate aim of turning over its responsibilities to an appropriate German office.[12] Inasmuch as the political situation had prevented the acceptance of the American plan for an "Allied Export-Import Bureau of Germany," the Byrnes-Bevin Agreement now assigned the initial responsibility for the development of German foreign trade in the Bizone to "a Joint Export Import Agency or such other agency as may be established by the two Commanders in Chief," with the proviso, however, that its mission would be transferred to a German agency for foreign trade under joint American-British supervision "as soon as circumstances would permit."

The difficult question of the anticipated annual deficit of the Bizone and of the respective financial responsibilities of the United States and Great Britain was settled in the course of direct negotiations between Secretary Byrnes and Foreign Minister Ernest Bevin. According to the original calculations of the two Military Governments, the deficit for the first year had been estimated at $200 million for the American Zone and $400 million for the British Zone.[13] It was believed that the deficit could be progressively reduced and that after three years the merged area would become self-supporting.

The American Military Government had taken the position that the respective financial responsibilities should be related to the population

11. Dodge to Draper, 26 Nov. 1945 (OMGUS records, 202-3/11).
12. Statement on U.S. Proposal for Export Import Bureau of Germany Submitted to Trade and Commerce Commttee ACA, 11 Feb. 1946 (OMGUS records, 123-2/3).
13. Byrnes, p. 196.

figures of the two zones, a proposal which would have favored the United States. The British, on the other hand, hard pressed for the dollars needed for the importation of food and raw materials, insisted that the United States should carry 60 percent of the burden. Since Clay and Robertson were unable to settle this point, it was finally referred to the higher governmental level, where Bevin reiterated that Great Britain did not have the necessary dollars to meet the expected deficit and again suggested an unequal sharing of expenses. Byrnes, in reply, pointed out that because of the anticipated larger deficit in the British Zone the United States actually would be assuming a larger share anyway if an even division was agreed upon. With implied reference to the Second Quebec Conference at which, under British pressure, the United States had relinquished its claim to the occupation of northern Germany, he then added that the United States was prepared to pay 60 percent of the total deficit if Britain would be willing to exchange zones. As expected, Bevin declined, and although later estimates envisaged a somewhat larger deficit than originally anticipated, an even division was eventually agreed upon.[14]

The economic merger of the two zones united an area which had a well diversified manufacturing capacity but insufficient resources of basic raw materials and food. Before World War II, the Bizone had been responsible for more than half of Germany's industrial production; it was also Germany's principal source of coal and steel, as well as of numerous industrial products—agricultural machinery, automotive vehicles, etc. The only major natural resource of the area, coal, had always been one of its primary export items. Its iron-ore resources, on the other hand, were of poor quality, its nonferrous metals and ores came from abroad, and the textile industries of the region depended entirely on imported fibers and, in the case of synthetic fibers, on foreign pulp. Before the war about two thirds of the exports from the Bizone had been metal products, machinery, optical goods, and chemicals, whereas only about one third had come from coal, textiles, and other consumer goods. It was therefore clear that the last three categories would not suffice to reach the prewar level of exports and that eventually the heavy industries would have to make a substantial contribution. The primary deficiency of the area, of course, was in the field of agriculture. Before the war it had produced only about 40 percent of Germany's domestic food, but in 1947 it contained almost 60 percent of the total German popula-

14. Ibid., p. 196.

tion. Even if food production in the Bizone could be restored to prewar levels, the area would provide only 50 percent of the prewar per capita consumption. Consequently, in order to make the Bizone independent of foreign subsidies, extraordinary progress in the field of foreign trade would have to be made. It was anticipated that $1 billion would have to be spent in 1947 by the two governments for imports, while exports would total $350 million; imports for 1948 were expected to be in the vicinity of $975 million, as compared with expected exports of $675 million. In line with the principal objective of the merger, namely, "the achievement before the end of 1949 of a self-sustaining economy," it was expected that during the third year after the merger a balance of exports and imports at an approximate level of $935 million for each would be reached.[15]

Under the arrangements for the merger, imports in the Bizone were divided into category A and category B. The former, mostly food, fertilizers, and petroleum products brought in "to prevent disease and unrest," were to be financed by the governments of the two occupying powers, with the United States drawing on appropriated GARIOA funds. Category B imports on the other hand were raw materials required by bizonal industry and expected to be funded from the proceeds of exports. The original capital of the Joint Export Import Agency (US/UK) consisted of the proceeds from exports of the American Zone accumulated during the first eighteen months of occupation; a sum of $29.3 million due to the American Military Government under the original British-American pooling arrangement;[16] and a U.K. obligation to match the total of this American contribution either in needed goods from the sterling area or in pounds sterling convertible into dollars on demand. Accordingly the initial paid-in capital of the agency, as recorded by Clay, was in the vicinity of $90 million,[17] a slightly larger amount than the one shown in a JEIA balance sheet of January 1, 1947, retained among the OMGUS records.[18] Additional amounts needed for the purchases of category B imports were to be provided by the two governments on an equal basis and in a mutually agreeable manner.

The Joint Export Import Agency (US/UK) was to be responsible for determining import requirements. The procurement of category B im-

15. Hutton and Robbins, p. 4.
16. Authorized by JCS W-85123, as reported in "Export-Import Aspects of Civilian Supply Problems" (OMGUS records, 355-1/5).
17. Clay, *Decision in Germany*, p. 173.
18. The amount shown as a starting capital in JEIA's balance sheet is $72,706,767.62 (OMGUS records, Gen. A. G. File 091.31).

ports and of those category A imports which could not be financed by appropriated funds also became a JEIA responsibility. The agency, furthermore, was given the mission of promoting and expanding German exports and of assisting in the removal of all barriers to German foreign trade as quickly as world conditions permitted. At the earliest possible date a fixed exchange value for the mark was to be established and a financial reform was to be effected. Normal business channels were to be restored, foreign buyers were to be given free access to the Bizone, and business communications between Germany and other countries were to be facilitated. In sum, there should be a speedy return to normal business practices. Also, in order to promote bizonal foreign trade, a joint Foreign Exchange Agency was created and authorized to open accounts in the name of the two Military Governments with approved banks of the countries where JEIA was to operate; all proceeds from bizonal exports were to be paid into these accounts. In recognition of the calamitous German food situation, the Byrnes-Bevin Agreement finally indicated that the current normal consumer ration of 1550 calories was to be raised to 1800 calories "as soon as the world food supply and the availability of funds would permit such an increase."

The Joint Export Import Agency (US/UK) or JEIA, as it was called, was formally established as of January 1, 1947, by the two commanders in chief. Its first headquarters was located in Minden, Westphalia, also the seat of the British economic administration and of its German counterpart, the Verwaltungsamt für Wirtschaft (VFW). As constituted by the Bipartite Board, the new agency consisted of an integrated American, British, and German staff headed by two chairmen to be appointed respectively by the commanders of the American and British Zones. At the outset the staff was composed of seventy-five Americans and Britons and thirty-five Germans. At the same time there were eighty-one Germans working in the foreign-trade section of the VFW.[19] The first two chairmen were Dr. Roy Bullock, formerly head of the Export-Import Section, OMGUS, and J. F. Cahan, an official from the British Treasury.

While American-British negotiations regarding the bizonal merger were still in progress, General Clay had initiated another consequential step aimed at the promotion of German exports. Recognizing that the established export procedure under OMGUS, whereby all transactions were channeled through Berlin, had caused a time-consuming bottle-

19. JEIA Monthly Report, Jan.–Feb. 1947, p. A.

neck, he ordered the delegation of certain procedural authorities to Military Government offices in the *Länder*. Accordingly, when the bizonal merger came about, the Export-Import Section at OMGUS, Berlin, was dissolved and part of its staff transferred to the new JEIA headquarters in Minden, whereas the remaining staff members were given assignments with the Export-Import Sections in the field. An almost simultaneous establishment of JEIA Branch Offices (January 20, 1947) in Munich (Bavaria), Stuttgart (Württemberg-Baden), Wiesbaden (Hesse), Bremen, and in the U.S. sector of Berlin, as well as their prompt amalgamation with the respective Export-Import Sections, completed the reorganization of foreign-trade responsibilities in the American Zone.[20]

The results of the decentralization were most beneficial and promptly noticeable, since the new branch offices were authorized to approve and license most export transactions without any further reference to higher headquarters. Furthermore, since nontransactional mail between German exporters and foreign buyers had been approved somewhat earlier, direct contacts between German and foreign firms had again become possible. German suppliers and foreign buyers were now able to agree on and prepare tentative export orders. After the proposed contracts had been screened by the German Aussenhandelskontore, they were passed to the JEIA Branch Office for final approval and the issuance of an export license. Although the procedure still had onerous bureaucratic aspects and hardly corresponded to peacetime trade practices, it probably was the best that could be done under the prevailing conditions and an important first step toward the elimination of the countless obstacles obstructing German export trade.

One of the new agency's first moves was a study of the type of foreign-commerce and foreign-exchange controls which the two Military Governments would have to retain for some time even after most of the responsibilities had been turned over to German governmental agencies. The study also involved an examination of the physical, legal, and administrative barriers to a revival of foreign trade. From this analysis a blueprint of JEIA's future course of action was drawn up with the aim of gradually eliminating the numerous obstacles and bottlenecks in this general area. Next, a three-step action program was prepared providing for a geographic decentralization of foreign-trade controls, the turning over of control to German governmental agencies as quickly as condi-

20. Instruction: Office of Military Governor to *Land* Directors, 20 Jan. 1947: Subject: Export Import Bipartite Arrangements (OMGUS records, 37-3/1).

tions would permit, and finally the removal of trade barriers in order to establish normal business practices at the earliest possible moment.[21]

In the British Zone, where all foreign trade had been centralized in a Zonal Commerce Office, progress was initially slower, and during the first part of 1947 business was still conducted on a government-to-government basis. There was no contact between German exporters and foreign buyers, and the German governmental agencies also played no part. Subsequently, in accordance with the new policies, the organizational pattern of foreign trade as established in the American Zone was extended to the British Zone, and JEIA Branch Offices were also opened in Düsseldorf (Nordrhein-Westfalen), Hannover (Niedersachsen), Kiel (Schleswig-Holstein), Hamburg and in the British Sector of Berlin.

In order to establish a uniform trade procedure, JEIA on April 8, 1947, issued its Instruction No. 1 entitled "Export Procedure for US/UK Zones of Germany to Be Observed by German Exporters." Composed of fifty paragraphs and twelve annexes, the document stated in its preamble that the agency's authorization was based on the Byrnes-Bevin Agreement, which had given JEIA the responsibility of supervising German foreign trade with the aim of achieving a self-supporting economy in the Bizone by the end of 1947. "In order to insure maximum foreign trade," it further indicated that "it was JEIA's intent to make every effort to return to normal commercial practices."

Instruction No. 1 also required the economic ministries of the *Länder* to draft export-import programs for their respective areas and to forward them to the Verwaltungsamt für Wirschaft in Minden, which in turn was responsible for their coordination and subsequent submission to the main office of JEIA. Initially only German exports, not imports, were decentralized, with the additional limitation that export applications involving contracts for amounts exceeding $50,000 or requiring more than nine months to execute, or contracts involving the processing of goods whose ownership remained with the foreign customer, required the approval of the main office in Minden. In July the authorization of branch offices to approve export transactions was extended to include not only contracts up to $250,000 but also those entailing an execution up to eighteen months. On the other hand, because of "international considerations including the allocation of scarce raw materials," a second JEIA instruction of April 25, 1947, limited the authority of the branch offices with regard to a number of basic commodities such as

21. Hutton and Robbins, p. 4.

coal, hops, lumber, potash, refractory material, cement, salt, aluminum, rolled iron, and steel. The first instruction also directed the branch offices to advise the Aussenhandelskontore concerning the new procedure and to assist German firms in export negotiations.

German exporters were specifically required to charge world market prices for their goods and services because it was "the purpose of the export program to obtain maximum proceeds from exports within the framework of sound long-term commercial policy." At the same time, they continued to receive only the legal domestic price of the exported product, plus legitimate additional expenditures such as special packing and transportation charges.

Also attached to JEIA Instruction No. 1 was a list of Reichsmark conversion factors to be utilized for the establishment of minimum export prices in U.S. dollars. Divided into nine categories, the list provided a conversion factor for each individual product. Under "Ceramics," for instance, a conversion factor of 0.40 was established for crucibles; 0.42 for ceramic rings, and 0.57 for chinaware, including figurines. In the other eight categories conversion factors ranged under "Machinery and Parts" from 0.44 to 0.52, under "Electrical Equipment" from 0.30 to 0.57, under "Semi-manufactured Products" from 0.40 to 0.53, under "Chemicals, Dyestuffs, Etc." from 0.38 to 0.80, under "Optical Equipment" from 0.48 to 0.57, under "Textiles" from 0.40 to 0.42, under "Consumer Goods" from 0.40 to 0.45, and under "Miscellaneous" from 0.42 to 0.52. The Branch Offices of JEIA were responsible for the screening of export prices, for ascertaining that maximum world market prices had been obtained, and for checking that dollar export prices divided by the controlled domestic Reichsmark price did not give lower than authorized conversion factors.

It soon became apparent that pricing according to an inflexible list entailed unnecessary complications, and a few months later JEIA Headquarters rescinded the list while delegating full pricing authority to the field.[22] Branch offices were now required to "take all necessary action to determine the fair market value measured by sales of comparable products outside Germany, and to coordinate such prices with prices already established by the Agency." Written evidence had to be kept on file in support of each price determination and "particular care was to be exercised to insure that evidence is on hand to refute possible future charges of selling below recognized market levels."

22. JEIA Instructions no. 1 and no. 2, amendment D, 21 July 1947 (OMGUS records).

As readily seen, the task was difficult and highly complex since it involved market research in many countries and concerned a great variety of industrial products. The writer, who had this responsibility in JEIA's branch office in Munich, can still recall some of the extraordinary problems connected with the collection of valid price data for specialized products—diesel engines, turbines, electrical equipment, locomotives, spinning machinery, optical instruments, etc.

The instruction also listed a number of approved German banks (Aussenhandelsbanken) which were authorized to make payments for export deliveries and which in turn were to be reimbursed by a central office, the Gemeinsame Aussenhandelskasse in Frankfurt am Main. A list of accounts included in one of the annexes to Instruction No. 1 pertained to joint accounts in the name of "Military Government for Germany (US/UK), Joint Export-Import Official Account" established by the national banks of Europe as well as by the Federal Reserve Bank of New York.

Although decentralization of export procedures and the gradual establishment of direct commercial contacts were useful steps in promoting foreign trade, the basic problem of the lack of incentives remained as a major obstacle. As the situation presented itself, the JEIA branch offices therefore were obliged to channel their efforts in two directions. On one hand, it was their task to help overcome whatever anti-German feelings there were in foreign countries, to solicit inquiries for German products, and to see to it that prices for German goods were the best obtainable; on the other hand, it was also JEIA's mission to generate interest in exports among German manufacturers, who more often than not considered each export transaction an outright loss, since it involved the exchange of real values against credit entries in Reichsmark bank accounts of questionable utility.

When JEIA announced that exported goods would be replaced by appropriate quantities of imported raw materials, the promise at first was not believed. When JEIA made good and the raw materials actually arrived, a number of "sharp" manufacturers engaged in the practice of delivering minimum amounts of export goods while extracting from the Military Government a maximum of raw materials to be hoarded against the day when the generally expected currency reform would again establish a sound accounting basis for the German economy. Needless to say, the task of policing these transactions was difficult and unrewarding. The same applied to the area of possible price collusion between German sellers and foreign buyers. Unless the German firm was farsighted enough to see that an unwarranted low dollar price today would establish an undesirable precedent for the exports of tomorrow, it had no direct interest in the dollar side of the export transaction; consequently, there was always the temptation of a special deal whereby, in addition to a low official export price, a specified amount would be paid into a numbered account in Switzerland. As Soviet-American tension grew and many Germans thought they could discern the clouds of a new war on the horizon, the desire for a hard-currency nest egg abroad grew quite rapidly.

German mistrust of the occupying authorities was another obstructive factor. The writer well remembers a meeting with a Bavarian producer of spinning machinery to discuss the prices of an impending export transaction to Switzerland. Specially designed products were involved, and it had not been possible to obtain meaningful price data from the American Embassy in Berne. The writer, therefore, could only stress to his visitor that the negotiation for an adequate price was in the last analysis a German problem. If the exporter sold too cheaply, he probably would spoil his future market when exchange rates again had become meaningful. The German expressed his appreciation, but left with a somewhat bewildered expression on his face; as we later learned, he had come to the meeting firmly convinced that he would be coerced into an unfavorable deal. It seemed almost inconceivable to him that here was a Military Government organization with his legitimate interest at heart.

It was easy to see that progress would be slow and the established export targets difficult to reach unless a system of incentives could be designed with the aim of overcoming the hardly disguised resistance of the German producers. Accordingly, after prolonged bizonal deliberations, the Bipartite Board in July 1947 approved an Export Foreign Exchange Currency Bonus which provided for the setting aside of 10 percent of the foreign-exchange proceeds from all export deliveries made after June 30, 1947.[23] A number of commodities such as coal, pig iron, scrap, timber, potash, electric power, gas, and water were excluded. The incentive was divided into two equal accounts of 5 percent each, thus encompassing an exporter's bonus as well as a labor fund. The exporter's share was expressed in the form of a certificate issued by the Aussenhandelsbank at the time the export payment was made. The face value of the certificate was expressed in the currency of the export

23. Hutton and Robbins, p. 12.

contract and could be used for the procurement of imports which directly or indirectly would tend to increase the volume of German exports. Because of the exporter's frequent dependence on supplies or services from subcontractors, he was authorized but not required to share these benefits with them. The bonus could be utilized for the importation of special machinery in order to improve, replace, or enlarge existing plants and buildings, as well as for purchases of spare parts and raw materials from abroad; it also authorized the financing of foreign representation and the travel of sales representatives in foreign countries. The utilization of the bonus for labor engaged in the production of export goods was covered by an interim plan announced as Amendment No. 1 to JEIA Instruction No. 6 of February 16, 1948. The plan entailed the establishment of an Export Bonus Office in Frankfurt am Main responsible for "the selection of the goods to be imported with due regard for the wishes of the workers of the export establishments and the existing possibilities of import." By the time the interim plan was announced, the bonus fund for workers in export industries had grown to a value of $2.5 million from its inception in July 1947.[24]

Another major impediment to a free flow of foreign trade was the problem of communications. During the first years of the occupation even the transmission of official Military Government correspondence was slow. Letters from Berlin to Minden, for instance, unless hand-carried by a traveling officer, took several days, but still were faster than telegrams. Communications with foreign countries were even slower. As the first monthly report of JEIA indicated, while Allied facilities were bad "those open to Germans are far worse. Their internal mails are improving but international mail takes days and weeks to travel only a few hundred miles. There are for all practical purposes virtually no long distance telephone and telegraph facilities. There is no outgoing airmail. These conditions must be improved before German exporters have to compete seriously with exporters in other countries. Few buyers will long continue to put up with the delays now imposed on them." [25]

After protracted negotiations on a quadripartite level, JEIA finally was able to announce a procedure whereby the branch offices were authorized to issue permits to German export firms for the use of international telephone and telegraph facilities. These services were considered approved imports within the framework of bizonal foreign-trade instructions, and dollars from the proceeds of exports were made

24. Meurer, p. 74.
25. JEIA Monthly Report, Jan.–Feb. 1947, p. B.

available to meet the resulting obligations outside Germany.[26] Another quadripartite ruling sanctioned, as of June 15, 1947, transactional mail with foreign countries provided the correspondence pertained to transactions permitted under the laws of the Allied Control Authority. It was expressly stipulated, however, that all proceeds from such transactions would have to go into the accounts of the Military Governments concerned. While formerly all export papers such as contracts, invoices, and shipping documents had to be transmitted through the branch offices of JEIA, under the new policy German exporters were permitted to deal with their customers directly.[27]

During the first years of the occupation, as a safeguard against carpetbagging, the borders of the Bizone had to remain closed to foreign visitors unless they traveled on official business. In order to facilitate normal trade practices, a new procedure for handling foreign businessmen was now worked out, providing for direct clearances and entry permits by Military Permit Officers stationed in the principal European capitals. In view of the logistical problems involved, quotas based on the respective volume of business were assigned to each country that engaged in trade with Germany. It was not an entirely satisfactory solution, however, and caused some unfavorable publicity. OMGUS—continuously in the middle of conflicting pressures—once was obliged to cable to Washington:

> Our facilities are taxed to the utmost to receive the official visitors who you are sending us in large numbers and to receive our agreed businessmen quotas. Hence, we are not in a position to offer adequate facilities to unofficial theater visits by special groups. We have neither the transportation nor the accommodations, and each such visit represents a special difficult problem. Failure to properly care for the unofficial visitors always results in creating severe critics of the U.S. Army.[28]

In the fall of 1947 a "Procedure for Arranging Travel of German Businessmen Abroad" was established. Branch offices of JEIA were given the authority to sponsor the travel abroad of German businessmen and to pay for their travel out of JEIA's foreign-currency funds. Criteria to be observed were the importance of the proposed journey to the

---

26. It is indicative of the obstacles which had to be overcome that the procedure had been drafted as early as January 1946; see memorandum Winant to Brig. Gen. Meade, 26 Jan. 1946 (OMGUS records, 123-2/3).
27. Hutton and Robbins, p. 7.
28. 7 July 1947, CC-9787 (OMGUS records, 38-1/1).

economic objectives of the two Military Governments and the inability of the traveler to use export bonus funds.[29] Although the gradual removal of travel restrictions was a step in the right direction, the transition from wartime controls to normal trade practices by necessity was complicated and very slow, as the following quotation from an official JEIA report demonstrates:

> As outlined in the instruction, Branch Offices will approve all instances of travel in conjunction with the *Land* Economic Ministries and will prepare a letter of sponsorship for each applicant to the consulate of the country to be visited. After the applicant has obtained clearance for travel from his local *Buergermeister* and Liaison and Security Office, and upon receipt of a letter from the country to be visited assuring the granting of a visa, the appropriate Branch office of the Combined Travel Board will issue the applicant a Temporary Travel Document with a Military Exit and Re-Entry Permit. The JEIA Branch Office or the applicant himself will then obtain the consulate's visa in the applicant's Travel Document.[30]

Considering this example of bureaucratic procedure it is hardly surprising that the Joint Export Import Agency (US/UK) had a bad press in occupied Germany as well as in most European countries. An American economist summed up the situation when he referred to JEIA as the "unhappy agency whose efforts in the face of impossible odds deserve greater recognition than they have received" and added that "JEIA found itself cast in the role of an export monopoly for an economy that had neither the means nor the incentives to export." [31]

As far as the German businessmen were concerned, their generally negative reactions to American-British efforts in the area of export promotion were based in part on a deep-seated distrust of the motives of their former enemies and in part on an understandable annoyance with complicated and burdensome export procedure. Inadequate public relations on behalf of the two Military Governments and the fact that foreign sales initially appeared contrary to German interests compounded the perplexity of the situation. To business firms abroad the bureaucratic formalities and a host of miscellaneous restrictions were equally annoying and the initial insistence by JEIA on dollar sales most

29. Hutton and Robbins, p. 8.
30. JEIA Instruction no. 8 (OMGUS records).
31. Wallich, pp. 230–31.

provocative. A document disseminated under the heading "Export and Import Problems" by the Military Government of Hesse on November 26, 1947, described the conditions with great perceptiveness and is therefore quoted almost in full:

> There appears to be a growing tendency to criticize Military Government and the German authorities on the part of German businessmen who claim that red tape, taxation, travel restriction, delays in correspondence, etc., have stifling effect on German business and initiative. Particularly violent exception is being taken to the manner in which exports and imports are being handled. The details of exporting and importing, the businessmen claim, are so complicated that they act as severe deterrents to prospective importers. LSO Wiesbaden reports there are numerous such businessmen who earnestly believe the Allies have no intention to allow Germany to get back on its feet economically. LK Offenbach businessmen recently alleged exports are intentionally rendered difficult by the German "bureaucracy" and the JEIA. For one small export, it was stated 51 forms must be filled out; the cost of labor, paper, translations, etc., was so immense that many businessmen refused to export. By trading on the black market or selling to members of the Occupation Forces, claimed the businessmen, much higher profits are realized than through export. As long as existing regulations continued to be in force, German merchants would not have the inclination to export.

> A review of export procedures and regulations reveals many of the complaints registered by the businessmen as unfounded. As to the amount of paper work involved, 28—in some cases 34—sheets must be filled out. However, in reality only seven separate forms are prepared—in cases of contracts over $5000, eight forms. The rest of the paper work consists of copies. This corresponds closely to the amount of paper work connected with exports made by German businessmen ever since 1933. (During the Nazi regime, an exporter had to prepare five, in some cases eight, forms.) Translations of the instructions and forms are unnecessary since all instructions are printed in both English and German, and English forms have German subtitles.

> The two or three days needed by the local JEIA to process an export application could hardly be described as delay or red tape. Slightly exaggerated are also the claims that it takes approximately

eight weeks, in the absence of airmail facilities, for a single exchange of correspondence with foreign buyers. The latter have the possibility of forwarding airmail to Germany—even ordinary first class surface mail from most European countries takes no more than four or five days—and the JEIA has made provisions for forwarding exporters' mail by air to foreign buyers. Telecommunication facilities are also available upon request. The only delay experienced by a German exporter is in payment receipts, which is not caused by JEIA or German agency "red tape" however, but by transportation difficulties within Germany. By the time a shipment reaches the port and shipping documents are cleared, at least eight weeks elapse. A local JEIA official has estimated that daily processing of shipping documents by German agencies (customs officials, *Aussenhandelskontore,* etc.) could perhaps reduce this by several days.

However, more important than complaints about red tape, excessive paper work and delays are the numerous allegations that German exporters are forced to sell their wares at prices lower than those on world markets. In this way it is often claimed—especially by political parties—that the U.S. makes large sums of money, driving German economy from world markets and subjugating Germany to the economic domination of the U.S. The influence of such systematic accusations on small uninformed businessmen is only too obvious. Instead of risking a loss through an unfavorable rate of exchange or low prices, they naturally prefer to hoard their products or to trade on the black market which requires no extra paper work and momentarily offers all the advantages of foreign trade. The fact that a conversion rate no longer is used in exports but has given ways to the practice of selling at world market prices seems unknown to the majority of potential exporters.

JEIA representatives believe competent German authorities could render German manufacturers and the German economy invaluable service by arranging a series of talks and discussions on export regulations. Many prospective exporters are influenced by rumors and unfounded complaints and deterred by the lengthy, legally phrased regulations governing exports. Such talks would help refute unfavorable and often erroneous charges and point out the advantages of export trade.[32]

32. OMGUS records, 26-2/7.

While JEIA's principal problems were indeed caused by the fact that the German economy had neither "the means nor the incentives to export," some obstacles to a free flow of foreign trade were traceable to the military restrictions connected with wartime controls, while still others resulted from the miniature crusades which unavoidably seem to accompany American foreign-policy moves. Among the former, the Trading with the Enemy Act of October 1917 initially played a major role, since it prevented German suppliers from dealing directly with foreign countries. After many months of prodding by OMGUS, the United States Government in March 1947 lifted the regulations under the Act as they applied to the American and British Zones of Germany. Among the latter, traditional policies against the restriction of free trade caused some problems, since they prompted the War Department to advise against exclusive contracts which "ultimately might lead to agreements to restrict trade." Accordingly OMGUS was told that "its exports should be pro-rated among available consignees with a view to broadest practical distribution"; furthermore, sales contracts were not to include firms which fixed prices, allocated markets, or otherwise operated to restrict free trade. Whenever OMGUS considered it necessary to authorize exemptions, it was instructed to consult with the Departments of State and War before approving a contract. For the same reasons OMGUS was asked not to permit contracts which would have the effect of "creating exclusive outlets in any country for any product where consignee owns or controls facilities for same or closely similar products." [33] Fortunately, and thanks to the common sense of the working levels, this crusade against the restriction of free trade had only minor consequences as far as the promotion of German exports was concerned, although it caused some difficulties at the time.

While most of these impediments were of a temporary nature, the American policy of free multilateral trade on a hard-currency basis became one of the key economic issues of the occupation. As indicated before, OMGUS had some very valid practical reasons for insisting from the start on export sales in dollars. Since the Reichsmark had become useless for purposes of international exchange, it seemed a logical alternative to utilize the most stable currency available. While the appropriate dollar funds of OMGUS at the beginning of the occupation were small, they could be used anywhere in the world and thereby permitted

33. W-86314, 28 Nov. 1946 (OMGUS records, 427-2/3). OMGUS in reply pointed out that it was "no longer in position of government selling agency with choice of determining with whom it will do business." 2 Jan. 1948, CC-2752 (OMGUS records, 355-1/5).

purchases at the lowest world market prices, which frequently meant in the United States.

In addition, the respective historical background of American and European foreign trade in the thirties was to be considered. In the United States after the passing of the Reciprocal Trade Agreement Act of 1935, Cordell Hull had negotiated numerous trade agreements built around the most-favored-nation clause. These resulted in a multilateral lowering of obstructive tariffs and a substantial increase of American exports.[34] Hull defended the principles of international free trade as he saw them persistently and often fanatically, while opposing the spread of the quota system which had actually become the key instrument of intra-European commerce in the decade prior to World War II. In his memoirs Hull tells a dramatic story of how President Roosevelt came perilously close to violating his secretary of state's economic policies by a barter agreement with Nazi Germany, a contingency which Hull considered "a supreme tragedy." [35] In Europe, on the other hand, most countries were obliged to resort to rigid currency controls after the economic crisis of 1930 and to apply great efforts toward an achievement of autarky in their respective enclaves. Once the separating walls had been erected, an introduction of bilateral barter with a firm quota system seemed the best possible method to facilitate at least a trickle of international commerce. Not only was the principle of quotas distasteful from the standpoint of international free trade as espoused by America, but its Machiavellian utilization for purposes of German conquest by Dr. Schacht had made it anathema to the government of the United States. By contrast, the traditional European trading partners of Germany, while well aware of the possible pitfalls of bilateral barter, had only limited dollar resources at the end of the war. They saw no choice but to trade with other European countries on a bilateral basis while using their dollars in the most advantageous fashion for the purchase of competitive American goods.

As it eventually turned out, the United States' attempt to introduce its liberalized system of foreign trade entailing the exchange of freely convertible currencies into Europe was premature, and the supporting efforts of the American Military Government actually were self-defeating.[36] It took a Marshall Plan and several years of carefully planned intra-European cooperation to bring about a positive solution. In the meantime, the European countries, led by the Netherlands and Belgium,

34. Hull, 1:375.   35. Ibid., 1:371–74.
36. Wallich, p. 232.

waged a vigorous campaign with every means at their disposal to effect a change in the dollar policy of American Military Government. Their protests and related recommendations were presented at top governmental levels in London and Washington, and there was hardly an economic meeting of the wartime Allies where these dissenting voices of Germany's neighbors could not be heard. Eventually they even found support among the miscellaneous American economic advisers stationed in U.S. embassies in Europe who met in Paris in 1946 and resolved that European countries with a severe dollar shortage were not able to contract for German exports. According to their recommendations it was desirable that "the dollar requirements be eased as soon as possible and plans developed for the acceptance of other currencies in payment for European exports." [37]

Although General Clay himself was one of the staunch defenders of the United States dollar policy,[38] the principle eventually had to be weakened and compromise solutions sought because of the force of circumstances. As a first step in this direction, a series of trade agreements were signed providing for offset accounts in European banks in the currency of the country concerned. The agreements said that the Bizone would be credited for its exports and debited for its imports, while its respective trading partners were to be similarly treated in these accounts. The provision was made that each quarter the portion of the net balance of the account representing items entered into the account two months before or earlier and still not offset by corresponding credits would become payable in cash immediately upon request of the party due payment, either in U.S. dollars or sterling. The agreements also stipulated that if at any time the balance of the offset account was in excess of a maximum specified amount, the excess portion of the balance would be payable in U.S. dollars or sterling immediately upon request.[39]

The first such agreement was signed with the Netherlands in January 1947. Additional offset accounts for the Bizone were established in the course of the same year with Norway, Sweden, Hungary, Bulgaria, and Greece. Usually during the first phase after the signing of the agreements there was a considerable upsurge of German exports, since at the outset no dollar payments were required. However, when the time approached for the settlement of a balance, the dollar clause still proved to be a serious handicap preventing additional increments. Most European

37. Winant to Draper, 15 Feb. 1946 (OMGUS records, 123-2/3).
38. Clay, *Decision in Germany*, p. 225.
39. Hutton and Robbins, p. 10.

countries continued to curtail their import licenses, a trend, as JEIA's monthly report for November 1947 mentioned, resulting directly from the nonconvertibility of the sterling and the small dollar resources of the importing countries. New pressures for an unlimited acceptance of bilateral barter on a quota basis were resisted by Clay and his financial advisers, who argued that "offset agreements fell short of being a commitment to bilateral barter and therefore had to be carefully administered to avoid such a commitment." [40] The impasse was only slowly resolved during the following years through a number of innovations in the area of international finance such as compensation of bilateral trade balances, the introduction of dollar-backed drawing rights, and the establishment of the European Payments Union, developments to be discussed in the next chapter.

In the meantime, in order to overcome some of the shortages of raw materials, JEIA began to encourage processing transactions in which foreign firms supplied raw materials or other commodities to be processed by German enterprises. The contract usually stipulated that all of the raw material was to be re-exported in the form of finished products and that payment for the processing would be made in U.S. dollars. Other contracts had a proviso whereby a portion of the finished products could be retained in payment for services. The fifty thousand bales of cotton brought into Germany under the auspices of the U.S. Commercial Company and mentioned above were handled in this manner. In the summer of 1947 JEIA also entered into an agreement with the American Cotton Supply Corporation in Dallas, Texas, and the Export Import Bank in Washington, to finance the import of $20 million worth of cotton and related materials into the two zones of Germany.[41]

At the time this agreement went into effect (June 13, 1947) JEIA was preparing a decentralized import licensing procedure to allow German textile mills to make direct purchases of raw cotton, cotton waste, and necessary related processing materials unobtainable domestically. Initially, it had been necessary to procure all imports centrally, so that only the most essential items were imported, because the funds available to JEIA for imports were relatively small while the need for all kinds of raw material was great. However, it soon became evident that while a centralized control was appropriate for the import of bulk commodities, it made the procurement of important spot requirements almost impossi-

40. Tennenbaum, p. 8.
41. One year later the 80th Congress under P.L. 820 established a revolving fund of $150 million for the sale of cotton to the occupied area.

ble. As a result many potential sales were lost because small quantities of needed import materials could not be obtained by the manufacturers in time.[42]

It was for the purpose of breaking this bottleneck that JEIA Instruction No. 4 in August 1947 put into effect a decentralized procedure authorizing branch offices to issue import licenses for raw materials and semiprocessed goods. German importing firms were now required to submit their import application through the *Land* ministry of economics to JEIA, with the proviso that expected foreign exchange from the sale of the finished product had to relate to the cost of the imported raw material on a 3-to-1 basis or better. Furthermore, the export of the finished product had to be realized within a maximum period of nine months after receipt of the imported raw materials. The branch offices of JEIA were responsible for checking import prices and for determining the salability of the resulting export in predetermined foreign markets. After approval of the import application by the JEIA branch office, an import license was issued to the German firm. Payment was arranged by the Joint Foreign Exchange Agency in the form of letters of credit.

As indicated, the new decentralized procedure pertained to all imports, including the so-called programed imports (i.e., raw material imports under inventory advance programs designed to produce specific exports), but not to stockpile imports nor to centralized general imports of coal, pulp, pulpwood, food, fertilizers, seeds, petroleum products, jute, timber, raw rubber, cork, copper, aluminum, and tin. (Stockpile imports, as defined by JEIA, were raw materials imported under custom bond prior to allocation to specific programs or for use as general imports. Provision was made that there should not be an amount in excess of $3,750,000 invested in stockpile imports at any one time.) [43] In an additional move toward the re-establishment of normal commercial practices, JEIA Instruction No. 10 of November 1947 authorized the issuance of import licenses to German importers and thus enabled them to procure centrally the imports which up to that date had been purchased by the main office of JEIA. Under this instruction, German importers could again negotiate for procurement, sign contracts, and

42. JEIA Monthly Report, July 1947. In a conversation with the writer, Dr. Roy Bullock referred to the difficulties which his staff encountered when trying to obtain raw materials from abroad. It was the question not only of dollar availability, he said, but also of overcoming the manifold obstacles created by miscellaneous national bureaucracies. As a result there were times when the officers in JEIA's main office had to devote even more time to negotiating import contracts than to the promotion of exports.
43. Hutton and Robbins, p. 10.

handle the acceptance and distribution of goods on arrival in Germany.

Some more spadework was done when JEIA arranged with the military the derequisitioning of a number of German hotels for visiting businessmen and tourists. These hotels were to operate under German management with the proviso that payment would be made in foreign-exchange vouchers. On the same basis a special taxi service was introduced in Frankfurt am Main, Munich, and Berlin. In Berlin alone the service produced $300,000 in hard-currency revenue during its first year of operation. The well-attended export fairs in Hesse, Schleswig-Holstein, and Lower Saxony may also be mentioned in passing for giving foreign merchants an opportunity to see German products again and to renew or make the acquaintance of German manufacturers. After many years of separation the free exchange of information between German suppliers and buyers from abroad seemed to promise a better future for Germany's foreign trade.

The statistical data reflecting the results of JEIA's first year of operation must have been viewed by the two military governors with mixed feelings. Actual export shipments for 1947 totaled $222 million and encompassed among other items $122 million of coal exports, $38.8 million of timber shipments, and $36.4 million of general exports. On a percentage basis, the breakdown of exports was as follows:

Coal	55.0%
Forestry and	
wood products	17.6
General exports	16.2
Invisibles	11.2
	100.0%

The $36 million of general exports, while still a very small amount, was well ahead of the very minute export deliveries of about $14 million in 1946. The total of $222 million, on the other hand, fell considerably behind the target of $350 million established by the Byrnes-Bevin Agreement, a development which JEIA with considerable justification ascribed to the "world shortage of dollars which forced Germany's traditional customers to restrict their purchases to absolutely essential items." [44]

The countries which were the principal recipients of German exports in 1947 are listed in Table 5.1. Worthy of note here are the insignificant

44. JEIA Monthly Report, Dec. 1947, p. A.

TABLE 5.1. Recipients of German exports in
1947 [45]

United Kingdom	$ 55,430,000
Netherlands	23,727,000
France	22,822,000
Austria	21,413,000
Luxembourg	20,070,000
Belgium	14,743,000
Denmark	14,499,000
Italy	10,083,000
Norway	8,282,000
Sweden	6,918,000
Switzerland	6,686,000
United States	6,249,000
All others	11,111,000
	$222,033,000

shipments to the United States, as well as an almost exclusive concentration on European purchasers.

During the same period export contracts totaling $195 million were signed, a figure which excluded coal, timber, and all services for which no formal contractual agreements had been entered. The primary sales covered by the contracts were cotton goods ($33 million), machines ($29.6 million), vehicles and vehicle spare parts ($19.2 million), electrotechnical products ($11.6 million), chinaware ($10.6 million), hops ($7.6 million), and cameras ($6.5 million).[46] These contracts covered transactions with the countries listed in Table 5.2. One notices here that the United States as well as Switzerland moved into a leading position among Germany's buyers, whereas purchases by France and Austria appear considerably curtailed. Of more permanent significance was the increase in the number of contracting countries, a trend which was to continue at an accelerated speed during the following years.

If one adds to this total of $195 million a reasonable estimate of $200 million for expected exports not covered by contractual agreements (coal, timber and invisibles), one arrives at roughly $400 million of total anticipated exports for 1948, that is, at a level which indicated good progress but by no means a rapid recovery.

The figures for category B imports in 1947, by contrast, were disappointingly small. Actual shipments received totaled only $36,721,000,

45. Ibid., p. 10.   46. Ibid., pp. 7–8.

Table 5.2   Contracts signed for German exports in 1947

United Kingdom	$ 36,548,000
Switzerland	27,203,000
United States	26,685,000
Denmark	13,944,000
Netherlands	13,712,000
Belgium	13,516,000
Sweden	10,125,000
France	7,883,000
Norway	7,145,000
Turkey	4,838,000
Yugoslavia	3,729,000
Czechoslovakia	2,842,000
India	2,744,000
Austria	2,724,000
Luxembourg	2,712,000
Finland	2,573,000
Iran	2,254,000
Italy	2,189,000
Poland	1,154,000
All others	10,480,000
	$195,000,000

whereas import commitments amounted to $125,000,000, including $24,413,000 of import contracts signed as late as December 1947. Inasmuch as all the proceeds of commercial exports were supposed to be available for the payment of category B imports, the gap appears surprisingly vast. The difficulty of obtaining raw materials in the world markets in 1947, even against cash payment in dollars, undoubtedly had something to do with the delay.[47] Another cause for the lagging imports was probably the previously discussed gradual transfer of purchasing authority to German importers, a transition which could not help but delay matters further. A critical observer of JEIA, therefore, concluded quite plausibly that since the minimum ratio of export values to import costs was three to one, $100 million of additional raw materials on hand in 1947 would have meant an increment of at least $300 million in exports.[48]

47. Ibid., pp. B, 1.   48. Meurer, p. 89.

The story of the slow but steady development of German exports in 1947 is dramatically presented by Fig. 5.1. The reversal in coal exports during the summer is attributable to a concurrent decline in the food rations; the upsurge of the black line in October, on the other hand, reflects the miners' expectation of a special bonus in the form of CARE

FIGURE 5.1   Exports from the western zones, 1947: contracts signed and deliveries. [After the Report of the Joint Export Import Agency (US/UK), Dec. 1947, p. 13.]

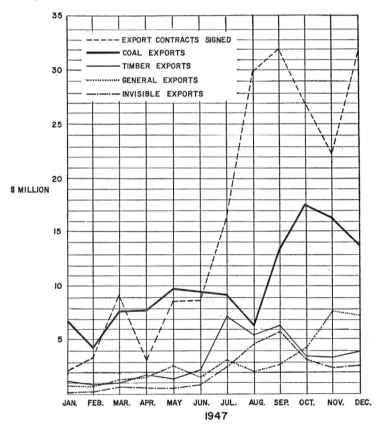

packages with an inevitable relapse after the bonus had been distributed. As can further be seen, export shipments had a slow but fairly steady rise, whereas the curve for export contracts performed most erratically, demonstrating the problems of JEIA's dollar policy in the form of "valleys" which corresponded to the lows of the importing countries' dollar funds. The final upsurge in signed contracts in December was attributed by JEIA to a change in the agency's policy authorizing the acceptance of contracts in sterling provided they were for sterling-area countries.[49] In conclusion, it seemed encouraging that the curve representing export contracts ended at the highest level of 1947, thus holding out the promise of greater progress in the years to come.

49. JEIA Monthly Report, Dec. 1947, p. A.

CHAPTER SIX

A PROLOGUE TO THE
EUROPEAN RECOVERY PROGRAM

The ink was hardly dry on the Bevin-Byrnes Agreement when serious difficulties arose with regard to the implementation of its financial provisions. It will be recalled that the British government initially had attempted to persuade the United States to settle for an allocation of financial contributions to the Bizone on a 60/40 basis, with the United States carrying the major share of the burden. When this attempt failed, the British representatives reluctantly agreed to an equal sharing of expenditures, a solution which, in view of the larger food deficit of the British Zone, still favored the United Kingdom. It was clear that their reluctance was prompted not so much by doubt as to the fairness of the arrangement, but rather by the apprehension of the British Treasury about assuming additional dollar responsibilities.

As it soon turned out, these fears were indeed justified. Great Britain found it increasingly difficult to furnish the dollars required for the initial capital of the Joint Export Import Agency (US/UK), as well as for the subsequent funding of purchases of food, fertilizers, and seed on the world markets. Accordingly, General Sir Brian Robertson, the British military governor, tried to utilize whatever legal angles could be found to substitute sterling for hard-currency commitments, an approach seriously resisted by Jack Bennett of the U.S. Treasury, who served as Clay's financial adviser.[1] Frequently General Clay leaned over backwards to accommodate the British, and on several occasions he actually overruled the technical reservations of his staff.[2] Nevertheless, when exports from the Bizone progressed more slowly than anticipated and

1. Keating to Clay (Moscow), Cable CC-8451; also Bennett to Clay (Moscow), undated cable (OMGUS records 40-3/2).
2. Clay (Moscow) to Keating, 26 March 1947, cable MA-51145 (OMGUS records, 149-1/3); Clay (Moscow) to OMGUS, 31 March 1947, cable MA-51185 (OMGUS records, 37-2/1).

the food situation continued to demand an increasing dollar outlay, it became evident that the weakness of the pound sterling would make it impossible for the British government to fulfill its part of the original bargain. In accordance with paragraph 12 of the Bizonal Fusion Agreement of December 2, 1946, American and British representatives, met, therefore, in Washington in the fall of 1947 to negotiate for an amendment to the original understanding. The resulting Revised Bizonal Fusion Agreement of December 17, 1947, signed for the United States by the Acting Secretary of State Robert A. Lovett, and for the United Kingdom by Sir William Strang, acknowledged that since "the Government of the United Kingdom has represented that they are unable to continue to make payments in dollars in respect to such [bizonal] imports," Great Britain would no longer be liable to pay dollars for category A imports and services imported into the bizonal area. As far as the pending obligations were concerned, the amendment authorized Great Britain to arrange, if possible, for procurement from Sterling Area sources and, whenever such arrangements could not be made, to pay the appropriate dollar equivalents to JEIA in sterling. For 1948 Great Britain took on the obligation of supplying the Bizone with category A goods and services worth £17.5 million, mainly by providing British ships to carry freight. The remainder of category A requirements for the Bizone for the period from November 1, 1947, to December 31, 1948, was to be provided by the government of the United States. With regard to sterling held by JEIA, the British government reaffirmed its earlier commitments to convert it into dollars on demand, while the United States "in recognition of the serious dollar difficulties of the United Kingdom," pledged that no more than the equivalent of $40 million would have to be converted prior to January 1, 1949.

In view of the larger contributions to be made by the United States, the British government acknowledged that the American government would be entitled to "a larger measure of authority with respect to the Joint Export Import Agency (US/UK) and the Joint Foreign Exchange Agency." In conformity with this basic consideration, each of the two agencies was to be governed by a Board of Directors to which the two military governors would appoint an equal number of members; they were to vote as a group with the proviso, however, that the relative voting strength of the two groups would reflect the proportion of appropriated funds made available to the Bizone by the two governments. Paragraph 5E of the revised agreement, furthermore, authorized the

Bipartite Board, i.e., the two military governors, to review controversial decisions of JEIA and JFEA; but any disapproval or modification of such decisions had to be unanimous. The Lovett-Strang Agreement also authorized the two military governors "to delegate to the JEIA and the JFEA full power and authority necessary for the conduct of the import trade including the authority to contract for imports and exports through such agencies as it may designate, to borrow and lend money, to pay and collect accounts, and to utilize and distribute foreign currency, and such other necessary authority as is essential to the rehabilitation and promotion of peaceful trade and commerce." The agreement furthermore emphasized that JEIA's responsibility for bizonal foreign trade was a temporary one, and that "it should be transferred to German Administrative Agencies under the supervision of the JEIA to the maximum extent permitted by the restrictions existing in foreign countries at any given period."

Probably the most consequential change of former export policies was contained in paragraph 3 directing JEIA "to maximize trade in both directions between the Bizonal Area and the Sterling Area." All trade between these two areas was to be conducted in sterling, and in order to implement this policy the Joint Foreign Exchange Agency was to open an account with the Bank of England to be known as "the Joint Foreign Exchange Agency Number 1 Account." All payments to residents of the Sterling Area for goods imported into the Bizone and all payments for exports sold to residents of the Sterling Area were to go through the Number 1 Account. In order to limit the debit or credit balances in the Number 1 Account, the Washington agreement provided for quarterly statements and settlements of credit balances exceeding a sum of £1.5 million by the Bank of England in U.S. dollars, and in the case of debit balances exceeding that sum by the Joint Foreign Exchange Agency in pounds sterling. The Sterling Area was defined as encompassing Great Britain and Northern Ireland, Australia, New Zealand, the Union of South Africa, Eire, India, Pakistan, Southern Rhodesia, Ceylon, Burma, Iraq, Transjordan, Iceland, the Faroe Islands, all British colonies, and any territory under British protection. The special position of the Sterling Area was additionally underlined in paragraph 8 (II) which said that Sterling Area sources for imports should be selected to the fullest extent practicable "so as to minimize the drain on the dollar resources of the Government of the United Kingdom." [3]

While the revised agreement gave the United States the right of final

3. OMGUS records, 147-1/3.

decision in financial and economic matters, it left intact the American-British parity in political affairs. As Clay writes, there had been some pressure from the American side to insist on a predominant voice, but the American Military Government had strongly and successfully argued against this. As he saw it, "by and large, British and American objectives in Germany were close and our own success in accomplishing them depended on genuine cooperation with the British. To insist on lowering their status to that of a junior partner . . . would have damaged British prestige in Europe, and was not really to our interest." [4]

Ostensibly, the Lovett-Strang Agreement went far to accommodate the British and to facilitate the development of foreign trade between the Bizone and the Sterling Area. It also was a realistic move which recognized the facts of European economic and financial life at the end of the war and thereby provided an opening wedge for the gradual liberalization of intra-European foreign trade.

One of the first consequences of the revision of the Bizonal Fusion Agreement was a merger of the Joint Export Import Agency (US/UK) and the Joint Foreign Exchange Agency, and the drafting of a new charter for the successor organization, the Joint Export Import Agency. Under the charter the new JEIA became a corporation with complete authority to deal with all matters pertaining to the Bizone's foreign trade in compliance with the provisions of the Revised Bizonal Fusion Agreement and the general policies of the Bipartite Board. It was understood that for some time the foreign trade of the Bizone would have to be controlled by an Allied rather than a German agency because German governmental authorities were still unable to hold foreign assets without incurring the risk that they would be seized or blocked under the wartime laws of Germany's former enemies. The agency was therefore instructed to ensure that maximum export progress be developed "consistent with the accomplishment of overall objectives in Germany and in conformity with the policy of the two governments to transfer responsibility to a German Administration as rapidly as is feasible."

The charter provided that the board of the agency would consist of the financial and the economic advisers of the two military governors, as well as of a director general and a deputy general of the agency. The former was to be appointed by the American and the latter by the British military governor. The Board of Directors was to meet at least once a month and was responsible directly to the Bipartite Board. All matters of policy were to be directed by the JEIA Board of Directors.

4. Clay, *Decision in Germany,* p. 178.

The director general was to "ensure closest collaboration between the agency and the Bipartite Control Office in all matters concerning relations with German governmental organizations and in questions affecting the interests of the various Bipartite Groups in Frankfurt." The Bipartite Control Office was to assist the JEIA in the preparation of its budgets and to make sure that the German administration under its control provided the necessary detailed data and recommendations. The agency furthermore was instructed to employ and train professional German personnel "with a view of replacing Allied personnel" and to prepare a plan for an early transfer of its responsibilities to a German administration. The Joint Export Import Agency was to continue "for the time being" as its own fiscal and accounting agent, but as soon as possible the Bizonal Länder Union Bank was to take over these responsibilities, including "the opening and operating of accounts with foreign banks into which proceeds of exports would be paid."

The new organization of the Joint Export Import Agency provided for two divisions, one under the supervision of a comptroller concerned with budgeting controls and accounting, the other under the management of a director of foreign trade responsible for the actual operations. The latter encompassed four branches, namely, Exports, Imports, Trade Negotiations, and Policy and Plans, to which at a later date a fifth branch, ERP Planning and Statistics, was added. Dr. Roy J. Bullock, the first American chairman of the Joint Export Import Agency (US/UK), had resigned in October 1947 and had returned to the United States. He was replaced by W. John Logan, a retired New York banker, who during the war had served as a director of the Distribution Bureau of the War Production Board and who was now appointed to serve as director general of the Joint Export-Import Agency. J. F. Cahan, an official of the British Treasury and the U.K. chairman of the old JEIA, was appointed as his deputy. The key position of director of foreign trade was held by a New York business executive, George J. Santry, who had joined OMGUS at the beginning of the occupation, with Brig. M. E. L. Robinson serving as his deputy. Dr. Ethel Dietrich, formerly a professor of economics at Mount Holyoke College, was responsible for Trade Negotiations. At the time of its reorganization the Joint Export-Import Agency including all its branch offices had a staff of 1457, composed of 204 British, 223 American and 1030 German nationals.[5]

As mentioned before, the promotion and control of bizonal exports

5. JEIA Organization and Personnel Authorization, 21 Jan. 1948 (OMGUS records, 146-1/3).

had been delegated to the JEIA branch offices operating with relative independence in Berlin, Bremen, Düsseldorf, Hamburg, Hanover, Kiel, Munich, Stuttgart, and Wiesbaden. Since some of the bureaucratic impediments to the development of foreign trade had been removed in the preceding year, it appeared reasonable to expect a considerable upsurge of German exports under the reorganized Joint Export-Import Agency. German businessmen were again able to reach their customers and suppliers abroad quite easily, and their directly negotiated export contracts, after a screening by the *Land* economic ministries, usually were promptly approved by the branch offices. One of the criteria for approval was that the ratio of export proceeds to the cost of imported raw materials had to be at least three to one; furthermore it was required that delivery would be made within fifteen months from date of approval. Contracts exceeding this time limit, or in excess of $250,000, required the additional approval of JEIA's main office, which in the course of 1948 was moved from Minden to Höchst and subsequently to Frankfurt am Main. As far as imports were concerned, bulk purchases were still made centrally in order to avoid the bidding up of prices and to obtain the advantages of large purchases. However, the importation of raw materials and semiprocessed goods for the production of specified export items also had been decentralized. The principal obstacle to a normalization of foreign trade was still the absence of a meaningful currency, especially since it was clear to everyone in Germany that a reform could not be delayed much longer.

It will be recalled that at the time of the bizonal merger the American and British military governors had taken some cautious steps toward the gradual establishment of a German administration. As long as the unification of the four zones still seemed a practical possibility, any appearance of a political amalgamation had to be carefully avoided. Notwithstanding administrative inconveniences, the German administrative agencies for Economics, Food and Agriculture, Transportation, Communications, Civil Service, and Finance therefore had been set up in four bizonal towns. In the early stages each of these agencies was headed by an executive committee composed of one representative from each of the eight German *Länder*. The committees had the authority to elect one additional member to serve as chairman and chief executive of the respective agency.

In the course of the Moscow Foreign Ministers Conference in the spring of 1947 it had become clear that there was no point in delaying much longer the gradual transfer of responsibilities and authority to

German hands, and the two military governors therefore had been told to proceed with a strengthening of the embryonic German administration.[6] They were still to avoid, however, any impression of German governmental authority and the creation of a West German capital. As a result of this change of policy, a German Economic Council was created which was to convene in Frankfurt am Main and to consist of 52 delegates elected by the Landtage of the eight *Länder* on the basis of one delegate for every 750,000 persons. The council's actions were subject to the approval of the two military governors. It was responsible for promulgating ordinances in the fields of economics, transport, finance, communications, food and agriculture, and civil service. The decisions of the council were to be carried out by an Executive Committee composed of one representative from the eight *Länder* to be designated by the respective *Land* government. The committee was to make recommendations for legislation to the Economic Council and to coordinate and supervise the six Administrative Agencies. Whereas at the beginning these agencies had been headed by committees, the latter were now replaced by executive directors nominated by the Executive Committee and confirmed by the Economic Council.[7]

After the abortive London Foreign Ministers Conference in December 1947, the American and British military governors were instructed to step up further the formation of a German economic administration. As Clay reports, he and General Robertson were ready to come out with appropriate public announcements when they were stopped in their tracks by an unexpected French *aide-memoire* presented simultaneously in Washington and London protesting against what Paris considered "a prelude to a powerful centralized government." [8]

Clay, when offering his views about the French move to the Department of State, stressed that

we are in a critical position in Germany and either have to move forward to give the Germans increased responsibility in the Bizonal Area to insure their proper contribution to European recovery, or we must move backward to increase our own forces to run a more colonial type of government. . . . Unless we are willing to establish a working organization in which the Germans are given real responsibility, we would have to expand our organization

6. Clay, *Decision in Germany*, p. 174.
7. American Military Government, Proclamation 5 and Appendix A (OMGUS records).
8. Clay, *Decision in Germany*, p. 178.

many times to take care of additional export trade which we fully hope will materialize in the coming months.[9]

Evidently the American and British governments were of a similar opinion, because, after assuring Paris that the contemplated provisional German administration would in no way prejudice a future German government, the two military governors were told to proceed. Accordingly, on February 9, 1948, two identical proclamations, drawn up with the assistance of German key officials,[10] were published in the two zones.[11]

Under the new setup the Bizonal Economic Administration was to encompass an Economic Council, a Länderrat, and an Executive Committee, as well as a number of old and new agencies (see Chart 6.1). The reconstructed Economic Council was to consist of the former 52 members and an additional 52 members to be elected by the Landtage on the basis of one for each 750,000 population. The Länderrat was to be composed of two representatives from each *Land,* one of whom could be the ministerpräsident to be appointed by the *Land* government. Finally, the Executive Committee was to consist of a chairman selected by the Economic Council subject to confirmation by the Länderrat, as well as the directors of the Bizonal Departments to be elected by the Economic Council. All appointments to the Executive Committee required the approval of the two military governors (the Bipartite Board).

The Economic Council was authorized to enact ordinances regulating bizonal finance, foreign and internal trade, production and distribution of goods, price formation, price control, the production, importation and collection of food, transportation, communications, and customs. The Länderrat, on the other hand, was given the power to initiate legislation on any matter within the competence of the Economic Council other than with respect to taxation or the appropriation of funds, and also the right to veto Economic Council legislation unless the veto was overridden by an absolute majority of the council. The members of the Executive Committee were responsible for the administration of their respective departments and for the implementation of legislation enacted and policies laid down by the Economic Council and the Länderrat. In summary, it was the machinery of a government, although its authority was limited to fiscal and economic matters and its acts were subject to Military Government approval.[12]

9. Ibid., p. 179.   10. Ibid., p. 180.
11. American Military Government, Proclamation 7; British Military Government, Ordinance 126 (OMGUS records).
12. Clay, *Decision in Germany,* p. 181.

BIPARTITE ORGANIZATION
U.S./U.K. AGENCIES

BIZONAL ORGANIZATION
GERMAN AGENCIES

LÄNDERRAT
(MEMBERS SELECTED BY LAND GOVERNMENTS)
STANDING COMMITTEES
ECONOMICS
TRANSPORT
FOOD, AGR., & FORESTRY
POSTS & TELECOMMUN.
FINANCE

ECONOMIC COUNCIL
(MEMBERS ELECTED BY LANDTAGE)
STANDING COMMITTEES
GENERAL (STEERING)
ECONOMICS   TRANSPORT
FOOD, AGRICULTURE   POSTS & TELECOMM.
& FORESTRY   MANPOWER
POLITICAL SCREENING CREDENTIALS
LEGAL   FINANCE   SENIORS

EXECUTIVE COMMITTEE
CHAIRMAN
EXECUTIVE DIRECTORS OF BIZONAL DEPARTMENTS

REGULATIONS IMPLEMENTING ECONOMIC COUNCIL ORDINANCES

BIZONAL DEPARTMENTS
TRANSPORT
POSTS & TELECOMMUNICATIONS
ECONOMICS
FINANCE
FOOD, AGRICULTURE & FORESTRY
ADDITIONAL AGENCIES
PERSONNEL OFFICE
BIZONAL STATISTICAL OFFICE

LÄNDER GOVERNMENTS (8)
LANDTAGE
CABINETS
MINISTRIES

U.S.
U.K.
GERMAN
U.S./U.K. INTEGRATED
COMMAND CHANNEL
FUNCTIONAL CHANNEL

BIZONAL HIGH COURT
(MEMBERS APPOINTED BY BIPARTITE BOARD FROM NOMINATIONS OF ECONOMIC COUNCIL)
OFFICE OF SOLICITOR GENERAL

BANK DEUTSCHER LÄNDER

ALLIED BANK COMMISION OF U.S./U.K. MIL. GVTS.

GERMAN COAL MINES ADMINISTRATION

LAND CENTRAL BANKS

JOINT EXPORT IMPORT AGENCY

JEIA FIELD OFFICES

(JEIA TO ECONOMICS DEPT. ON EXPORT IMPORT MATTERS)
(EACH GROUP TO CORRESPONDING DEPARTMENT)
(TO ECONOMICS MINISTRIES ON EXPORT-IMPORT MATTERS)

BIPARTITE BOARD
SECRETARIAT
ADVISORS
ECONOMICS   COMMUNICATIONS
FOOD &   FINANCE
AGRICULTURE   CIVIL SERVICE
TRANSPORT   CIVIL AVIATION

BIPARTITE VETTING PARTY

JOINT AUDIT OFFICE

POLICY

(ADM) U.S./U.K. COAL CONTROL GROUP

BIPARTITE CONTROL OFFICE
CHAIRMEN
SECRETARIAT
ADVISORS
BIPARTITE GROUPS
TRANSPORT
COMMUNICATIONS
FINANCE
FOOD & AGRICULTURE
COMMERCE & INDUSTRY
CIVIL SERVICE
BIPARTITE STATISTICAL COORD. OFFICE

U.S. ZONE LAND DIRECTORS OF MILITARY GOVERNMENT

U.K. ZONE REGIONAL COMMISSIONERS

ON ECONOMIC MATTERS

Simultaneously, another Military Government proclamation established a German High Court for the Combined Economic Area with its seat in Cologne. The court was independent of executive control and responsible for the interpretation and the enforcement of bizonal legislation.[13]

In order to complete the economic reorganization of the combined zones and to put more financial responsibility into German hands, the two Military Governments on March 1, 1948, approved the charter of the Bank Deutscher Länder, which was to act as the central bank in a new West German banking system. The bank was to serve as the fiscal agent for the German administration and also as a clearinghouse for all the central banks and Aussenhandelsbanken of the *Länder*. The new bank also took over the operations of the Joint Foreign Exchange Agency and eventually the functions performed by the comptroller's office of the Joint Export Import Agency. In many ways the organization of the bank corresponded to that of the Federal Reserve System of the United States. The initial capital was subscribed to by the central banks of the *Länder* in proportion to their deposits and monetary reserves. The Bank Deutscher Länder furthermore was authorized to discount bills of exchange and to grant credit to the Bizonal Economic Administration and to its member banks. In accordance with the American pattern, it had the authority to determine interest and discount rates, to prescribe the reserve requirements of commercial banks, and finally to enact open-market operations, i.e., to buy or sell bizonal securities and thus to control the volume of currency in circulation as well as the availability of credit to industry and government.[14]

The gradual transfer of governmental responsibilities into German hands tended to insure a more active German cooperation, but also brought forth latent German discontent and criticism of occupational policies. Not only were there valid reasons for discontent, but the German people, having spent some time under Anglo-Saxon rule, had also become confident that they could speak up without risk to life or limb. While most of the critical observations expressed through German official channels were helpful, responsible, and constructive, there were others, such as the so-called Harmssen Report or the widely publicized Semler speech at Erlangen, which belonged more to the sphere of a re-emerging political propaganda.

---

13. American Military Government, Proclamation 8; British Military Government, Ordinance 127 (OMGUS records).
14. Meurer, pp. 96–97.

The Harmssen Report, or as its original title went, *Reparationen, Sozialproduct, Lebensstandard: Versuch einer Wirtschaftsbilanz,*[15] was the work of a team headed by Senator Gustav W. Harmssen of the Free City of Bremen. Published in November 1947 as one volume with twelve annexes, it had an official character, since it was prepared at the request of the ministerpräsidents of the eight *Länder* in the Bizone and was supposed to supply the economic and financial data for a negotiated peace settlement. Actually the book did none of this because, on one hand, it was based on the abstract concept of a unified Germany and, on the other, it offered concocted data on alleged reparations payments said to amount to $71 billion by the end of 1947! Nevertheless, since Senator Harmssen presented the thesis of the "illegality" of reparations, carefully avoided mentioning the Hitler era, and was one of the first German officials who publicly dared to challenge the authority of the victors, his opus attracted wide and favorable attention within Germany. The London *Economist* in a commentary wrote that the document should be taken seriously "not because it is moral, objective, accurate and realistic —it has none of these qualities—but because it may become the *Mein Kampf* of the new German nationalism." [16] Looking at it in retrospect, however, it appears that the Harmssen Report was too far off the mark to make a lasting impact, so that the *Economist*'s apprehension proved to be unfounded.

A speech delivered by the director of the Economic Administration, Dr. Johannes Semler, to his party friends of the Christian Democratic Union in Bavaria had similar sensational aspects. While his comments on the food crisis, the deplorable conditions in the coal mines, the slow progress of the steel industry, the delayed currency reform, and the barter economy were supported by facts and were well justified, Dr. Semler, for reasons of his own, apparently felt that to prove his German patriotism he had to challenge the integrity of the American and British Military Governments. He criticized American emphasis on the duty of German farmers to deliver their quotas and questioned whether this was done only to relieve American taxpayers of their burden and "whether Mr. Clay possibly desires to make a good exit at our expense." He then added:

The [food] imports which we could now have received, we were unfortunately not permitted to buy. Corn was sent and chicken

15. Bremen, Trüjen Verlag, 1947.
16. *Economist* 154 no. 5455 (13 March 1948): 410.

feed and we are paying for it dearly; it is not a present. We pay for it in dollars gained by German work and German exports and are expected to say thank you for this in addition. It is high time that German politicians cease to say "thank you" for this supplementary food.

At a later point, addressing himself to the British Military Government, Dr. Semler took credit for a recent increase in the German export price for coal and remarked:

When I took office we sold a ton of coal for $10 and made a present of $5 per ton to some interested persons. That is today's recognized European price. We shall act the same way in other cases. After three years we shall have to get the English out of the habit of plundering [*ausplündern*] the German economy any further.[17]

The deplorable aspect of the speech was not that it was made, but that it had been presented by a man who, because of his position, knew the falsehoods which it contained. The speech caused enough of a stir to prompt OMGUS to come out with a press statement describing in considerable detail the bizonal pricing policies for the export of coal and demonstrating that it was indeed in the interest of American and British taxpayers to collect the highest possible export prices.[18] A week later, in a similar effort, the director general of the Joint Export Import Agency, William J. Logan, went on the air defending his Agency's export policies:

The success of the export-import program is a matter of life and death for Germany. It is therefore our intention to turn its management over to qualified German officials as soon as possible. Just how long will that be? Well, as long as the bizonal area does not have sufficient foreign exchange to feed its people adequately and keep its factories going, that is, as long as the American and British taxpayers must make up the deficit out of their own pockets, it is appropriate that Allied Authorities should exercise final control to see that the limited supplies of foreign exchange are wisely used. But responsibility for planning and day-to-day admin-

---

17. Johannes Semler, speech at Erlangen, 4 Jan. 1948 (OMGUS records, 150-3/3). John Gimbel, pp. 191–93, discusses the Semler incident in great detail.
18. Statement for F. Taylor Ostrander, Chief Price Control Section, OMGUS Public Information Office (OMGUS -1-C-55), 29 Jan. 1948 (OMGUS records, 148-2/15).

istration of the program can be put into German hands as quickly as experienced and capable personnel are available for the job. . . .

There has already been considerable misunderstanding about where JEIA gets its money and what it does with that money. JEIA funds come from the sale abroad of German exports. To date these have not been as great as many people believe. Sales and export deliveries for 1947 amounted to only $222 million, and all of this except $36 million was from the sale of coal and timber instead of from the sale of manufactured goods. Obviously, this is only a beginning. But you can rest assured, the greater the export, the greater will be the imports of raw materials for making more exports or for revitalizing the internal economy and thereby strengthening the export program. . . .

It is natural that the German people are going to have many questions to ask about the plans and accomplishments of the JEIA. They will want to follow JEIA progress reports just as a doctor studies the fever chart of a very sick patient. . . . So it was not unexpected when a German manufacturer asked me recently: "Why doesn't Military Government permit German businessmen to go abroad to renew old business contacts? They could do more for the export trade than all the regulations and plans Military Government could possibly create."

The answer to such a question is that Military Government encourages German businessmen going abroad if the trip is likely to justify the necessary expenditure of foreign exchange. The main barrier to foreign travel is that every country in Europe still has strict rules on the admission of German nationals. Despite these difficulties, however, we are now sending comparatively small numbers of businessmen to the U.S., Great Britain, Scandinavian and other countries. And it is our hope that their numbers will be rapidly increased.

It is naturally a great temptation to criticize a government agency for real or suspected faults and failings. We do not mind fair and constructive criticism. The fair-minded person will acknowledge our efforts to make Germany a "going concern" again and will assist and abet our efforts by offering constructive suggestions for improvement.

But it will take more than criticism, even constructive criticism. These are trying times. Right now you need our money and our business know-how. We need your historic ability to organize, produce and export. We have a job to do which must be done together. We stand ready to assist you in this task with men, money, and a large share of the world's food.[19]

About the same time, in an indirect reference to Semler's speech, General Clay remarked in the course of a meeting with German officials:

I have heard a great deal about our unwillingness to buy food with export proceeds. Actually there are a few low-caloric luxury foods that could be bought with export proceeds. Added all up, they would add very little to the individual diet. The U.S. Congress is being asked to appropriate $720 million for food for Germany next year. . . . In obtaining these appropriations General Robertson and I committed ourselves to this kind of program; that our governments would underwrite the cost of bringing food into Germany but that on the other hand Military Government here in Germany would see that German exports were developed and were utilized so that the entire proceeds could be plowed into raw materials and consumer goods to build up the German economy. We had to make a strong case because it is quite obvious that it is difficult for the American and British taxpayer to understand why he is paying money for food to go into Germany while these export proceeds do not become his property. . . . The Dutch want to sell their cabbages for dollars. They will advertise to the German population that cabbages are available. The whole total lot of them wouldn't add five calories a day to the German diet, but the several million dollars would bring in raw materials that could be converted into a good many millions of dollars of exports. . . .[20]

Fortunately, the voices of Harmssen and Semler were representative of only a small minority, whereas the majority of the German people would have agreed with Dr. Ludwig Erhard, who, in summing up the economic situation before the Economic Council, remarked:

If you keep in mind that as a result of our chaotic currency conditions our economy has been deprived of any standards of

19. William J. Logan, "Streamlining the German Export Program," radio address on the Geramn network in the U.S. Zone, 5 Feb. 1948 (OMGUS records, 108-3/11).

20. Extracted from Verbatim Record of Meeting of the Military Governor with the President of the Economic Council and the Chairman of the Executive Committee on 14 Feb. 1948 (OMGUS records, 111-1/1).

value and comparison, that in every purchase and sales transaction we are operating with quite unpredictable monetary values and are living in a world of fiction, if you bear in mind what it means to have to reduce a highly developed modern monetary system to the level of primitive barter, then what we really need is not scapegoats but—and the need is urgent—the restoration of sound monetary values.[21]

Patience was running out not only in Germany and Europe, but even more quickly and decisively in the United States. There had been a widespread misconception in America as to the nature and extent of Europe's problems after the end of the war. As Dean Acheson, then an Under Secretary of State, remarked, no one in the United States had been aware of the complete disruption that had taken place. America had operated on a theory of taking care of hunger, disease, and unrest, "until one or two good crops would come in; but the problems were much more far reaching and it grew upon us toward the end of 1946 that we were heading for very bad trouble." [22]

The syndrome of inadequate industrial and agricultural production, of inflation, and of a nonconvertible currency was by no means confined to Germany. The related problems actually affected most of Europe. At the beginning of 1947, industrial production in western Europe had reached only 78 percent of prewar volume and still was far below the 1938 level in France, Greece, Italy, and the Netherlands.[23] Wartime destruction and the obsolescence of machinery naturally played an important role here. Other elements were insufficient supplies of basic raw materials and fuel, especially German coal, as well as the general undernourishment of the working population. Agricultural yields in many areas were not yet up to 80 percent of the prewar volume, while market demands had become greater. The population had grown by about 8 percent between 1937 and 1947 and continued to increase.[24] The unusually severe winter of 1946–47 accentuated the crisis.

Inflation was another factor. In France, for instance, wholesale prices had risen by 80 percent in 1946. When the workers demanded and obtained higher wages, wholesale prices rose by an additional 50 percent in the subsequent year. A series of strikes for higher wages followed. The bread ration had to be cut to 200 grams per day, i.e., as low as

21. Ludwig Erhard, speech at the fourteenth plenary session of the Economic Council, 21 April 1948.
22. Price, "The Marshall Plan and its Meaning," p. 9.
23. ECA, *Third Report to Congress*, p. 126.
24. United Nations, *World Economic Report*, 1948, p. 220.

during the worst war years. Furthermore, Europe's foreign-exchange reserves had been exhausted and it was no longer able to buy food and raw materials from overseas.[25]

Oddly, although understandably, the turning point came in Moscow, where Secretary of State George Marshall, in the course of the Foreign Ministers Conference, attempted once more to revitalize the wartime alliance with the Soviet Union and to find a common meeting ground for American-Soviet cooperation in Europe. Marshall reports that he became convinced, in a private and stormy session with Chairman Joseph Stalin and Foreign Minister Vyacheslav Molotov on April 15, 1947, that the Soviet government was only stalling for time while doing all it could to make matters in Europe more difficult.[26] Thus, since it had become clear that new constructive approaches had to be sought, Marshall upon his return to Washington instructed the Department's newly formed Policy Planning Staff to come up with a plan of action.

The resulting proposals, in the main prepared by George F. Kennan, expressed the belief that the European crisis resulted in large part from the disruptive effects of the war on the economic, political, and social structure of Europe and from a profound exhaustion of physical plant and spiritual vigor. According to the Planning Staff, American efforts in aid to Europe should be directed not to the combatting of communism as such but to the restoration of the economic health and vigor of the European society. "It is necessary to distinguish clearly," the paper continued,

> between a program for the revitalization of Europe on one hand and a program of American support of such revitalization on the other. It would be neither fitting nor efficacious for this Government to undertake to draw up unilaterally . . . a program designed to place Europe on its feet economically. The formal initiative must come from Europe; and the Europeans must bear the basic responsibility for it. . . . The role of this country should consist of friendly aid in the drafting of a European program and of the later support of such a program. The program which this country is asked to support must be a joint one, agreed to by several European nations. . . . The request for our support must come as a joint request from a group of friendly nations, not as a series of isolated and individual appeals. . . . The European pro-

25. Price, p. 31.   26. Price, p. 4.

gram must envisage bringing Western Europe to a point where it will be able to maintain a tolerable standard of living on a financially self-supporting basis.

As Marshall saw it, it was not too difficult to propose a good plan, "but exceedingly difficult to manage the form and procedure so that it had a fair chance of political survival."[27] The subsequent steps of the Administration therefore had to be carefully planned and well coordinated.

The opening shot was Secretary Marshall's speech at Harvard University, in which he stated:

> Europe's requirements for the next three or four years . . . are so much greater than her ability to pay that she must have substantial additional help or face economic, social and political deterioration of a very grave character. . . .
>
> Aside from the demoralizing effect on the world at large and the possibilities of disturbances arising as a result of the desperation of the people concerned, the consequences to the economy of the United States should be apparent to all. It is logical that the United States should do whatever it is able to do to assist in the return of normal economic health in the world, without which there can be no political stability and no assured peace. Our policy is directed not against any country or doctrine but against hunger, poverty, desperation, and chaos. Its purpose should be the revival of a working economy in the world so as to permit the emergence of political and social conditions in which free institutions can exist. Such assistance, I am convinced, must not be on a piecemeal basis as various crises develop. Any assistance that this Government may render in the future should provide a cure rather than a mere palliative. . . .
>
> It would be neither fitting nor efficacious for this Government to undertake to draw up unilaterally a program designed to place Europe on its feet economically. This is the business of the Europeans. The initiative, I think, must come from Europe. The role of this country should consist of friendly aid in the drafting of a European program and of later support of such a program so far as it may be practical for us to do so. The program should be a joint one, agreed to by a number, if not all European nations.[28]

27. Price, p. 25.   28. Price, pp. 25-26.

A week later President Truman reiterated in Ottawa the basic concept of the Harvard address and again stressed the importance of a European initiative.[29]

The American suggestion was promptly taken up by the French and British governments, which discussed it in the course of a brief conference with Foreign Minister Molotov. However, since the two Western nations insisted upon a cooperative approach, whereas the Soviets contended that this would entail meddling in the internal affairs of sovereign nations and that each country should negotiate for economic aid with the United States directly, the meeting broke up. A week later the British and French foreign ministers issued a joint communiqué inviting twenty-two other European nations to send representatives to Paris to discuss a European recovery plan. The subsequent six months brought about the emergence of a Committee of European Economic Cooperation (CEEC) and its early transformation into a more permanent Organization of European Economic Cooperation (OEEC) encompassing the sixteen participating countries as well as the three Western zones of Germany. In compliance with the basic American concept of European responsibility, the CEEC drafted a plan of action aiming at:

(i) A strong production effort by each of the participating countries especially in agriculture, fuel and power, transport and the modernization of equipment.

(ii) The creation and maintenance of internal financial stability as an essential condition for securing the full use of Europe's productive and financial resources.

(iii) The development of economic cooperation between the participating countries.

(iv) A solution of the problem of the participating countries' deficit with the American continent particularly by increased exports.[30]

Later and also in accordance with the American concept, the OEEC assumed the responsibility for recommending the division of aid among the participating countries.

In the United States, at the same time, three governmental committees headed respectively by W. Averell Harriman (then secretary of com-

29. Price, p. 26.
30. CEEC (Committee of European Economic Cooperation), *General Report* (Paris, 1947), 1:6.

merce), Julius A. Krug (secretary of the interior), and Edwin G. Nourse (head of the Council of Economic Advisors) began to analyze the fundamentals for the drawing up of a program for Congressional approval. Whereas the first committee examined the policies which were to guide an aid program and the requirements and capacities of the European countries, the Krug committee analyzed whether the American economy had the resources for a substantial program of foreign aid. Finally the Council of Economic Advisors scrutinized the probable effects of a large, government-financed export program on domestic prices, consumption, and production.

By November, as a result of the groundwork by European and American experts, the tentative outlines of the Marshall Plan had been completed, and President Truman on December 19 submitted to Congress a "Program for U.S. Support to European Recovery." Against a background of generally favorable American public opinion and the active support of some leading members of House and Senate, among whom Senator Vandenberg played a decisive role, the European Recovery Act was passed by both houses and became law on April 3, 1948. While Congress refused to make definite financial commitments for more than one year at a time, total funds made available for the European Recovery Program during the four years of its existence exceeded $12 billion, encompassing $4.97 billion for the 1948–49 fiscal year; $3.78 billion for 1949–50; $2.3 billion for 1950–51; and $1.02 billion for 1951–52.[31]

The refusal of the Soviet government to participate in the European Recovery Program made it clear that the United States and the Soviet Union had come to a parting of the ways and that it could not be long until the final breaking point would be reached. If there were any hopes that the Soviet Union might modify its position at a late date, they were dispelled by Molotov at the Foreign Ministers Conference in London, which adjourned *sine die* after seventeen abortive meetings filled with bitterness and increasing mutual distrust. There were two significant developments in the early months of 1948 directly related to the unsuccessful London Conference. In Berlin the Allied Control Council broke up after the chairman, Marshal Vassily Sokolovsky, and his entire delegation unceremoniously walked out of the meeting. In London, on the other hand, the three Western Allies convened to prepare the political merger of their zones and the establishment of a West German

31. U.S. Department of Commerce, "Foreign Aid by U.S. Government, 1940–51" (FOA, Admin. Records), pp. 110–15.

government. In the course of their deliberations, the Western Allies approved the participation of the three Western zones of Germany in the European Recovery Program and recommended similar approval by the other participating countries.

The Organization of European Economic Cooperation (OEEC) was formally established on April 16, 1948. During the subsequent eighteen months the three Western zones were still represented at the OEEC by officials of the occupying powers; nevertheless, the fact that members of the German economic administration actively participated in the deliberations and that Germany was able to take part in an international undertaking for the first time since its surrender provided a considerable boost to German morale. (Not all the European nations were anxious to welcome Germany back in their midst, yet few went as far as the Norwegian representative, who, while reluctantly concurring with the German participation, commented that he, personally, was still in favor of the Morgenthau Plan.) [32] On October 31, 1949, after the formation of a West German government, the Military Government representatives were replaced by delegates of the Federal Republic, and West Germany became a full-fledged member of the OEEC.

The Economic Cooperation Agreement between the United States and the Bizone, signed on behalf of the two Military Governments by General Clay and General Robertson, recognized in its preamble that a strong and prosperous European economy was essential for the attainment of the purposes of the United Nations. The achievement of such conditions, it added, called for "a European Recovery Plan of self-help and mutual cooperation open to all nations which cooperate in such a plan, based upon a strong production effort, the expansion of foreign trade, the creation or maintenance of internal financial stability and the development of economic cooperation including all possible steps to establish and maintain valid rates of exchange and to reduce trade barriers." The terms which would "govern the furnishing of assistance by the Government of the United States under the Economic Cooperation Act of 1948 and the receipt of such assistance by the United States–United Kingdom occupied areas" were then established in eleven articles dealing with "Assistance and Cooperation," "General Undertakings," "Guarantees," "Local Currency," "Consultation and Transmittal of Information," etc. The most important sections of the first two articles are extracted herewith.

32. U.S. Department of State to HICOG, 17 March 1950, cable HICOG 1952, quoted in Schmidt, *Liberalization*, p. 10.

ARTICLE I

Assistance and Cooperation

1) The Government of the United States of America undertakes to assist the United States–United Kingdom occupied areas, by making available to the Military Governors or to any person, agency or organization designated by the latter such assistance as may be requested by them and approved by the Government of the United States of America. The Government of the United States of America will furnish this assistance under the provisions, and subject to all the terms, conditions and termination provisions, of the Economic Cooperation Act of 1948, acts amendatory and supplementary thereto and appropriation acts thereunder, and will make available to the Military Governors only such commodities, services and other assistance as are authorized to be made available by such acts.

2) The Military Governors, acting directly and through the organization for European Cooperation signed at Paris on April 16, 1948, will exert sustained efforts in common with other participating countries speedily to achieve through a joint recovery program economic conditions in Europe essential to lasting peace and to enable the countries of Europe participating in such a joint recovery program to become independent of extraordinary outside economic assistance within the period of this agreement. The Military Governors reaffirm their intention to take action to carry out the provisions of the General Obligations of the Convention for European Economic Cooperation, to continue to participate actively in the work of the Organization for European Economic Cooperation, and to continue to adhere to the purposes and policies of the Economic Cooperation Act of 1948, etc.

ARTICLE II

General Undertakings

1. In order to achieve the maximum recovery through the employment of assistance received from the Government of the United States of America, the Military Governors will use their best endeavors to assure:

   a) the adoption or maintenance of the measures necessary to ensure efficient and practical use of all the resources available to the United States–United Kingdom occupied areas etc.

b) the promotion of industrial and agricultural production on a sound economic basis along healthy non-aggressive lines; the achievement of such production targets as may be established through the Organization for European Economic Cooperation . . .

c) the stabilization of the currency, the establishment and maintenance of a valid rate of exchange, the balancing of governmental budgets as soon as practicable, the creation or maintenance of internal financial stability, and generally the restoration or maintenance of confidence in the monetary system; and

d) cooperation with other participating countries in facilitating and stimulating and increasing interchange of goods and services among the participating countries and with other countries and in reducing public and private barriers to trade among the participating countries and with other countries.[33]

In order to prepare for the cooperation of the American and British Zones with the European Recovery Program, the German Bizonal Administration established a European Recovery Program Group under the president of the Economic Council. At the same time the JEIA set up an ERP Planning and Statistics Branch which had the mission of serving as the controlling and planning office for JEIA operations in connection with the European Recovery Program. The German and Allied offices cooperated in the preparation of statistics and analysis for a "1948/49 Plan for the Reconstruction of the Bizonal Area" envisaging an import program of $1,959,878,000 for the first ERP planning year in order to attain 60 percent of the 1936 production level. Export proceeds for the same period were estimated at $695,750,000, thus leaving a foreign-trade deficit of $1,264,128,000.[34] It was furthermore anticipated that about $730 million would be provided in the form of direct contribution from appropriated funds through the U.S. and U.K. Treasuries,[35] leaving an uncovered deficit of about $530 million to be funded by ECA. Since the division of the ERP funds among the participating countries had been delegated to the OEEC, the military governors were obliged to

33. ECA, *First Report to Congress,* supplement, pp. 198–209.
34. JEIA Monthly Report, April 1948, p. 2.
35. BICO/ERP/SEC (48) 34/1, appendix (OMGUS records).

negotiate with Paris for the allocation of the bizonal share, a task which according to Clay was not always an easy one. The first tentative allocation of the OEEC to the Bizone seemed especially inadequate and necessitated a spirited and energetic intervention on the part of the military governor.[36]

Even before the first ECA-financed shipment arrived in Germany, the beneficial effects of the impending large-scale aid program had become noticeable, especially since the Joint Export Import Agency in expectation of the expected flow of funds had instructed the German Economic Administration to prepare category B import programs for 1948 on the basis of an expenditure of $400 million. At the same time, the German authorities were told to commit $100 million for each of the first two quarters and $50 million for each of the last two quarters of 1948. The figures for the latter two were to be revised and adjusted at the beginning of each quarter against the background of actual export performance. Since a minimum ratio of three to one relating export proceeds to import costs prevailed, it was clear that JEIA thus had taken an important step toward its statutory task "to ensure that a maximum export program shall be developed."

For a short while bureaucratic procedures delayed the first deliveries of ECA-financed raw materials, and it almost seemed that JEIA had acted too hastily. OMGUS felt obliged to cable to Washington and Paris:

It should be understood clearly that JEIA in anticipation of ECA Program as outlined before the Congress has already committed almost its complete available assets to import programs in the expectation that shortly after April 1, when the first one billion was made available to ECA, purchases of industrial raw materials, transportation, equipment, etc., would be authorized and pipe line be kept full by ECA financing. The fact is that JEIA is now practically out of dollars and can make no further commitments except as collections come in. This means unless the procedures are quickly simplified and actual contracts written and letters of credit or cash actually made available by ECA, the pipeline will dry up and the present favorable basis for increase in production and recovery generally may be stopped in its tracks. . . .[37]

36. Clay, *Decision in Germany*, pp. 217–18.
37. Clay to Chief of Staff for Secretary Royall, 3 July 1948, cable CC-5020 (OMGUS records, 84-1/1).

As far as bizonal exports were concerned, the cooperative efforts of the participating countries to reduce European trade barriers were probably as important as the financial ERP aid itself. It will be recalled that the trade agreements which the Bizone had signed in the course of 1947 were only temporary palliatives and that their effects waned when the pound sterling could not be converted and quarterly settlements of the offset balances in dollars became necessary. There was some improvement in the effectiveness of the trade agreements negotiated after January 1948 because by that time the contracting parties had agreed to issue export-import licenses for the quotas listed in the respective agreements. This, of course, did not mean that the commodities listed had to be bought, but it did mean that whenever contracts could be negotiated by German and foreign firms, the governments concerned were pledged to grant the necessary licenses.[38]

In October 1948 a significant step was taken toward the development of a multilateral system for the clearance of international payments through the "Agreement for Intra-European Payments and Compensations," which was negotiated in the framework of the OEEC and which produced two new methods of international settlement. First, a scheme of multilateral compensations was established whereby each country's credits with other participants could be used to offset its debits with third participating countries. With Bank for International Settlements in Basel, Switzerland, acting as the clearing agency, a system of periodic clearances of outstanding balances was thereby established. Second, the Intra-European Payments Agreement devised a system of "drawing rights" whereby ERP dollars received from the United States were used to eliminate the remaining net creditor or debitor positions. Under this system "conditional" dollar funds were made available above and beyond the normal ECA aid, provided that the recipients among the participating countries offered the equivalent amount in their own currency to their prospective debtors. When the first Intra-European Payment Agreement expired on June 30, 1949, it was replaced by a second agreement extending until June 30, 1950, and this in turn gave way to the Intra-European Payment Union. In order to stave off the risk of establishing a soft currency area, it became possible under the second agreement to utilize the drawing rights outside the OEEC. With the arrival of the European Payment Union, the drawing rights were abolished and instead a scheme was set up with quotas of credits and debits

38. Meurer, p. 104.

vis-à-vis all countries. At the same time the United States ceased to grant aid to the individual participating countries and instead directed its financial support to the Union itself.[39]

While it could not be determined to what extent drawing rights were actually responsible for the substantial increase in intra-European trade that followed, they were used for the settlement of almost two fifths of the gross deficits and surpluses incurred by the participating countries during the operation of the agreements.[40] As far as Germany was concerned, the significance of the new mode of internaional settlements is reflected in the fact that the three western zones of Germany granted drawing rights to the extent of $97.4 million during the period 1948/1949 and at the same time received drawing rights totaling $114.2 million. During that time Germany was a net creditor vis-à-vis Austria, Denmark, France, Greece, and the Netherlands and a debtor to Belgium, Italy, Norway, Sweden, Turkey, and the United Kingdom.[41]

The first trade agreement under the reconstructed JEIA was made with Greece in January 1948. After August 1949 a pattern of more liberalized trade agreements developed whereby most quotas were abolished and the contracting countries established monthly global amounts up to which export and import licenses had to be granted regardless of the type of products involved. As of spring 1948, officials of the German Economic Administration participated in all trade talks at every level, from subcommittee deliberations to final negotiations.[42] By the time the responsibility for foreign trade was turned over to the German Federal Government, JEIA had concluded trade and payment agreements with thirty countries, including twenty-one in Europe and nine overseas.

The break up of the Allied Control Council opened the way for the long-delayed currency reform in the three western zones as well as in West Berlin. It will be recalled that early in 1946 an American committee of financial experts had recommended the prompt introduction of a new currency, the Deutsche Mark, and submitted a detailed program, usually referred to as the Colm-Dodge-Goldsmith Report, for that purpose. Although the absence of a meaningful currency undoubtedly was the most detrimental factor obstructing an early revival of the German economy, the United States and Great Britain, recognizing that any bilateral action in this regard would shatter all hopes for German political unification, had delayed the fateful step as long as possible.

39. Price, pp. 124–27.   40. Price, p. 101.
41. Diebold, *Trade and Payments in Western Europe*, p. 40.
42. Dietrich, "Bizonal Trade Agreement Program," pp. 3–5.

After the Soviet walkout there obviously was nothing to hope for, and the United States and Great Britain decided to proceed promptly with the unduly delayed reform.

In anticipation of the reform, JEIA established as of May 1, 1948, a new procedure which did away with the system of multiple exchange rates for bizonal exports and replaced it with a pegged rate of 30 cents for one Reichsmark. The new procedure applied to the export of goods (except coal) and services, as well as to imports. Until the currency reform, payment to German exporters and by German importers had to be made in Reichsmarks on the basis of this exchange rate.[43] After the currency reform the pertinent JEIA Instruction was amended to read: "in Deutsche Mark" instead of "in Reichsmark."

The new currency had been printed in America and held in readiness for some time. The original American proposals for the currency reform were discussed with and refined by Allied and German experts. Literally at the last moment, the French government decided to join in the bipartite venture, a welcome decision, although it caused some additional delay.[44]

The reform was announced on June 20, 1948, in the form of several separate laws.[45] All currency and savings, including both time- and demand-deposits, had to be registered and converted into the new currency, the Deutsche Mark, on a ten-to-one basis. Half of the new balances were blocked and 70 percent of the blocked accounts were eventually canceled. The final result of the reform was a radical contraction of the money supply since it actually entailed a conversion rate of 6.5 Deutsche Mark for 100 old Reichsmark. Debts were simultaneously devalued at the rate of ten to one. One of the laws empowered the Bank Deutscher Länder to issue and control the new currency while establishing an upper limit of 10 billion DM. Furthermore a six-day moratorium was declared and the exchange of 60 Reichsmark per person for new Deutsche Mark on a one-to-one basis was authorized.

The success of the currency reform was instantaneous. In fact, for those who had an opportunity to observe the sudden change on the German scene, it was astonishing. Consumer goods not seen in Germany for years emerged practically overnight, and empty shop windows and shelves were rapidly stocked with hoarded merchandise. Everyone had been aware that a great deal of hoarding had taken place in expectation

---

43. JEIA Operations Memorandum no. 25, BIP/P (48) 41 (OMGUS records).
44. Clay, *Decision in Germany,* p. 213.
45. American Military Government Laws 61–64 (OMGUS records).

of the currency reform, but the actual extent of it took most people by surprise. Although the necessity for equalization measures to distribute losses fairly had been emphasized in the Colm-Dodge-Goldsmith Report, the first law of monetary reform stipulated that "the task of equalizing burdens is laid on the appropriate German legislative bodies as one of the greatest urgency to be accomplished by December 31, 1948." It actually was four years before the pertinent German legislation was promulgated, but nevertheless it appears appropriate for Military Government to have left the drafting of equalization measures, with all their sociological and economic implications, to German authorities.

Whether a fair equalization was eventually achieved seems at least debatable. During the three years preceding the currency reform numerous German industrialists and businessmen had been able to build up incredibly large inventories, Allied and German controls notwithstanding. The real value of these, of course, was maintained, and it seemed to anyone observing these developments from close by that the subsequent legislation left the resulting huge profits largely intact.

There can be no doubt that the effectiveness of the currency reform was greatly enhanced by the promise of early and substantial ERP aid. Although at the time of the reform no ERP shipments had actually arrived, everyone was aware that with a large supply of commodities in the offing, the new currency would be backed by an increasing and adequate German production. As a result the demoralizing effects of a meaningless public accounting system quickly vanished, while traditional German characteristics such as industriousness, orderliness, and thrift reappeared.

During the months following the currency reform considerable progress was made toward the unification of the three western zones. Although it had been decided that there would be no economic fusion of the bizonal area with the French Zone prior to political unification, important steps were taken to insure better economic cooperation.[46] They involved the establishment of a tripartite Allied Banking Commission, a common customs policy, and the taking over by JEIA of the foreign-trade operation of the French Zone previously conducted by an Office of Foreign Commerce (OFFICOMEX). Accordingly, some French representatives were added to JEIA's Board of Directors, whereas American and British representatives were assigned to Baden-Baden, the headquarters of OFFICOMEX, which now became another

46. Clay, *Decision in Germany*, p. 396.

JEIA branch office. Henceforth new trade agreements with other countries were negotiated in the name of a trizonal Germany.[47]

As one would expect, the drastically changed economic situation prompted the Joint Export Import Agency to proceed quite rapidly with its basic mission of normalizing German foreign trade. Accordingly, the quota system for the entry of foreign businessmen into the Bizone was abolished and individuals interested in trading with the bizonal area were admitted for repeated journeys for a period of thirty days. In addition, the branch offices were authorized to grant necessary extensions. At the same time, additional German hotels were released by American and British military authorities and made available to JEIA for the accommodation of foreign businessmen, with the result that by 1949 several hundred hotels were at the disposal of visitors from abroad.[48]

Among the industries particularly useful for German export trade were textiles and ceramics, since both of them yielded high export proceeds on the basis of relatively small import expenditures. In order to give these industries an inducement to step up their export business, JEIA authorized a new procedure as of June 1948 whereby exporters of textiles and ceramics received a "40 percent foreign exchange credit which could be used for all purposes directly or indirectly connected with the promotion of exports." Under a simplified procedure these two industries were able to use their 40 percent foreign-exchange credit for the importation of raw materials, machinery, and spare parts, as well as for the purposes of export promotion.[49]

Of a more general significance was the revision of the existing export controls and the issuance of a new liberalized export procedure for the Trizone by JEIA in November 1948.[50] The stated purpose of the new regulations was "to reduce the amount of documentation and to offer the German exporters the opportunity to export without former interference and clearances required by the Military and German trade bureau." [51] Under the new procedure applications for export were no longer required except for a few restricted items, and the branch offices of JEIA were relieved of the licensing function. Export transactions from then on could be carried out by German businessmen directly in accordance with

47. JEIA Instruction no. 1, revision 1, effective 1 Dec. 1948 (OMGUS records).
48. JEIA Monthly Report, May 1948, p. 5.
49. JEIA Instruction no. 20, effective 21 June 1948 (OMGUS records).
50. JEIA Instruction no. 1, revision 1, effective 1 Dec. 1948.
51. JEIA Monthly Report, Dec. 1948, p. 6.

the general customs of international foreign trade. The new procedure required only an export control document submitted to one of the numerous foreign trade banks (Aussenhandelsbanken) in the Bizone prior to the shipment of goods. If the export control document was found in order, the German Aussenhandelsbank issued an export license on behalf of JEIA. JEIA was still required to examine all approved export control documents. If JEIA thought that an exporter had not complied with the terms and conditions governing German export trade, he could be asked for an explanation; if the explanation was found unsatisfactory, the exporter's future transactions became subject to more stringent controls. Under the new procedure the export control document and the license were combined in a single form replacing the numerous export documents previously obligatory for each transaction. In a pertinent press release OMGUS at about the same time answered the vociferous criticism about "JEIA's red tape and involved procedures." As the announcement pointed out:

> "The responsibility [for the delays] was not due to the burdensome procedures of JEIA but was inevitable with the commercial banks of Germany not being in a position to handle export and import transactions. Therefore the work of hundreds of commercial banks was being carried on the shoulders of the staff of JEIA in its head office and 10 branches. At the present time all the export transactions are taken directly by the exporter to the commercial banks instead of to the JEIA offices. That means there are 175 available places to deposit documents instead of 11. . . . This procedure could not have been initiated before as the facilities of the banks were not available.[52]

A few months later the liberalized export procedures were followed by a similar move aimed at the revision of import-licensing procedures. Under the provisions of a new JEIA instruction, the former import-licensing procedure was revised to facilitate and expedite the import of commodities needed for export production as well as for the internal economy. Any importer, manufacturer, or industry group was eligible to import approved commodities subject to the supervision of and approval by a newly formed Industry Advisory Committee consisting of Allied and German representatives. At the same time a budget office was established which was responsible for maintaining records of budgetary

52. OMGUS Release no. 396, 5 Jan. 1949 (OMGUS records).

allocations in accordance with instructions issued by the JEIA Comptroller.[53]

As imports were turned over to private industry, central procurement by JEIA ceased. Nevertheless, since foreign exchange was still limited, imports still had to be controlled. The pertinent German economic offices were therefore instructed to prepare a quarterly budget and import program for JEIA's approval. Once approval had been obtained, the German economic and agricultural administrations were required to publish weekly lists of commodities approved by the Industry Advisory Committee announcing the quantity and amount allocated for each commodity plus special instructions if there were any.

Under the new procedure, importers could then proceed with their purchase negotiations as long as they were in accordance with the published lists and did not exceed 20 percent of the announced quantities. After completion of the purchase, the importers were required to apply for an import license at one of the foreign-trade banks, which had to ascertain that the foreign-trade funds were still available before issuing the license. Any notification of approval or disapproval had to be given within twenty-four hours. The importer had to arrange for payment in accordance with the customs of the trade but not before presentation of the shipping documents. Upon receipt of these documents, he could ask the foreign-trade bank to establish a letter of credit in the foreign currency or to make other payment arrangements. At the same time the importer was required to pay to his bank the Deutsche Mark equivalent of the purchase price.

It stands to reason that the simplification of the foreign-trade procedures by JEIA in 1948 and the gradual restoration of normal export-import channels were important factors in the spectacular revival of German exports. Other important elements were the arrival of substantial GARIOA-financed food supplies, the participation of the three western zones in the European Recovery Program, the Intra-European Payment Agreement with its compensation and drawing-rights arrangements, a series of active trade agreements, and finally the currency reform.

Actual exports for the year totaled $598 million as compared to $225 million in the preceding year. Whereas coal and solid fuels had been responsible for 54 percent of the bizonal exports in 1947, the percentage dropped to 47 in the following year. Concurrently the share for exports of finished and semifinished products rose from 12 to 35 percent, a trend

53. JEIA Instruction no. 29, effective 8 Feb. 1948 (OMGUS records).

which was continued during the following year. By the end of August 1949, the last month covered by the reports of the JEIA, the annual rate of West German exports had risen to $1 billion, with a 32 percent share for exports of coal and solid fuels and a 56 percent participation by finished and semifinished products.

Actual imports into the Bizone in 1948 totaled $1.4 billion, including $797 million for food and other imports financed by U.S.-appropriated funds, $417 million financed from export proceeds, $101 million provided by ECA, and the balance supplied by the United Kingdom's contribution of $70 million.[54]

Another breakdown of imports for the year 1948 gives the following figures: $990,752,000 for food, $251,544,000 for raw materials, $94,800,000 for semifinished products, and $37,839,000 for finished products; grand total, $1,375,000,000.[55]

As an OMGUS press release of January 5, 1949, indicated, eighteen months earlier the Bizone had been exporting at a rate of a little over $200 million per year. Seventy percent of this figure represented the proceeds of the sale of coal. As of December 1948, exports were moving at a rate of $800 million per year, which was well over 3.5 times the annual rate of June 1947. Imports of raw materials from the proceeds of exports during all of 1947 were not more than $60 million; in 1948 imports paid by exports were well over $400 million, or about seven times the 1947 figure. Imports of food and other essentials paid for by American and British taxpayers had amounted to $800 million in 1947 and to about $1 billion in the following year. (In 1947 Germany's exports could have paid for only about a quarter of this bill, whereas in 1948 they equaled almost half of the value of the larger volume of imports.) See also Figs. 6.2, 6.3, and 6.4.

During 1949 the rate of production and of foreign trade continued to increase. Industrial output, which prior to the currency reform was 47 percent of the 1936 level, rose to 89 percent in March 1949. Exports averaged $89 million per month in the first three months of 1949, reflecting an expected annual export rate of $1 billion, which was actually exceeded.

The ground had been laid—West Germany was on the road toward a complete economic and financial recovery in the framework of the European Recovery Program. In the spring of 1949 the first West German government was formed, an occupational statute was signed,

54. Clay, *Decision in Germany*, p. 220.
55. JEIA Final Report, p. 37.

TABLE 6.1 Industrial production index
in the Bizone of Germany: all goods
(1936 = 100) [56]

Year and quarter	Production
1936	100
1945	Not available
1946	
1	28
2	32
3	37
4	36
1947	
1	30
2	39
3	42
4	43
1948	
1	46
2	48
3	65
4	76

and the work of Military Government terminated. Accordingly the job of JEIA came to an end and the responsibility for German foreign trade was transferred to the appropriate agencies of the German federal government.

A military government imposed by a foreign power can never be popular. From the record it would appear, however, that the Joint Export-Import Agency as an instrument of the occupying powers incurred more than its share of German wrath. In this context an epitaph to JEIA offered by the London *Economist* provides a most appropriate appraisal.

THE PASSING OF JEIA

A landmark on the path back to German sovereignty was passed on October 15th [1949] when JEIA handed over all its administrative functions with one exception, to the German foreign trade authorities. Until it is dissolved, JEIA will retain advisory and

56. Research Analysis Corp., McLean, Va., Technical Paper RAC-TP-352, April 1969, p. 60.

FIGURE 6.2   The foreign trade of bizonal Germany, 1947–1948.
[After JEIA *Monthly Report,* Dec. 1948, p. 5.]

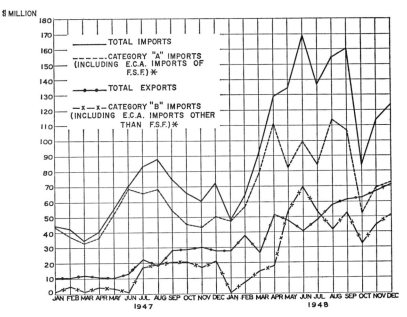

* F.S.F. — FOOD, SEED, FERTILIZER.

supervisory rights and will control, or attempt to control, the
exports of restricted goods to the Russian sphere. After it is
dissolved a committee of the High Commission will assume this
limited role in the sphere of German trade.

During its lifetime, JEIA was regarded by the Germans as the
sinister embodiment of Allied ill-will, and by traders of all nations
as a synonym for red-tape. In justice to JEIA it must be said that
its task was extraordinarily complicated. At the outset, German
exports had to be forced out of a prostrate economy. Prices had to
be fixed at a level which would both secure contracts and yet
satisfy British and American competitors that the Germans were
not dumping. Until the currency reform of June 1948, the German
Mark and the internal price level bore no relation whatever to
external conditions and the Agency had to operate a complicated
system of individual price-fixing which gave full scope for bureaucratic muddles and national suspicions. The tangle became still
worse owing to the American insistence on decentralized government, which gave the local German State Ministries the right to put

FIGURE 6.3 Export deliveries, 1947–1948. [After JEIA *Monthly Report,* Dec. 1948, p. 10.]

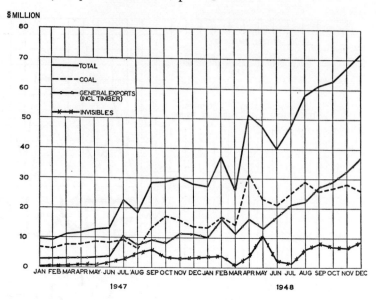

FIGURE 6.4 Bizonal Germany: the road to viability, 1947–1953: three months' moving average. [After JEIA, *Final Report,* p. 22.]

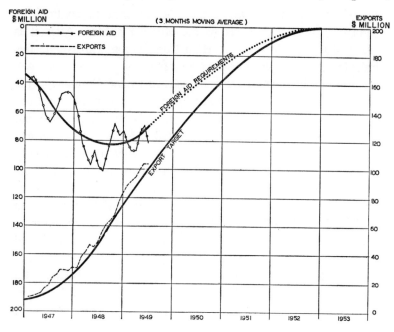

a finger into the foreign trade pie. Lastly, the obligation to settle balances in dollars which until recently formed the basis of all JEIA's trade pacts, acted as a brake and irritant on all sides.

Nevertheless German exports have multiplied under the JEIA regime. In 1947 they totaled only $222 million, in 1948 they reached nearly $600 million and during the first six months of this year they had already passed the total for 1948. In 1947 Germany was paying for only a third of its imports; it has now doubled that proportion in spite of the fact that imports have risen from $734 million in 1947 to $1400 million in 1948 and to over $1000 million in the first six months of the year.

During this time, the American and British heads of JEIA have constantly cut their own red-tape. Exports have been largely freed from licensing controls, and the importing procedure has been simplified. JEIA's last work has been to negotiate new types of bilateral trade pacts which it is hoped will serve as a model to the Organization for European Economic Cooperation. In the last few months agreements have been concluded with Switzerland, Holland and Norway which go a considerable way toward freeing German trade from quota limitations. The latest German pacts specify commodities—a small but important list—which are still restricted; leaving the rest free; and in the agreements with Holland the dollar clause is eliminated altogether.

The manner of JEIA's passing is therefore becoming to an organization in which the American vote predominated. Already German merchants are finding that the local bureaucracy which has taken its place is the worse of two evils.[57]

57. *Economist,* 157 no. 5540 (29 Oct. 1949):937.

Chapter Seven

Summing Up

On August 13, 1941, only a few weeks after the invasion of Southern Indochina by Japan, the U.S. House of Representatives approved the extension of the Selective Service Act by a majority of one. Four months later, the United States was at war with Germany and Japan, facing the two most powerful war machines of any age.

A school teacher in the year 2000, wishing to demonstrate to his class the peaceful sentiments of the American people on the eve of World War II, could hardly make his point more effectively than by citing this Congressional action. The majority of a single vote reflected fairly well the feelings of a disillusioned America which long ago had given up hope of making the world safe for its own particular brand of democracy. While an earlier generation had accepted the Kaiser's exclusive war guilt and believed in fabricated stories of German atrocities, the abatement of war hysteria and postwar scrutiny, as well as the vengeful attitude of America's Allies at Versailles, St. Germain, and Trianon, had brought about a reappraisal of the events leading to World War I and had left Americans convinced that the rest of the world was beyond saving and that the United States should refrain from further involvement in European affairs.

In 1941, even the "hawks," at that time the liberal element, opposed the war and did not go further than endorsing a policy of "Defend America by Aiding the Allies." The conservative "doves," on the other hand, had banded together and organized an influential "America First Committee" that, among other things, endeavored to prevent Congress from enacting legislation that might jeopardize the peace of the United States. According to the views of the America Firsters, National Socialist Germany could not be defeated and the wisest course of action for the United States would be to come to terms with the Axis powers. Such views were strongly expressed by the committee's most prominent member, Charles A. Lindbergh, who, as Göring's guest, had inspected the German Air Force and become convinced of its invincibility. In the same vein, his wife, Anne Morrow Lindbergh, had depicted Hitler's national socialism as the forces of the future which could not be fought and were about to conquer the world.[1]

Pearl Harbor, with the subsequent German declaration of war on the United States, presented the American people with a *fait accompli* ending, at least temporarily, their internal debate and prompting conservatives and liberals alike to rally to the flag. America's attitude toward the war, however, differed greatly from that of World War I. With the exception of some emotional anti-Japanese propaganda on the West Coast causing the relocation of more than 100,000 Japanese-Americans in "detention" camps, there was no war hysteria comparable to that of the first world conflagration.

Twenty-four years earlier, George Creel's Committee for Public Information had "waged a battle of words in a fight for the minds of men for the conquest of their convictions" and "the battle had run through every home in the country." Creel's assertion that there was no medium of appeal that he did not utilize was no exaggeration; among many other activities his committee published more than fifty pamphlets for distribution to 75 million Americans and mobilized 75,000 speakers, who delivered more than 750,000 speeches in support of the war effort. Most of the information distributed in this manner was rather crude propaganda attempting to create a "black top enemy image"[2] of the Central Powers and attributing nothing but good to the Allies. In its efforts to shape the American mind, the Wilson Administration did not limit itself to persuasion. With the support of two wartime statutes, the Espionage Act of June 15, 1917, and the Sedition Act of May 16, 1918, it carried out widespread arrests of all citizens considered disloyal. In these actions democratic process often was not observed, and while the American army had been sent abroad to carry the torch of liberty to Europe, the country was impairing the safeguards of democracy at home.

By contrast, World War II saw nothing of the kind, and while the Roosevelt government endeavored to promote an active prosecution of the war, no attempt was made to control public opinion and to conduct domestic propaganda in a fashion similar to that of the Creel Commit-

1. Anne Morrow Lindbergh, *The Wave of the Future,* p. 34.
2. A term coined by Ralph White, *Nobody Wanted War,* p. 24. It refers to the tendency to regard all enemy leaders as distinguished from the population as "evil."

tee. Accordingly, soft- and hard-liners alike, while loyally following their government, continued to express their own views as to the causes of the war the United States was engaged in.[3] There was no widespread hatred of the German people in evidence, and the national emergency was generally regarded as a necessary evil that it was hoped would come to an early end. Public support of the war effort seemed more than adequate, but nevertheless the Roosevelt Administration could not help being aware of the underlying distaste for the war.

In addition, it faced a most precarious military situation, especially at the beginning of the war. The well-trained, superbly equipped German armies overran most of western Europe in a matter of weeks and after taking close to four million Russian prisoners, were fighting at the outskirts of Moscow and Leningrad. It seemed as though nothing could stop Germany's military might. In addition, there were other imponderables—including the question of whether the Soviet Union would be willing and able to continue the war or whether, in case of a military deadlock, a Soviet-German peace might be negotiated. While such a course of events did not appear likely, there were the precedents of the Molotov-Ribbentrop agreement, of Rapallo, and of Brest Litovsk, all of which ruled against completely discounting such an eventuality. Finally, enough of the scientific breakthrough toward unleashing atomic energy had taken place in Germany to create the threat that Germany might be first in developing the bomb. While the superiority of America's industrial-military potential could not be questioned, it nevertheless was also clear that either a separate German-Soviet peace settlement or the production of a German atom bomb would change the chances for a successful termination of the war. In the Far East, at the same time, the ferocious military power of Japan had just succeeded in eliminating half of America's Pacific Fleet. Taking all these elements into account and disregarding the easy wisdom of hindsight, it is understandable that the Roosevelt Administration devoted all its energies and talents to the effective prosecution of the war and was admittedly reluctant to devote much time to postwar plans.

For the lower military echelons at SHAEF this reluctance created a most difficult situation, especially when the fortunes of war turned in favor of the Allies. When, in the spring of 1944, the possibility of a

3. "Am liebsten hätte man mit gekreuzten Armen zugesehen wie die Europäischen Dictatoren einander umbrachten. Pearl Harbor und Hitlers Kriegserklärung zwangen zur Aufgabe dieser Haltung. Nachdem sich die Nation im Krieg befand, suchte die Rechte loyal und nach besten Kräften zum Sieg beizutragen, liess sich aber von der ideologischen Begeisterung der Progressiven nicht anstecken." Schwarz, p. 97.

German collapse became quite real and instructions from Washington, in spite of urgent requests, were not forthcoming, SHAEF had to proceed on its own by preparing a policy directive for the first phase of the occupation. The result of these efforts was the original version of the *Handbook for Military Government of Germany,* which was completed just in time, i.e., four or five weeks before the first elements of the U.S. Army entered Germany.

Contrary to rumored allegations,[4] there is no reason to assume a collective pro-German bias on the part of the officers responsible for the *Handbook.* It is true that one or another may have agreed with General Patton, who later remarked that he saw little difference between the Nazi Party and the two major political parties in the United States. (In a similar vein, a war crimes officer of the 82d Airborne Division, when presented with the evidence of a German war crime near Cologne, refused to initiate prosecution and commented to the writer: "After all, we have such thugs also in America.") In this connection it seems worthy of note that conflicting allegations, namely, that many key positions in OMGUS were staffed with Treasury representatives who toed the Morgenthau line, were equally unfounded. Colonel Bernard Bernstein, who is usually mentioned as an example, returned to Washington in the summer of 1945 "to protest, to fight for his views, and to resign." [5]

In other words, the officers at SHAEF who drafted guidelines for the occupation, as well as those who later were to be charged with their implementation under Military Government, naturally reflected a cross section of America. They included liberal hard-liners who wanted to do away with the last vestiges of Nazism, as well as conservative America Firsters who were often more suspicious of the Russian ally than of the German enemy. The underlying conflict and official reactions thereto were also reflected in some documents. One of them was distributed by the U.S. Group Control Council several months before the end of the war:

Subject: Advocacy of JCS/1067

Memorandum to: Division Directors (Personal)

1. The importance of JCS/1067 as an expression of U.S. policy, and the necessity of following the letter and spirit of it in our

4. "Rumors of Fascists in Military Government School in Charlottesville prompted the President to request information concerning the background of its trainees." Hammond, p. 320.
5. Ibid., p. 438.

planning, has been called to your attention on frequent occasions. In this connection, the following is quoted from a recent letter from General Hilldring, Director of Civil Affairs Division of the War Department:

> "I have sensed a lack of willingness among certain of your people in London to accept and follow the clearly laid down policies established in Washington on the highest levels. . . .
>
> "I would like to suggest that you employ every means to make certain that the officers under your command understand that the policy of the United States with respect to the military government of Germany is presently laid down in JCS/1067, and must be followed in letter and in spirit. It is particularly important that your officers should be *advocates* of 1067 and under no circumstances critical of its policies. . . .
>
> "There is no friction or discordance between the Departments of the Government back home on these issues, and so far as I know, no differences between responsible U.S. officials in London and their home agencies. I am sure you will agree with me that any public impression to the contrary must be disastrous to our cause."

2. It is desired that the foregoing information be brought to the personal attention of every officer in your Division. The importance of JCS/1067 will be re-emphasized to the end that they will become thoroughly indoctrinated with the full understanding that this document is not merely to be followed in our planning, but that each officer must be a sincere advocate of 1067, and under no circumstances critical of its policies.

3. It is further desired that new officers reporting for duty be given similar indoctrination, so that it cannot be said that any member of this Command does not give full and active support to JCS/1067, and to all other approved U.S. policies.

C. W. WICKERSHAM
Brigadier General U.S.A.
Acting Deputy [6]

Another document referred to the opposition by the hard-liners. The relevant paragraph has been extracted from General Clay's letter of September 16, 1945, to John J. McCloy:

6. OMGUS records, 16.

In a few days Colonel Bernstein is returning to the United States for temporary duty with the Treasury Department. On the exact nature and origin of his request I am not entirely clear. In view of the changes over here, you might do well to keep in touch with Mr. Vinson [the secretary of the treasury] to make sure that the purpose and the character of the changes is not misunderstood. There is no need to tell you that they have no relation to "soft peace" or "hard peace," but some people less well informed might be led to conclude that there was some connection. If so, it would be helpful for you to correct any such erroneous conclusions.[7]

As to the content of the first *Handbook,* it must be recognized that it was a rather astute document reflecting a high degree of perceptive analysis and a sound appraisal of things to come. The U.S. Army was about to complete its mission of winning the war in Europe and as a matter of course it prepared for its next task, namely, the occupation of Germany, in a businesslike and efficient manner. Since the health experts had ruled that 2000 calories were the minimum daily ration for a working population, and because it was fairly clear that indigenous food supplies in Germany would not suffice, provisions for the importation of food would have to be made; since Germany always had depended on imports of industrial raw materials, this contingency also had to be taken into consideration; and since it was well known that most key positions in government and industry had been occupied by members of the Nazi Party, it seemed appropriate to use their services initially in order to establish an effective governmental apparatus under the supervision of the U.S. Army.

While all this reflected good judgment from a strictly military point of view, it is equally understandable that Morgenthau and his hard-line associates, when they learned of the army's pragmatic approach, lost their composure. The two developments which followed actually canceled each other out. On the one hand Morgenthau, by alerting the White House, was able to curtail the distribution of the first *Handbook;* on the other hand, his "plan" for a pastoral Germany came to naught when, as a result of a vocal opposition by the American press, Roosevelt disavowed his previous approval. The net result was that the United States by October 1944 had neither a short- nor a long-range policy for the postwar treatment of Germany, a hiatus which was extended by Roosevelt's refusal to get into detailed planning "because we are not

7. OMGUS records, 410-2/3.

there yet and we don't know what we will find." While the wisdom of Roosevelt's abstention has been and will be challenged,[8] it is noteworthy that Churchill a few months later expressed a similar view to Eden: "It is a mistake to try to write out on little pieces of paper what the vast emotions of an outraged and quivering world will be either immediately after the struggle is over or when the immediate cold fit follows the hot. . . . There is therefore wisdom in reserving one's decisions as long as possible and until all the facts and forces that will be potent at the moment are revealed." [9]

The War Department in Washington, as John McCloy emphasized to the writer, was in the middle of the dispute. Since the army was to be responsible for running the show in Germany, there had to be early policy guidances; at the same time, while the considerations encompassed in the *Handbook* were perfectly valid, the political climate most definitely precluded high-level endorsement. Once again, to quote McCloy, "we could not follow a soft or even an objective line . . . in this atmosphere we could not spell out a constructive program . . . we had to go along with a generally negative approach." [10] This was the rationale for the much maligned JCS/1067, a document that reflected the antagonistic pressures under which it was composed but nevertheless served its purpose well. It excluded the worst extremes of Morgenthau's proposals, namely, the plan for a pastoral Germany, the wholesale destruction of German industries, and the breaking up of Germany into several parts. On the other hand, it did include the general hard-line approach of the liberals, and therefore secured the concurrence of White House, Treasury, and State. Probably its most practical aspects were the preamble which made it an interim directive, as well as the disease-and-unrest formula which even the most fanatic German haters could not challenge. It was this escape clause that permitted circumvention of most of the directive's tough economic terms. Finally and most important, the document gave the army at literally the last minute a policy guidance without which it would have been unable to operate.

It will be recalled that the final version of JCS/1067, classified as secret, was released for appropriate distribution in May 1945. By the middle of August several of its key provisions in the area of economics had been modified or superseded by pertinent paragraphs of the Pots-

8. George F. Kennan, contrary to the criticism expressed by other distinguished scholars, holds the view that the theories of possible postwar cooperation with the Soviet Union in Germany were mere "pipedreams." *Memoirs, 1925–1950,* p. 178.
9. Churchill, *Triumph and Tragedy,* pp. 350–51.
10. Interview, 30 Nov. 1967.

dam Agreement, an important correction which most historical appraisals of the period have failed to make clear. Inasmuch as JCS/1067, after
its belated declassification, became available to the press only in October
1945, i.e., several months after the signing of the Potsdam Agreement, it
is evident why the relation between these two sets of documents was
never understood by the general public. It is nevertheless surprising that
even as well-informed an observer as Harold Zink could present the
view that it was left to Clay's discretion to choose between the two
documents in the case of conflict.[11]

After Clay's initial shock over JCS/1067 had worn off and he had
appraised the ramifications of the escape clause which the War Department had devised, he began to organize the re-establishment of the
German economy as JCS/1067 authorized and the Potsdam Agreement
requested him to do. Indigenous German food rations were supple-
mented by food imported from abroad on an increasing scale; domestic
food production was stepped up through the importation of fertilizers
and seeds; destroyed railways, bridges, and harbors were repaired;
canals and rivers were opened for traffic; the postal service was put back
into operation; telephone and telegraph services were restored; coal
production was increased, industrial production stepped up, and an
export program organized. After the initial phase of pump priming had
produced some exports, their proceeds were used to organize the import
of raw materials on a steadily increasing scale, a development that was
expedited by the device of so-called self-liquidating imports. Initially all
this was done quietly and without much fanfare, since it implemented
the policy stated in the escape clause rather than the announced policy
guidance stipulating that "no steps were to be taken leading toward the
economic rehabilitation of Germany or designated to maintain or
strengthen the German economy."

In view of the complete collapse of the German economy after five
years of warfare, the breakup of Germany into four parts, and the
critical shortages of food and raw materials on the world markets,
progress was bound to be slow. Consequently, when one food crisis
followed another and industrial production remained far below prewar
levels, vociferous, steadily mounting criticism arose to question and
challenge the real intentions of the American Military Government.
During the first phase of the occupation, however, little substantive
information was forthcoming, and publicity in behalf of the American
reconstruction efforts in Germany in subsequent years remained ineffec-

11. Zink, p. 94.

tive. The resulting communications gap seriously affected the image of the American Military Government not only in Germany but also most regrettably in the United States.

Both the general public and competent observers—since they were rarely told differently—were compelled to draw their own conclusions. Connecting announced policy directives with economic conditions that often seemed to deteriorate rather than to improve, they saw a causal link which, although nonexistent, nevertheless appeared highly plausible. When there was not sufficient food and only 1200 or 1300 calories could be distributed, the fact that half of it was imported from the United States hardly came into focus. The missing 700 or 800 calories below an acceptable 2000 calories level attracted all the attention, leading to the conclusion that the deficiency was caused by an American policy of revenge. When indigenous food production in Germany lagged, it was not the depleted German soil and lack of incentives for the farmer which were held responsible but the alleged dismantling of fertilizer plants for reparations. When industrial raw materials could not be brought in from abroad, it was not the result of Germany's lack of hard currency, but the consequence of an imaginary Allied embargo devised to keep Germany down. And finally, when industrial production failed to pick up, it was not the lack of coal, electricity, and raw materials or the absence of all incentives for the workers which caused the prolonged stagnation; instead it was the Allied Level of Industry Plan in accordance with JCS/1067 and the Potsdam Declaration that prevented a revival of the German economy.

These misinterpretations could still be taken lightly if they had been temporary and confined to the daily news media. Regrettably, though, in accordance with America's muckraking traditions,[12] this kind of evaluation crept into numerous professional writings on the subject, so that even a recent publication of the U.S. Senate's Judiciary Committee has asserted: "During the first two years of the Allied occupation the Treasury program of industrial dismantlement was vigorously pursued by American officials." [13] One therefore usually encounters the view that in accordance with Treasury-inspired directives from 1945 until 1948 the United States not only took a hands-off attitude as far as the

12. A recent report of the American Foreign Service Association. "Toward a Modern Diplomacy," refers to the American penchant for self-criticism as the "masochistic streak that feeds on the American tendency to downgrade its accomplishments abroad." *Foreign Service Journal* 45, no. 11, pt. 2 (Nov. 1968): 14.

13. *Morgenthau Diary*, p. 76.

problems of the German economy were concerned, but actually proceeded with a broad-scale reduction of its level of production. According to the same negative appraisal, America, in belated recognition of Germany's importance for the European economy, finally underwent a change of heart in 1948, and the active reconstruction of Germany began.

As the preceding chapters have attempted to demonstrate, the actual reconstruction of the German economy began under the most difficult conditions in the summer of 1945, i.e., right after the German capitulation. The change of policy guidances which took place in 1947 had little if any bearing on the constructive efforts of the Military Government; in conjunction with a changing political climate, however, the new policy helped to set the German stage for the European Recovery Program which, thanks to the groundwork of the preceding years, could pursue the same objectives at a much accelerated pace.

The question finally arises whether a more vigorous reconstruction of the German economy could not have been pursued earlier and whether the slow economic revival could not have been expedited during the first years. The obvious answer is that eighteen to twenty-four months probably could have been gained if, as suggested, there had been a currency reform in the summer of 1946 rather than two years later and if General Draper's proposal in 1946 to make $1 billion of industrial raw materials promptly available could have been implemented. The reasons why neither of these two steps could be taken at that time have been discussed in some of the earlier chapters. It may be added that the wisdom of General Draper's suggestion was implicitly recognized in the European Recovery Program, proposed in 1947 and effective the following year.

The political situation changed dramatically in the course of these three postwar years. The alliance with the Soviet Union broke down and West Germany was readmitted to the family of Western nations. As the record indicates, the policy guidances prepared by the War Department for the occupation fortunately were flexible enough to permit the Military Government to continue its work in the interests of peace through the years of transition in an enlightened and progressively more effective manner.

BIBLIOGRAPHY

Items referred to OMGUS records are available in
Record Group 260 at the Federal Records
Center, Suitland, Maryland.

Balabkins, Nicholas. *Germany Under Direct Controls: Economic Aspects of Industrial Disarmament, 1945–1948.* New Brunswick, N.J.: Rutgers University Press, 1964.

The Businessman's Guide to the Combined US/UK Area of Germany. Berlin: Office of the Economic Advisor, 1947.

Byrnes, James F. *Speaking Frankly.* New York: Harper, 1947.

Cahan, J. F. "The Recovery of German Exports," *International Affairs,* 26 April 1950, pp. 172–79.

CEEC [Committee of European Economic Cooperation], *General Report, 1948.*

Churchill, Winston S. *Triumph and Tragedy.* Boston: Houghton Mifflin, 1953.

Clay, Lucius D. *Decision in Germany.* Garden City, N.Y.: Doubleday, 1950.

Colm-Dodge-Goldsmith Report. "A Plan for the Liquidation of War Finance and the Financial Rehabilitation of Germany." OMGUS records, 14-3/5.

"Comparative Readings in Basic U.S. Policy Directives on Germany." Prepared by Program Control Branch, OMGUS. OMGUS records.

Davidson, Eugene. *The Death and Life of Germany: An Account of the American Occupation.* New York: Knopf, 1959.

Dennison, F. S. V. *Civil Affairs and Military Government: Northwest Europe, 1944–1946.* London: H.M.S.O., 1961.

Diebold, William, Jr. *Trade and Payments in Western Europe.* New York: Harper, 1950.

Dietrich, Ethel. "Bizonal Trade Agreement Program," *OMGUS Weekly Information Bulletin,* 24 Aug. 1948, pp. 3–5. OMGUS records.

Dorn, Walter L. "The Debate Over American Occupational Policy in Germany, 1944–1945," *Political Science Quarterly* 72 (Dec. 1957): 482.

ECA [Economic Cooperation Administration]. *First Report to Congress,* June 1948.
———. *Third Report to Congress,* Dec. 1948.
Erhard, Ludwig. *Prosperity Through Competition.* New York: Praeger, 1958.
Fay, Sidney. *The Origins of the World War.* 2 vols. New York: Macmillan, 1930.
Feis, Herbert. *Churchill, Roosevelt, Stalin.* Princeton, N.J.: Princeton University Press, 1957.
———. *Between War and Peace: The Potsdam Conference.* Princeton, N.J.: Princeton University Press, 1960.
"Food and Agriculture in the Bizonal Area of Germany." Manuscript, 1 Oct. 1947. OMGUS records.
Foreign Relations of the United States; Diplomatic Papers: Conference of Berlin (Potsdam), 1945. U.S. Dept. of State Publication 7015. Washington: U.S. Govt. Printing Office, 1960.
Foreign Relations of the United States; Diplomatic Papers: The Conferences at Malta and Yalta. U.S. Dept. of State Publication 6199. Washington: U.S. Govt. Printing Office, 1955.
Friedmann, Wolfgang. *The Allied Military Government in Germany.* London: Stevens, 1947.
Friedrich, Carl J., et al. *American Experiences in Military Government in World War II.* New York: Rinehart, 1948.
Gimbel, John. *The American Occupation of Germany.* Stanford, Calif.: Stanford University Press, 1968.
Gottlieb, Manuel. *The German Peace Settlement and the Berlin Crisis.* New York: Paine-Whitman, 1960.
Hammond, Paul V., "Directives for the Occupation of Germany, the Washington Controversy." In *American Civil-Military Decisions,* edited by Harold Stein. University, Ala.: University of Alabama Press, 1963.
Handbook for Military Government in Germany. 15 Aug. 1944. OMGUS records.
Harmssen, E. C. *Am Abend der Demontage.* Bremen: F. Trüjen Verlag, 1951.
———. *Reparationen, Sozialprodukt, Lebensstandard: Versuch einer Wirtschaftsbilanz.* Bremen: F. Trüjen Verlag, 1947.
Hill, Russell. *The Struggle for Germany.* New York: Harper, 1947.
"History of Military Government: VE Day to June 30, 1946. Chap. 8. Economics. Pt. 6. Food and Agriculture Branch." Manuscript. OMGUS records, 20-3/5.
Holborn, Hajo. *American Military Government: Its Organization and Policies.* Washington: Infantry Journal Press, 1947.
Hoover Report: "Food and Agriculture U.S.–U.K. Zone of Germany." Feb. 1947. Manuscript. Prepared by U.S.–British Bipartite Food and Agriculture Panel. OMGUS records 20-3/5.

Hull, Cordell. *The Memoirs of Cordell Hull.* 2 vols. New York: Macmillan, 1945.

Hutton, Edward L. and D. Walter Robbins. "Postwar German Foreign Trade." Manuscript, 15 Dec. 1947. OMGUS records.

JEIA [Joint Export Import Agency] Instructions. OMGUS records.

————. Monthly Reports. OMGUS records.

Kennan, George F. *Memoirs, 1925–1950.* Boston: Little, Brown, 1967.

Keynes, John Maynard. *The Economic Consequences of the Peace,* New York: Harcourt, 1920.

————. "The German Transfer Problem." Chap. 6 in *Readings in the Theory of International Trade,* edited by Howard S. Ellis and Lloyd A. Metzler. Philadelphia: Blakiston, 1949.

Klein, Burton H. *Germany's Economic Preparations for War.* Cambridge, Mass.: Harvard University Press, 1959.

Lindbergh, Anne Morrow. *The Wave of the Future.* New York: Harcourt, 1940.

Litchfield, Edward H. *Governing Postwar Germany.* Ithaca, N.Y.: Cornell University Press, 1953.

Lubin, Isador. "Reparations Problems," *Proceedings of the Academy of Political Science* 21, no. 4 (Jan. 1946): 68.

Mendershausen, Horst. "Fitting Germany Into a Network of World Trade," *American Economic Review, Proceedings and Papers,* May 1950.

Meurer, Hubert, "U.S. Military Government in Germany: Policy and Functioning in Trade and Commerce." Manuscript. OCMH. U.S. Military Government, European Command, Karlsruhe, Germany, 1950.

Morgenthau, Henry. *Germany Is Our Problem.* New York: Harper, 1945.

————. "Our Policy Toward Germany." *New York Post,* 26 Nov. 1947, sec. 1, p. 2; ibid., 28 Nov. 1947, p. 18.

Morgenthau Diary. U.S., Congress, Senate, Committee on the Judiciary, Subcommittee to Investigate the Administration of the Internal Security Act and Other Security Laws, *Morgenthau Diary.* 90th Cong., 1st sess., Nov. 1967.

Mosely, Philip E. "The Occupation of Germany: New Light on How the Zones Were Drawn." *Foreign Affairs* 28, no. 4 (July 1950).

Murphy, Robert. *Diplomat Among Warriors.* Garden City, N.Y.: Doubleday, 1964.

Notter, Harley A. *Postwar Foreign Policy Preparation 1939–45.* U.S. Dept. of State publication 3580. Washington: U.S. Govt. Printing Office, 1949.

Ohlin, Bertil. "The Reparations Problem." Chap. 7 in *Readings in the Theory of International Trade,* edited by Howard S. Ellis and Lloyd A. Metzler. Philadelphia: Blakiston, 1949.

OMGUS. "History of Economic Planning in the Bizone." Manuscript. OMGUS records 406-1/3.

OMGUS [Office of Military Government for Germany (US)], *Food and Agriculture.* Monthly reports of the Military Governor, U.S. Zone. OMGUS records.

OMGUS, Trade and Commerce. Monthly Report of the Military Governor, U.S. Zone. OMGUS records, 16-1/5 and 17-1/5.

OMGUS, Weekly Information Bulletin. OMGUS records.

Penrose, Ernest F. *Economic Planning for the Peace.* Princeton, N.J.: Princeton University Press, 1953.

"Plan of the Allied Control Council for reparations and the level of post-war German economy." OMGUS records.

"Planning for the Occupation of Germany." Manuscript. Office of the Chief Historian European Command. Office Chief, Military History, OCMH.

Price, Harry Bayard. *The Marshall Plan and Its Meaning.* Ithaca, N.Y.: Cornell University Press, 1955.

Ratchford, B. U., and W. D. Ross. *Berlin Reparations Assignment.* Chapel Hill, N.C.: North Carolina University Press, 1947.

"Review of Industry, May 1945–September 1947." Unpublished manuscript. OMGUS records, 358-1/5.

Revised Plan for Level of Industry in the US/UK Zones of Germany. Berlin, Aug. 1947. OMGUS records.

Schmidt, Hubert G. *Food and Agriculture Programs in West Germany.* Office of the U.S. High Commissioner for Germany, Office of the Executive Secretary, Historical Division, 1952.

———. *The Liberalization of West German Foreign Trade.* Office of the U.S. High Commissioner for Germany, Office of the Executive Secretary, Historical Division, 1952.

Schwarz, Hans Peter. *Vom Reich zur Bundesrepublik.* Neuwied, 1966.

Slover, Robert. *The Bizonal Economic Administration in Western Germany.* Cambridge, Mass.: Harvard University Press, 1950.

Snell, John L. *Wartime Origins of the East-West Dilemma Over Germany.* New Orleans: Hauser Press, 1959.

Statistisches Jahrbuch für das Deutsche Reich. 1936 Statistisches Reichsamt, 1937.

Stimson, Henry L. *On Active Service in Peace and War.* New York: Harper, 1947.

Stolper, Gustav. *The German Economy, 1870–1940.* New York: Reynal & Hitchcock, 1940.

———. *German Realities.* New York: Reynal & Hitchcock, 1948.

Tennenbaum, E. A. "Why Do We Trade for Dollars?" OMGUS, Office of the Finance Advisor, 15 Feb. 1948. OMGUS records, 84-2/1.

"Three Years of Reparations." Special Report to the Military Governor, 1948. OMGUS records.

"Toward a Modern Diplomacy," *Foreign Service Journal* 45, no. 11, pt. 2 (Nov. 1968).

United Nations. *World Economic Report.* Department of Economic Affairs, U.N. 1948.

Varga, E. "Vosmeshchenije ushcherba gitlerovskoi germaniyei i yeyo soobshchnikami [Reparations by Hitler's Germany and its accomplices]," *Voina i rabochi klass,* no. 10, 15 Oct. 1943.

Verwaltungsamt für Wirtschaft. "The Effect of Envisaged Dismantling on Germany's Economic Situation and its Role in European Reconstruction. Frankfurt am Main, 1948. Manuscript. OMGUS records.

von Oppen, B.R., ed. *Documents on Germany Under Occupation.* New York: Oxford University Press, 1955.

Wallich, Henry C. *The Mainsprings of the German Revival.* New Haven, Conn.: Yale University Press, 1955.

Welles, Sumner. *Time for Decision.* New York: Harper, 1945.

"A Year of Potsdam: The German Economy Since the Surrender." 1946. OMGUS records.

Zink, Harold. *The United States in Germany.* Princeton, N.J.: Van Nostrand, 1957.

INDEX

Talisman, Operation, 7
Time, 16, 17
Title #13, 119, 120
Trade and Commerce Branch
  (OMGUS), 106, 107
Trading with the Enemy Act, 147
Treasury Department, 9, 12, 15,
  16, 18, 19, 21, 24, 29, 93,
  116, 195, 197, 198, 200
Trizonia, 184
Truman, Harry, 27, 28, 29, 53,
  68, 174

United Nations, 9, 13, 23, 25, 37,
  70, 88, 128
United States Commercial Com-
  pany, 114, 124, 125, 150
United States Commodity Credit
  Cooperation, 114, 124
United States Congress, 50, 51,
  131, 150, 175, 192
United States Group Control
  Council, 39, 40, 195
USFET, 39, 40

Vandenberg, Arthur, 175
Varga, E., 63
Versailles Treaty, 10, 11, 31, 61,
  192
Verwaltungsamt für Wirtschaft,
  87, 90, 136, 138
Völkische Beobachter, 17

Wall Street Journal, 15
Wallich, Henry C., 12, 24, 38,
  88, 144
War Department, 4, 6, 7, 16, 18–
  21, 24, 25, 28–30, 50, 59, 82,
  93, 106, 147, 196, 198, 199,
  201
Washington Post, 10, 17
Welles, Sumner, 11
Western Zones, 44, 70, 71, 73,
  84, 174, 176
White, Harry, 9
White House, 9, 24, 58, 197, 198
White, Ralph, 193
Wickersham, C. W., 196
Wilkinson, Larry, 115
Wilson, Woodrow, 61, 193
Winant, Frederick, 107
Winant, John, 18, 19, 65
Wolf, George W., 84
Working Security Committee, 6
Württemberg-Baden, 43, 98, 137

Yalta Conference, 14, 65, 66, 67
Yalta Reparations Protocol, 67,
  69, 70, 72, 73, 88

Zink, Harold, 24, 199
Zones, 8, 107, 109, 130 (*see also*
  Western, British, American,
  Soviet, and French Zones)